1986

P9-AQV-213

# A WRITER'S GUIDE
## TO
# BOOK PUBLISHING

Second Edition
Revised and Expanded

# A WRITER'S GUIDE
# TO
# BOOK PUBLISHING

## RICHARD BALKIN
with two chapters by Jared Carter

Hawthorn/Dutton
*New York*

*To W.H.Y.H.,*
*who taught us both,*
*among many other things,*
*that publishing is more*
*than a business.*

The article entitled ''A PUBLISHING FABLE'' by Lachlan P. MacDonald originally appeared in the 1980 issue of *Publishing in the Output Mode*, a newsletter issued by Lachlan MacDonald's Padre Productions, San Luis Obispo, CA 93406. Copyright © 1980 by Lachlan P. MacDonald. Reprinted by permission.

Published in the United States by Elsevier-Dutton Publishing Co., Inc., 2 Park Avenue, New York, N.Y. 10016

Library of Congress Cataloging in Publication Data

Balkin, Richard.
  A writer's guide to book publishing.

  Bibliography: p. 229
  Includes index.
  1. Authors and publishers.   2. Publishers and publishing.   I. Carter, Jared.   II. Title.
PN155.B3   1981        808'.025        80-27256

ISBN:  0-8015-8925-8 (cl)
       0-8015-8926-6 (pa)

Published simultaneously in Canada by Clarke, Irwin & Company Limited, Toronto and Vancouver

10  9  8  7  6  5  4  3  2  1

Second Edition

# *Contents*

*written by Jared Carter

# *Preface*

As book publishing moves into the eighties, two main issues and their repercussions are of grave concern to publishers, and their consequences are having an impact on writers: inflation and—for want of a better phrase—conglomerate concentration and commercialization.

The effects of inflation, compounded by the high cost of borrowing money, have caused publishers to continually raise the list prices of their books to compensate for their own rising costs of composition, paper, book production, and so on. But as consumers are equally pinched, they are cutting back on *their* book purchases, and not only for expensive clothbound books. In 1979, for the first time in over thirty years, mass market unit sales (the quantity of books sold) declined, and this trend seems likely to continue. Exacerbating this problem are growing returns from booksellers—now averaging 20-25 percent for trade hardcovers and 35 percent for mass market books—more than double what they were a decade ago. Publishers no longer expect the growth they had been accustomed to, and in the process of cutting back on their expenses, such as in tightening budgets for advertising, reducing their staffs through attrition or firing, lessening the number of direct sales calls (in favor of telephone calls), and signing up fewer books, their authors are now feeling the pinch as well.

According to a P.E.N. survey conducted in 1978, the *median* income from writing was $4,700. The *average*, however, was an impressive $21,192. What this reflects in trade publishing is that the "big" books (those with advances of $100,000 and up) are skewing the statistics. There seems to be no dimunition of this practice: Big books are still garnering the large advances, eating up 80 percent of the promotional budget, and generally getting the big push from the publishing house. But owing to inflation, fewer middling books are being signed up, and less attention is winging them on their way: in editorial help, publicity, advertising, and sales (as stores, and chains especially, increasingly focus on best sellers). Furthermore, authors' advances are definitely not keeping up with the rising cost of living. Literary fiction in particular is suffering, and there seems scant indication that matters will improve.

The situation raises another issue now vigorously debated in publishing circles: Have publishers been publishing too many books? Is the crunch actually having a salutary effect, in that less chaff and more wheat will now be available in bookstores? This last position has fewer advocates in publishing than you might think. Most of us see more and more books on exercise, popular psychology, dieting, and romance glutting the marketplace, and fewer and fewer serious works of both fiction and nonfiction being published by major houses. Readers will undoubtedly have less current reading matter from trade houses to choose from in the 1980s—though whether the difference between 40,000 and 45,000 books is going to cause any consumer concern is moot—and writers will definitely have a harder time selling serious books to trade publishers.

One important reason for this brings us to the second major concern of many people in publishing: conglomerates and commercialization. The Authors Guild, among other publishing spokespersons, has been vociferous in its efforts to stem the increasing concentration of publishing houses, a result of conglomerate acquisitions. Testifying before the Senate Subcommittee on Antitrust and Monopoly, the Guild's counsel, Irwin Karp, pointed out that the effects upon authors are to reduce their already limited bargaining power and to diminish their opportunities to be published, especially because "the bottom-line interests of conglomerates inevitably abet the 'big book' or best-seller syndrome." Statistics seem to support this concern: In trade book publishing the eight largest publishers now account for almost 50 percent of books shipped, the eight largest mass market publishers have 80 percent of the paperback business, and the two largest book clubs have a market share of more than 50 percent. While a dose of hard-nosed business practices superimposed by the conglomerates might have a salubrious influence on some traditional publishing dilemmas, such as the chaotic state of book distribution, the other pressures they exert are not likely to have a beneficial effect on authors. As Herbert Mitgang of the *New York Times Book Review* reported in *Publishers Weekly* (2/8/80): "... you're not going to get many top editors or publishers to admit that the heat is on from the conglomerate. But it is. The fear is there at the very top. I've seen it."

Within publishing houses, I have been surprised to hear from a handful of editors during the past year: "I'm quitting; I just can't take it anymore." For the past five years, on the other hand, it was not uncommon to hear, on an average of once every two weeks, that yet another editor was being laid off. The new spate of resignations, however, suggests that the pressure cooker is working both ways. Now fewer editors are handling more books, so that the kind of individual attention authors used to receive in the form of substantive editing is diminishing —the "big books" notwithstanding—and may soon become a thing of the past. It is no longer uncommon for a book to pass through the editor's hands directly to the copyeditor's desk without receiving more than a perfunctory glance.

Two other effects of conglomerate acquisitions are expressed by two leading authors, E. L. Doctorow and Christopher Lasch. Testifying before a different subcommittee in Washington, Mr. Doctorow stated:

> There is a tendency of the publishing industry to be absorbed by the entertainment industry, with all its values of pandering to the lowest common denominator of public taste coming to bear. . . . Traditional publishing always reflected the tension between the need to make money and the desire to publish well. . . . This balance of pressures within a publishing firm is upset by the conglomerate values—the need for greater and greater profits.

That this tendency is extending even to an arena of publishing in which high standards and high purpose presumably prevailed is expressed by Christopher Lasch in a statement that accompanied his decision to reject the 1980 T.A.B.A. award for his book *The Culture of Narcissism*, in the "paperback current interest" category.

> [The] new selection process . . . gives priority to commercial success, [and] sanctions the worst tendencies in publishing today. . . . In the last twenty years more than three hundred mergers have taken place in the publishing industry. . . . These figures [huge advances] confirm what is already obvious from other evidence— that publishers prefer to publish blockbusters or would-be block-busters instead of taking a chance on a book that may take several years to find an audience. Instead of keeping books in print, they remainder a title as soon as its initial sale is exhausted. New authors find it more and more difficult to get published at all. . . . The trend towards economic consolidation can only have the same effects on book publishing that it has already had in other industries: destruction of craftsmanship; standardization; built-in obsolescence; and the promotion of shoddy products through media hype—including T.A.B.A.

The grim forecasts are countered by contrary, if less prevailing, opinions, from distinguished figures in publishing, such as John Dessauer and Townsend Hoopes, president of the Association of American Publishers. Reporting an increase in the past ten years of close to 50 percent in the number of book publishers (now well over 10,000, according to R. R. Bowker Co.), and a concomitant increase of more than 50 percent in the number of booksellers, Mr. Dessauer contends that "to continue claiming excessive concentration in the face of such evidence is perverse." He further notes the irony of authors such as Mr. Lasch being published by the very same imprints they condemn. Since we live in a pluralistic culture, he essays, it is an exercise in snobbery and a manifestation of contempt to condemn the tastes of 90 percent of the book-buying public (who buy the blockbusters by the millions). And Mr. Hoopes, appearing before the second senate subcommittee and citing the same statistics, concluded that "Book publishing today is a flexible, open industry characterized by ease of entry and vigorous competition. It is not overly concentrated and certainly not subject to improvement by government intervention."

The surprising increase in the number of publishers provides a measure of optimism, particularly for the first-book author. It has always been hard to crack the top two dozen houses, and while that problem is now intensified, the other end of the spectrum in publishing, the small and regional presses, are clearly flourishing. Although there is definitely less opportunity here to make much money from writing books, there is clearly now a greater possibility of seeing your book in print. For this reason, I have considerably expanded that section of the book. Correspondingly, because small presses attract poets and literary novelists, I have added sections on both genres to the first chapter to indicate the current state of affairs in trade publishing. Sections have also been added on translating, el-hi text publishing, professional and reference books, on preparing a revision, "special sales," book distribution, and paperback originals. My coauthor, Jared Carter, has attempted to keep up with the mushrooming use of computers in the areas of editing, composition, and book manufacturing, by adding information on new methods and developments. So much is taking place so fast that it is impossible to be *au courant* by the time this book appears in print (that is one area of book publishing that hasn't changed—it still takes about nine months to make a book).

Within all other phases of book publishing, I have attempted to supply recent statistics, information, and examples, and have added materials on current trends or developments. To try to authoritatively encompass the entire field of book publishing—even concentrating just on what, presumably, authors wish to know—is a presumption, and I must beg the reader's indulgence for errors and omissions.

# Acknowledgments

My education in publishing has been immeasurably enriched by a number of fine articles and books written by dedicated bookmen and bookwomen, without whom this book might not have been written. I have frequently dipped into their storehouse of knowledge for facts and explanations. *Publishers Weekly* has equally been an endless source for information and statistics; I salute the men and women who are responsible for maintaining its excellence.

During the preparation of the manuscript a number of people were kind enough to read portions of it and to make useful suggestions and comments: Andy Effrat (who gave me the encouragement to start it all), Frances and Bill Hackett, Ned McLeroy, Philip D. Jones, Gardner Spungin, Ceil Smith, Lloyd Scott, Georgia West, Nick Lyons, Jared Carter, A. Dale Timpe, Allan Lang, Sy Rubin, Nelson Richardson, and Arthur Abelman. I am grateful to them for their time and efforts. And thanks to my editor, Bob Oskam, whose skill and disposition has improved the book, won my respect, and generated a friendship.

I am deeply indebted to Felice Swados, who bore my fits and starts with equanimity, was constant in praise and encouragement, read and commented on a large portion of the manuscript, and believed when I doubted.

On the occasion of this revision I would like to thank the following people, who were kind and generous enough to spare their valuable time and share their expertise with me. Needless to say, they share no responsibility for any errors or omissions. Let me thank Daphne Abeel,

Harry Ford, Len Fulton, Ashbel Green, Jerry Gross, Bill Henderson, Elizabeth Knappman, Harry Lewis, David Lyon, Randall Marshall, Dick McDonough, Richard Marek, Shirley Sarris, and John Thornton. Unsung but not unappreciated are those whose articles and books I have unhesitatingly mined for information and opinions, as well as several dozen colleagues who responded generously to phone calls and let me pick their brains. Without the help of all these people, this edition would not have been written.

A portion of this book, chapters 5 and 6, were written by Jared Carter, a friend and former colleague. He would like to thank the following individuals for their helpful comments on early versions of his two chapters: Benton Arnovitz, Rick Balkin, William Bokermann, Frances Hackett, Bill Hackett, Edward Iwanicki, and Carol Stevens; Lou Keach, Harriet Curry, Ron Haldeman, and Walter and Edith Albee for their advice and comments concerning his revision of chapters 5 and 6.

# Introduction

John Creasey, a noted mystery and detective-story novelist who died several years ago, had received—according to his obituary—744 rejection slips before his first work was accepted for publication. To add to this *Guinness Book of World Records* statistic, he wrote and had published 560 novels during his lifetime. Though you may have some doubts about the authenticity of the first figure, the second is a matter of record. The moral of this story is not "you are bound to get published sooner or later"—for many books will never make it to the printer's, and both the industry and the reading public, in most instances, will be grateful—but, rather, "don't give up too quickly." A few rejection slips do not mean your book proposal or manuscript is a complete flop and that editors sit at their desks laughing at it before they ask their secretaries to send you a polite but standard rejection letter.

Much of the seemingly inherent conflict between publishers and would-be and published authors (95 percent of whom can regale you with their publishing horror stories) is the result of ignorance about the various stages between the submission of a proposal or manuscript and the receipt of an author's first royalty check. It is usually the author's ignorance, but sometimes—in this age of specialization, expansion, and technological change—the editor's as well.

But this is a guide primarily for authors, and it is called a guide because it presumes to contain most of what an author or a potential author might want to know about publishing. There are, however, several qualifications: This is not a book about how to write a book.

Many of these are available, from the humblest high school grammar to the most sophisticated style manuals, not to mention the many informal, anecdotal "how to's" turned out by both successful and unsuccessful writers. Nor is this book specifically concerned with the technical aspects of publishing, such as design, printing, and manufacturing; nor the internal aspects of publishing, as, for example, the economics of running a publishing house, new uses of technology in publishing, or the general administrative process.*

The decision on what to include in this book grows out of thirteen years of experience communicating with writers, both as an editor and as an agent. There are seven main areas of the publishing process that particularly interest writers, and they comprise the bulk of this book: how does a writer approach a publisher; what are the methods and criteria publishers use in evaluating proposals and manuscripts; how does a writer prepare a "final" manuscript; how does one read, understand, and negotiate a book contract; what is a publisher actually doing with the manuscript during its nine to twelve month gestation; how does the publisher promote and sell the book; and, finally, what alternatives are open to the writer of a "noncommercial" book. No one can expect to be an expert, or even well informed, in all phases of publishing, and I do not pretend that *all* you wish know will be found here. In fact, I have ignored several areas of publishing completely, such as Bible publishing, standardized texts, encyclopedias, and subscription sales—of the Time-Life variety—which taken together comprise a hefty portion of total U.S. book sales. I have little experience with them, and they are far afield of the average writer's concerns.

This book focuses primarily on general trade books (both cloth and paperback), but includes many references to and tips for writers of textbooks, mass market paperbacks, professional books, juvenile books, and other specialized areas of publishing. I have not distinguished religious books as a separate category, even though most of them are published by religious book publishers and distributed and sold primarily by the three thousand or so religious bookstores in the United States and Canada. Every other distinction is more or less immaterial, and they can be considered trade books as far as the writer is concerned—except that, obviously, a writer is generally advised to approach religious publishers if the book fits into that genre. (Apropos, contrary to what you might conclude from most best-seller lists, the leading best sellers are

---

*John P. Dessauer's *Book Publishing: What It Is, What It Does* (R. R. Bowker, New York, 1974) successfully and amply explores this realm, whereas Elizabeth Geiser's forthcoming *The Business of Book Publishing: 39 Experts on Every Phase and Function of the Publishing Process* (Westview Press, 1981), seems likely to become the definitive tome on the industry.

religious books—not just Bibles either—and mass market houses are now issuing paperback editions of these in increasing quantities.) The ground rules for these other areas are much the same: You have to write the book, you have to find and interest a publisher, and the publisher has to produce and sell the book—that's the A, B, and C of it.

The decision to include both trade and textbooks in the same volume grows out of the increasingly murky distinction between the two markets (the basic distinction from the bookseller's point of view is in the discount). According to a survey by the Association of American Publishers, only 57 percent of the book sales in college stores were for textbooks; more than 33 percent were for general trade books (cloth, quality paperbacks, and mass market paperbacks). Of this one-third, probably over 80 percent, is directly related to use in courses. Yet these statistics are somewhat misleading, since many trade paperbacks sell in greater quantities in colleges than they do in regular book outlets. Most well-known trade paperback lines, such as Penguin (Viking), Anchor (Doubleday), and Vintage (Random House) take in close to 50 percent of their revenues from high school and college bookstore sales, and in the past ten years these publishers have devoted considerable time, money, and personnel to expanding and catering to the high school and college market. The same virtually holds true for mass market paperback publishers, whose eyes were opened even before Eldridge Cleaver's *Soul on Ice* and *The Autobiography of Malcolm X* sold more than a million copies each year over a two-year period in college adoptions alone. Paperback sales have practically quadrupled since 1963, and even in the last few years have shown an average yearly increase.

As a consequence, trade publishers and authors keep their eyes on the educational market, and many teachers and professors are writing less technical and more trade-oriented books. The more scholarly the book, the more difficult it is to find a publisher (and this is especially true now for university presses, who are increasingly pinched for funds). This is not to say that textbooks or scholarly books are on their way out, only that more caution is exercised in signing and publishing them, and you as a potential textbook author will feel this competitive crunch.

In trade books an equally pessimistic note was recently sounded by the president of a major publisher: "It's harder to keep the middling book alive than it used to be. . . . It's because attention goes to the big books and that happens all the way down the line from the book clubs to the stores." In other words, finding a publisher who agrees to publish your book is not the end of your worries. When you consider that less than one out of every four books published earns a pretax profit for a publisher, and consequently not much in royalties for the author, you can understand why three out of four published authors are openly vocal about their gripes, and often feel overtly hostile toward their publishers. The publisher is the easiest target for the writer whose book doesn't sell. Surprisingly, though, you don't find the publisher maligning the author for the lack of sales, even though three out of four books don't pay their way (and the median posttax profit for the industry for the last few years hovers around a mere 3 percent).

The reason for these low sales is simple in the abstract: Either the book wasn't of sufficient interest to a large enough group of book buyers, or the publisher didn't "handle" the book properly. Practically speaking, and in most cases, it's a much more complex set of problems and there is no definitive answer to them. Publishing will remain a giant lottery, and perhaps that's the way it should be, so don't expect advice on how to turn your book into a best seller.

What this book offers instead is a realistic description of the publishing process, from the initial idea you have for a book to the receipt of your first royalty check. By describing all the phases in between, I hope you may not only develop a certain amount of respect for and understanding of the publisher's world, but also improve your chances of finding a publisher, getting a "good deal," and becoming the one-out-of-four author whose books earn a profit—for the publisher *and* you.

Most of the people in publishing, especially those engaged in editorial work, are underpaid, especially if one compares their education, skills, and experience to those of people in other industries. Most of them go into publishing because of an authentic interest in books and ideas, certainly not to get rich. They are not the enemy; quite the contrary, they are turned on by nothing so much as the first few pages of a fresh manuscript that they immediately feel must be published. Many a battle may have taken place about your book in an editorial meeting where it was "shot down" for reasons that have nothing to do with the quality or even sales potential of your book; or it could have been turned down as a result of a five-to-four decision.

So, don't be easily discouraged by a rejection slip; you never know what the next editor's reaction will be. A book published several years ago by Braziller had been rejected by many British publishers before it wound up in the bottom drawer of an editor's desk. It remained there for almost a dozen years, until it was finally returned to the author. Undaunted, she resubmitted it to an American publisher and fifteen years later, she was autographing copies.

## The Language of Publishing

In any profession or business, a body of words is either created or conscripted from the language of ordinary discourse to provide a common language for those who ply the trade or profession. This is also the case in publishing. Many writers, exposed to this language either in the media or through contact with agents, editors, or others in the profession, are sometimes confused, misled, or under the illusion that they understand a term or expression in the context of publishing when in fact they do not. For instance, *trade paperback*, which is synonymous with *quality paperback*, is a term for the slightly larger-format paperback books found primarily in bookstores, in contrast to the smaller-format "mass market" paperbacks found also in drugstores and variety stores. Thus a trade paperback is sold to the general consumer—but a "trade" magazine is published both for and within the specific industry or profession. To add to the confusion, I occasionally hear editors refer to the newer oversized paperbacks (circa 8½″ x 11″ and up) as mass market books.

Wherever possible, therefore, I have tried to define my terms, and in the interest of either variety or brevity, I have taken a number of liberties. For variety's sake, I have used *average, common, general, conventional, typical, and standard,* both synonymously and abundantly, since in any lengthy discussion of publishing procedures the exceptions are the rule, but had all of them been noted, this book might have turned into an encyclopedia. For brevity, I often use a single entity, such as *professional books*, in lieu of repeating that I include technical, scientific, business, medical, law, and engineering, under the same heading.

A more flagrant example is my adaptation of the term *publisher*. In the industry, the publisher is either the owner, the president, or the editor-in-chief, and the title is a term of respect generally reserved for the man or woman who runs the show, though it is no longer much in use today. A few firms, however, perhaps in place of adequate financial compensation, refer to their senior editors as publishers (*editor* is another label under which many different hats are worn for many different tasks). But I have sometimes used the term *publisher* in those situations or cases in which an aggregate decision is the rule, such as when the editor, editor-in-chief, sales manager, publicity director, and advertising director plan the promotional strategy for a specific book, and then merely said, "When the publisher decides . . ." Since joint decisions are more common than individual ones in many phases of publishing, I felt it would have been tedious to constantly list the participants (besides, they differ from house to house) and have therefore conveniently resorted to a single term.

Finally, like many of today's writers (and editors), I find myself stymied by the third-person-pronoun problem: Should I say *he* or *she*? Should I torture the sentence into an awkward shape in order to avoid the problem? Should I repeat a noun endlessly so that personal pronouns are unnecessary? No groundbreaker by nature, I have fallen back on the convention of using the masculine pronoun, with apologies to those it may offend, and with the hope that some brave and imaginative soul, be he a she or a he, will soon solve the problem for all of us.

# 1
# How to Approach a Publisher

> It circulated for five years, through the halls of fifteen publishers, and finally ended up with Vanguard Press, which, as you can see, is rather deep into the alphabet.
> —Patrick Dennis commenting on *Auntie Mame**

Publishers are always on the lookout for a good book. This is something to keep in mind no matter how discouraging the prospect of finding a publisher is, no matter how many rejection slips you get, and no matter how overwhelming the odds seem. And the odds *are* discouraging since unsolicited manuscripts, known as over-the-transom submissions, are put into the "slush-pile"; an optimistic guess is that only one out of every 2,500 books in the slush pile is eventually published.

An article published in *Writer's Digest* many years ago, "I've Turned Down More Best-Sellers Than You Have," surveyed more than a dozen well-known publishing executives and editors about the big one they let get away. Everyone recounted several anecdotes about books they turned down that eventually landed on the best-seller list, and had there been sufficient space the article could have grown into a book. Books like *Jonathan Livingston Seagull, How to Profit During the Coming Bad Years*, and *All Things Bright and Beautiful* had been turned down by over a dozen publishers before some house or editor "took a chance." The first two were submitted by agents, the third was a British import; but there are plenty of slush-pile success stories too, such as *I Heard the Owl Call My Name, Ordinary People*, or Rosemary Rogers' romances, one of which, *Dark Fires*, has sold over two million copies.

The reasons for turning down books are often more subtle than

---

*This and the successive epigraphs are gratefully borrowed from *The Writer's Quotation Book*, edited by James Charlton ($6.95, Pushcart Press, 1980).

negative answers to "Do I like it?" and "Will it sell?" even though they are the basic considerations. For instance, "it doesn't suit our list" is a very common reason for rejecting a proposal. A house that has not published cookbooks is unlikely to start with yours, though you may never find this out, since most form letters of rejection are very vague about the reasons behind the rejection. And where that reason is expressed, it may just be a polite way of saying maybe you should consider cutting out paper dolls for a hobby instead of writing. Most editors have no desire to dent a stranger's ego just for the hell of it; where they are unsure of or unimpressed with the writing style in a manuscript, they will rarely present that as an explicit reason for rejection.

Rejection letters are usually vague for three additional reasons: Since the number of proposals coming in each week is staggering, most editors or readers do not have the time to respond personally to each manuscript's problems—it's simpler just to say thanks, but no thanks. Another reason is that most negative decisions about a "maybe" book have been made after considerable reflection, and the editor feels it's time to go on to the next proposal. He doesn't wish to stir up a correspondence with the author, who will probably try to counter or rebut any detailed analysis of the flaws of the manuscript, the small market, etc. There just isn't time for this kind of Ping-Pong, and anyway a good editor can usually spot a diamond-in-the-rough. The third reason is illustrated by a tale I heard from a seasoned editor-in-chief who resolved at the beginning of his career to be absolutely candid with authors whose manuscripts he rejected. He held to this policy until one day he read of the suicide of an author who had just received from him a brutally frank opinion of his work.

The point is, whether an editor takes a week or six weeks to turn your book down, you may never know exactly why, so it is senseless to jump to the conclusion that your book is awful, or that the editor is a fool for not recognizing a masterpiece. The reasons may be complex and varied, or it may just be as haphazard as the fact that he put too much sugar in his coffee that morning and it's affecting his judgment. Since many books make the rounds of many publishers before they get signed up, and since factors beyond your ken may be responsible for any single publisher rejecting it, the moral is keep trying.

If the editor feels the proposal or manuscript is sound and is interested in the book for his list, but he thinks certain substantive changes in the form or content need to be made, he will say so. Then you have as options to revise and resubmit, to ask for a commitment before you make changes, or to go elsewhere. But it bears repeating to say that the market, the number of copies a publisher expects to sell in the first year or more is usually more important than the answers to such questions as: do we like the book; is it a solid, important, interesting, necessary, well-written book?

In 1979, in the U.S. alone over 45,000 books were published—an astounding figure.* If you have something worth saying, can write well, and have chosen a topic of interest to a book-buying audience of more than, say, 7,500 people (or 5,000 for a first novel; even less for university presses, scientific, technical, and reference publishers), your chances in this lottery aren't as dismal as the huge slush piles would lead you to think. What is required is just persistence, and maybe a bit of luck. The suggestions I have to offer in this chapter should narrow the lottery for you, since many writers are either haphazard in their preparation of a proposal or in their choice of publishers.

## Use Your Contacts

My first suggestion is that you attempt to exploit any and all possible contacts you have, however distant, in the publishing industry. Friends, relatives, acquaintances, teachers, colleagues, someone who knows someone, are all possible links, no matter how tenuous, to that editor or agent who may become interested in your work. Though your work has to stand on its own, overcoming the anonymity of the unsolicited, over-the-transom manuscript will often result in your proposal or manuscript getting a serious review. In any publishing house, with proposals constantly flowing in and out, a flag—something that will induce the editor to look more closely at your proposal—may be just the added nudge that will result in a contract. So do not hesitate to ask someone to call or write and establish a contact for you, or do it yourself by referring to the relationship: "my cousin, who published a book with your firm ten years ago," and so forth.

## Selecting the Right Publisher

One of the major reasons most beginning authors get enough rejection slips to paper their walls with is their choice of publishers. They start with Random House, Doubleday, or Harper & Row and work their way through the biggies, the two dozen or so largest, most well-known, and glamorous publishers. Since agents and "successful" writers are beat-

---

*Of these, more than half are trade books; the balance are text, professional, and so on. This figure also includes over 7,000 reprints.

ing at the same doors, the competition is terrific. The president of Doubleday has estimated, in a *New York Times Book Review* column, that Doubleday receives an average of 10,000 unsolicited manuscripts and proposals a year, out of which maybe three or four are chosen for publication. Give or take a few thousand, the other dozen leading publishers are getting the same number. Unless you have a book that is absolutely ideal for their list—fills an obvious vacuum, fits into a series, or perfectly complements one of their titles—skip them. There are approximately 1,500 trade book publishers; you are thus left with 1,475 or so likely publishers. *Literary Market Place* or *Writer's Market* have almost all of them listed. If this is your first book, you will improve your odds by avoiding the giants.

Though some of the larger houses publish in almost every field, most do not. It is important to understand that there are specific divisions in many houses, for instance, trade, college text, el-hi, juvenile, business, religious, technical and reference, scientific, law, and medical. As a very broad guideline, if it appeals to the general reader, it's a trade book; if it has a special audience, it may belong in another division. Each division usually has a separate editorial staff, and you should direct your proposal to the appropriate division. An additional limitation is that most publishers, even the large trade houses, have one or more areas in which they concentrate, for instance, history, biography, Americana, natural science, and how-to, even though many are nevertheless eclectic enough so that they will take on any trade title they want. You might also consider the one hundred or so "religious" book publishers, who account for 5 percent of the book industry's 6 billion dollars' annual sales. Though they are primarily interested in books with religious themes, whether they be fiction or nonfiction, many of their books—such as Marabel Morgan's *Total Woman*—fall into the general reader category, and they are not as overwhelmed with submissions as are many trade houses. Finally, there are many smaller houses that publish almost exclusively in one field, for example, psychology, military history, or gardening. Again, *LMP* or *Writer's Market* can supply you with all these distinctions.

Since you should already know which publishers are doing books in the area you wish to write about, they may be the logical choices to approach first. Editors and publishers have both commercial and personal interests, as evidenced by their choice of subject areas, series, and titles. By looking at your own shelves, writing the publisher for his current catalog,* and browsing in several local bookstores and the

---

*Almost all publishers print a fall and spring catalog; get the address from *Literary Market Place* and request a catalog from the Publicity Director. Or see *The Publisher's Trade List Annual* at your library. It contains the seasonal catalogs of many university presses and trade houses, as well as those of some regional presses.

library, you will be able to identify the publishers who are more likely to be receptive to your proposal.

If you are proposing a book that directly competes with a book on a publisher's list, you may think that he will not wish to compete with himself. This is true in some cases—a biography, a specific hobby craft, or a translation, for example—but not true in others. Publishers seem to vary in their attitudes toward the ethics and commercial wisdom of publishing a new book that directly competes with a previously published one of their own. If the market is large enough, say American history, business management, or introductory textbooks, most publishers will consider a directly competitive book. If the market is smaller, for instance, for a guide to the restaurants of San Francisco, the publisher probably will not consider a competing book. For translations, reprints, certain types of anthologies, and upper-level textbooks, you are obviously better off approaching a publisher who does not have a directly competing book on his list. Most new trade books, however, although they may compete for the same book buyer's attention, are more likely to complement rather than exclude or replace existing books on the publisher's list, and are thus fair game for consideration.

## *Why Prepare a Proposal?*

No matter what field or subject you are writing about, and no matter what category of publishing your book fits into—trade, text, reference, scientific, technical, religious, juvenile, law, medical, or business, you are going to need a proposal or prospectus. This is an outline and description not only of the projected or completed manuscript, but of other factors of interest to the publisher, such as the audience and the competition. The proposal is a more manageable document for an editor than a complete manuscript, not only because it is shorter, but because other people at a publishing house are normally consulted in the final decision-making process: an editor-in-chief, a sales manager, or any number of others depending on the particular house and its *modus operandi* and hierarchy. While the editor usually has the time and interest to scrutinize all the material you send him carefully—besides, it's his role as an editor—the others involved may only skim it. However carefully they read your submission, obviously a concise presentation simplifies their task, and since the amount of written material circulating at any publishing house is huge, a proposal is more functional than a complete manuscript; it is virtually a necessity. Fiction is the only exception, for neither an editor nor anyone else in the house will normally sign up a first novel unless at least one person has read the entire manuscript. And here, a synopsis accompanying the manuscript can perform the function of an outline.

## *The Query Letter*

One of the conventions in approaching an editor or an agent is called the query letter, which is basically the same as the covering letter we are about to describe. A query is merely a one-to-two page letter that permits the editor to decide quickly whether or not he is interested in pursuing the idea any further. If he is, he can then ask to see a sample of the manuscript. My recommendation is to submit a complete proposal with sample chapters, if it is a book rather than an article you are working on. If you follow the guidelines of this chapter, you will be choosing your target very carefully, so why waste time in adding another step to your first contact with an editor? If your covering letter excites him, he's got the material right there to decide whether you have been successful in turning conception into execution.

## *The Proposal*

**Basic Requirements.** Whatever the nature of your proposal, it should generally include a covering letter, a résumé of your previous publications and qualifications (if it is pertinent), a contents page if it is suitable (obviously you won't need a contents page if you are submitting a novel or proposing a new translation of Plato's *Republic*), an outline, and several sample chapters, particularly if this is your first book. Always type the complete proposal: Double-space the material not included in your covering letter, use decent margins, and check the spelling carefully. The proposal should be as neat as a letter sent to request employment or to a foundation requesting a $10,000 grant. Be sure your name is on all material in addition to your covering letter; it can easily go astray if you are using paper clips. While these suggestions may seem self-evident, an amazing number of proposals violate one or more of these basic procedures. Many editors will read no further than the covering letter if that is handwritten, littered with spelling errors and poor punctuation, or is marred by a flabby style.

Following these principles may not make the difference between an acceptance or a rejection, any more than they might make the difference in your getting a job or grant; but *not* following them certainly won't help, and since you are, in effect, urging a publisher to invest anywhere from eight to fifty thousand dollars in publishing your proposed book, you can at least assure him of the seriousness of your intentions by *not* sending him a sloppy proposal.

If you are submitting a novel, your covering letter need only include your previous publications, if any, and any pertinent biographical or vocational information, such as the fact that your novel about life on a submarine was inspired by a ten-year stint in the navy, or that the setting of your novel, Lapland, achieves its verisimilitude from your many years as a reindeer shepherd. Otherwise, just say hello and goodbye, but always submit a finished novel, unless you have already published one or more successful novels (meaning you earned back more than your advance). Partially completed first novels generally don't stand a chance, unless perhaps you are halfway through a 600-page commercial saga or romance, in which case the first 300 pages will do, or if you have an extremely novel novel idea with a hefty sample (the Iraqis are towing an iceberg to irrigate some part of their desert, but the Iranians manage to spike it with LSD, and then...). And, as mentioned, also include a two-to-four-page synopsis of the novel—when we discuss what happens to your proposal (or novel) at the publisher's, you will see the advantage of the synopsis.

Many proposals sent in over-the-transom are photocopied or mimeographed; the only thing personal about them is the publisher's address at the top of the covering letter. A lot of them go into the waste basket after the editor scans a few paragraphs. While this may seem unjust (and maybe they are discarding the next *Joy of Sex*), consider your own response to photocopied or mimeographed letters. Such letters suggest to an editor that the author is sending them to any or all publishers and that he is neither confident nor hopeful of receiving a positive response. A covering letter to an editor should be an original typed copy; additional material can be photocopied or mimeographed.

**The Covering Letter.** The information an editor finds useful in a covering letter includes: a brief description of the book, the reason you think the book ought to be published, why you have chosen that particular publisher (this is not expected, but for obvious reasons is useful), your own special qualifications to write or edit the book, the audience and competition (or lack of it) for the book, and the approximate length and special requirements for it.

*The Description.* A brief description of the book is simple enough. Consider it a kind of synopsis in which you describe the relevant features in one paragraph. For further information the editor can turn to your more extensive outline, contents page, or preface or introduction. Whether it is a guide to flowers of the northeast, a "how-to," a psychological self-help book, a sociology textbook, or a study of American Indian sign language, you are approaching your topic from a specific point of view and can explain this in a paragraph. Avoid jargon in your description.

*Why Publish It?* The fact that you are writing or editing a book implies that there are reasons that the general reader, the professional, the antiques collector, or the novice macramé enthusiast may want to buy it or read it—or, specifically for a textbook publisher, that other teachers or professors will want to use it in their classes. If you are breaking new ground, i.e., treating an area previously not explored—say, feminist communes—explain it. If you are applying a certain model (for example, Freudian, Hegelian, and structuralist) or taking a particular point of view for a topic already treated in other ways, justify it and explain its unique relevance. A new translation? Why is it necessary and superior to those already in print? If you wish to edit a book that is out-of-print, why do you think that now is the time for reissuing it? If you are putting together an anthology, what is unusual about your coverage or approach? If a proposed monograph fills a vacuum in the literature of a scientific or scholarly specialty, explain its topicality. There are scarcely any subjects you can think of that have not been treated in book form in one fashion or another. If your previous publications and reputation in that area are not sufficient in themselves to prompt a publisher to offer you a contract, then you will have not only to submit a well-written sample, but make a good case for it as well.

*Your Unique Qualifications.* It follows, then, by reason of either your own personal experiences, vocation or avocation, previous publications, research, the courses you teach, prior education, or current interests that you have some special competence to write the book. Whether you include a résumé or list of publications or not, you can and should describe in a paragraph what unique expertise and resources you bring to the book.

*Why That Publisher?* If your book fits in with his current list, or into one of his series, or seems to fill a gap on his list, point this out and explain why you think he is the ideal publisher for your book. If you have bought or read or are impressed with the books that he has published and this has influenced your decision to write to him, let him know it. Editors are not immune to praise or recognition of the success of their decisions. Choosing the right publisher can save you a lot of time and effort and will definitely increase your chances for publication; many publishers turn down books because they aren't right for their list. It will also decrease your chances of receiving a form letter of rejection.

*The Audience.* In most instances, the audience for your book is obvious: either just a general audience (as for a biography or a novel) or a readily identifiable specific audience (such as for a coin collector's manual), but in some cases it is broader than an editor might recognize at first glance, or otherwise difficult to ascertain. For instance, a general book on pocket calculators might have an audience that ranges from high school students to engineers. You undoubtedly know which audience(s) will be interested in your book. It can do no harm to point this out to the editor, even though his knowledge of the market may be equal to your own. Some textbooks—this is true in the social sciences particularly—may fit into several disciplines. If this is the case, the sociology editor, for example, may wish to consult the psychology editor to see if the book fits into both areas.

Many publishers have several divisions: trade, textbook, reference and technical, religious, and juvenile, as well as their own book club(s). If you think your book would have a secondary market for one of the other departments, that is, would also interest the clergy, doctors, scientists, or business executives, then mention this. Obviously a technical or narrowly focussed or jargon-laden monograph will not have "trade appeal," nor will a standard textbook, nor will most juvenile or young adult books. But you may have reasons to think that your book will interest both the general public and a more specific but not obviously identifiable special segment of it, and you should point this out. The various divisions of a publishing company sometimes collaborate on a book (depending on the firm), and they may decide to produce a trade cloth edition and a college text paperback, for example. A number of other options are possible, and an editor will try to exercise them if the book warrants it.

Many authors make blanket generalizations about the huge audience for their books. They project a grandiose and unrealistic estimate of the potential market and sales for their book. It is wise to restrain any impulse to make this sort of estimate. Textbook authors, for instance, often mention "guaranteed adoptions" of anywhere from 100 to 5,000 copies at their own school, but this has limited value because of academic mobility. Still, there's no harm in putting a *conservative* estimate in your letter. The editor not only has at his disposal the accumulated knowledge and intuition of his years in the business, but he will be aided by other editors, salesmen, and publishing personnel—and occasionally some informal market research—in estimating potential sales. Your exaggerations will be suspect; your realistic projections can be useful and may provide additional ammunition for getting your book approved at the weekly editorial meeting. (More about this later.) And beware of overkill; publishers do not welcome "instructions" on the size of first printings and other similar matters which are their domain.

*The Competition.* If your book competes directly with one or more already published, you should be able to list the distinctive merits of your own book, as opposed to the leading competitor(s). Your book may have a unique perspective, a broader or more detailed coverage, a particular thematic structure, unusual organization, or just be more up-to-date. Whatever the distinction, you should favorably compare your own book, especially if you think that a book buyer is going to have to make a choice between your book and another. Mentioning the leading competing books and pointing out the important differences and improvements of your own will not only show the editor that you have considered this carefully in your decision to send a proposal, and that you know your field well, but will inform him of additional merits in your book which neither he nor his colleagues might otherwise see. Perhaps current developments, discoveries, or research in the field render certain competing books obsolete; translations may be old-fashioned; "how-to's" can quickly become dated; some textbooks will no longer be suitable because of changing curriculum patterns. Whatever the reasons, you can place your book in the context of competition, especially if it provides new information and consequently has no real competition but is, rather, *related* to books in the same category. Of course, the book may just be a new entrant in the field. Some fields are so competitive or the market potential so great that competition is much less relevant. Nevertheless, it is likely that there are some significant differences between your book and others that you are aware of that can and should be described.

*Size and Special Features.* Whether you have finished writing the book or are merely outlining it—in which case you should state the completion or delivery date—some estimate of its size and special features should appear in your proposal. It is best to give the editor an approximate word count (including introduction, preface, appendixes, and even footnotes, if they are going to be plentiful), which he can translate into printed pages. If there are to be illustrations, charts, graphs, maps, or other sorts of "artwork," indicate the kind and number. The cost as well as the price of the book, obviously, will vary in direct ratio to the length and special requirements. Length should be considered carefully, particularly if your book may be a long one (say, over 75,000 words). Mounting plant, paper, and manufacturing costs now make it quite expensive to produce a book. Such costs will often have an influence on the publisher's decision to accept or reject the proposal. The longer your book, and the more artwork it requires, the more cautious the publisher's decision. He will need this information sooner or later, and you can save yourself some unnecessary correspondence by providing it sooner. If you don't know approximately how long your book will be, you may not be ready to propose it to a publisher.

An average single column of text has roughly 320 to 360 printed words to the page, versus the 250 on a double-spaced typewritten manuscript page. A manuscript of 75,000 words will produce a book of roughly 224 pages (most books are published in multiple units of 32 pages, called signatures). Any manuscript between 50,000 to 75,000 words is considered normal to a publisher; between 75,000 and 125,000 words he begins thinking about the higher cost estimate.* Above this amount is the beginning of mild indigestion, and any manuscript over 160,000 words can be a cause for an ulcer. Of course, this can be mitigated by several factors: the type of book, the extent of its coverage, the audience, the market, and the author's willingness to cut his manuscript. Most manuscripts have fat on them.

Selections for an anthology may require the payment of permissions fees to the various copyright holders, as may a translation, a book with artwork, or a reprint of an out-of-print book, provided the material for these is not in the public domain.** If your book requires the use of previously published material, it will be necessary to write to the *original* publisher or present copyright holder, describe precisely what you wish to use, and determine whether or not there is a fee for permissions. Many anthologies have extremely high permissions costs. An anthology of contemporary poetry or drama could cost upward to $15,000 in permissions alone. Every editor will consider these costs before making a decision, and they will definitely influence the final verdict on whether or not to sign up the book. From experience, an editor, or someone else in the house, can make a fairly accurate estimate of total permissions costs. There is no point in writing for permission until you have a contract, as you will see in Chapter 4 where both permissions and copyright are discussed in detail.

**Résumé, Contents Page, Preface, Introduction, Outline, Sample Chapters.** Most editors would like to know some facts about your personal or academic background (insofar as it pertains to your book)

---

*See Chapter 2 for a discussion of cost estimates, print runs, and pricing.

**Any book published prior to 1906 and any book published since that time but not copyrighted is in public domain.

and your previous publications. A brief résumé, if you have one, is the simplest way to provide this information, even though you may have mentioned some of it in the covering letter. It is particularly appropriate for textbooks and scientific, technical, or reference books. If you have published a book before, it will lend some weight to an editor's decision—articles too, but not quite as much.

In most cases, whether you are preparing a nonfiction trade book, textbook, a scholarly monograph, or an anthology, you should as a matter of course include a contents page. The other ingredients—preface, introduction, outline, and sample chapter(s)—will depend on the book itself and your own judgment.

Most nonfiction book proposals ideally should include an introduction, a preface, or an extensive outline and at least two sample chapters. If both your previous publications and rank in your field are sufficient to have garnered you a "reputation" of sorts, you may be able to get a contract without sample chapters; enclose relevant samples of earlier published work. An outline of a book could either mean a one-paragraph synopsis of each planned chapter, or a two-to-six-page description. For a translation, you can include a sample of ten to twenty pages. For an anthology, I would recommend including either a finished introduction, or a precise outline of the introduction, with some indication of how you plan to introduce the sections and the individual selections. Several representative sample selections should be included as well. For a reprint, an introduction (or outline of it) should suffice—or a preface, if an introduction already exists. If you are putting together an original collection, i.e., an anthology of hitherto unpublished essays by several authors, you definitely ought to include a synopsis in which each selection is described in a paragraph or two. If you are planning this kind of collection, you must have informal commitments from the contributors *in advance;* many of these proposals are planned and submitted without consulting the proposed contributors (sometimes listing second and third choices for individual selections). This kind of optimism is unwarranted; publishers know it and may not seriously consider such a proposal.

Each book is unique. It is impossible to generalize about which combination of these materials you should include. The main distinction between the covering letter and the proposal is that the latter fleshes out the former; don't be reluctant to repeat yourself, provided you are giving more detailed information. Whatever you decide to include, unless it is a novel, do not send a complete manuscript if your submission is unsolicited. Editors or readers who are examining twenty-five or more proposals a week will generally not read entire manuscripts. A sample is sufficient either for a contract or for a decision to request more of the manuscript.

**When to Send a Proposal.** Should you send a proposal before, during, or after you have completed a book? At least 50 percent of the proposals publishers receive that do not come from agents are for books that are already completed. But that does not mean you have to wait that long. If you have not published a book before, and have published only a few articles or none, an editor or publisher will wish to see at least a partial manuscript before the house makes a decision.

I would discourage an author from completing a nonfiction manuscript without a contract. Since almost all publishers (some university presses are an exception) will contract a book based on a sample or half a manuscript, it seems to me an exercise in unwarranted optimism to spend six months to five years completing a book that may not find a home. If you have previously published a book, you may be able to get a commitment from a publisher without sample chapters, but even this is not always true, especially if you are approaching the publisher, rather than vice versa.* If your first book was a financial success, by all means let the editor know.

For most books, a sample of 20 to 25 percent should be sufficient, though exactly how much of a completed manuscript you may need for a contract depends on several factors: past publications, how much the proposal interests the editor, the kind of book you propose, the reputation or expertise you have in your area, and the whims of the individual editor or publisher. In any case, if the editor is interested in your proposal, he will let you know how much more of the manuscript he wants to see in order to make a decision; some will insist on a complete manuscript. You can decide whether to do more writing or whether you want a publisher's commitment before you go further.

**Who Gets Your Proposal.** At every house, at least one or more "first readers" or editors review over-the-transom proposals. No matter whom you address the letter to, it will probably arrive at the right person's desk. Very few over-the-transom proposals are directly addressed to a specific editor. If yours is, there is a decent chance he or she will try to respond to it personally, if only to recommend the right publisher if the house is not interested or to comment on the proposal's strength or lack of it, though form letters of rejection are the most common response.

As a matter of fact, some houses now return unsolicited manuscripts or proposals unread, with a polite but mimeographed explanation. You will probably avoid this most disheartening of missives if you send your covering letter to a specific editor. Nothing stops you from calling a

---

*Be sure to check the fine print on your first contract; the publisher may have an option on your next book.

publishing house and asking who usually handles the "how-to's" or the cookbooks, though trade editors frequently insist on calling themselves "generalists." Some editors specialize in fiction, either mysteries, science fiction, romances, etc., so try to find out who does what. But do *not* try to discuss your proposal with an editor; they resent it unless you have a specific entrée, that is, someone who knows the editor has paved the way for you with a phone call or letter. Even then, writing is better than calling; until an editor knows whether you can write a decent paragraph, you are just a distraction.

The Bible for the publishing industry, *Literary Market Place (LMP)*, a Bowker publication, is updated every year and contains a listing of key personnel at almost all publishing houses, as well as listings of agents, advertising agencies, jobbers, distributors, and a host of other services and personnel. Small presses have their own catalog, *The International Directory of Little Magazines and Small Presses.*\*

*Writer's Market 1981* also has an up-to-date listing of publishers, though it is not quite as extensive or accurate as that in *LMP*. On the other hand, *Writer's Market* provides information, such as the kind of books a house is interested in, that is sketchy in *LMP*. You can find at least two out of these three reference tools at your local library. Unfortunately, they sometimes do not identify the editors by name, often listing only the editor-in-chief, executive editor, and other executives.

Instead of writing to "Fiction Editor" or "Nonfiction Editor" or "Sociology Editor," you are better off addressing your letter to the vice president, editor-in-chief, or executive editor of the appropriate division—trade, text, or professional. This person will reroute it to the right individual, who will usually give it the attention it deserves. In using *LMP* or *Writer's Market*, you will secure up-to-date information and frequently save yourself some time and energy, though because of musical chairs in publishing and rapid changes of ownership, these guides are already somewhat out-of-date upon publication.

**Multiple Submissions.** Many authors will send proposals to more than one publisher at a time. One can scarcely blame them, considering the treatment most over-the-transom proposals get: no response, a very tardy response, or a standard rejection letter. If you prepare your proposal carefully and send it to the right publisher, you will generally get a polite response within a month. Nevertheless, I believe it ethical to submit a proposal to more than one publisher at a time (not with novels,

\*This handy yearly is available in paperback for $13.95 from: Dustbooks, P.O. Box 100, Paradise, California 95969. It is particularly useful for poets and short-story writers, for whom commercial markets are scanty, to say the least.

though) provided you make it clear in your proposal that you have done so, both to keep your conscience clear and to be fair with the editor. Many authors submit to more than one publisher. A proposal is a probe, and since it could take you a year or more to get an offer if you were to submit it to one publisher at a time, you ought to have the opportunity to find out in less time than that if anyone is interested in your book.

One disadvantage to a multiple submission is that many editors feel only successful authors or agents are justified in following this procedure and even then only for a "hot" book. So your proposal may be turned down without consideration.

If an editor or publisher is interested, he may respond by saying that he wants to examine your proposal or manuscript carefully, but he wants some assurance that you will not make any other commitment until he has a chance to "check it out" and make an offer. This is only fair, considering that the editor may engage the services of his readers, consultants, or outside specialists, not to mention investing his own time and effort.

**Current Fashions in Proposals.** Certain subjects of topical interest become popular for a year or two. Then they either become permanent features, such as ecology, maintaining a long life, or they abruptly fade into obscurity. The publisher, during the period of intense interest, receives scores of proposals from authors who attempt to jump on this bandwagon, though many of these are hastily conceived proposals (often for anthologies and reprints) that arrive too late to be of real interest. In the past few years health and nutrition, the occult, feminism, pollution and ecology, and psychological self-help have been subject areas heading the fad list. While such topics may deserve the consumer and publishing attention they get, the average publisher can be overcontracted in those fields by the time the topic is nationally popular, or feel that the wave has crested.

There is always room for the serious, carefully researched, and well-written book that has permanent value, but many of the proposals that come in to publishers are one to three years out-of-date. For example, over the past few years I have received a number of proposals for books on home computers, home insulation, solar energy, running, pocket calculators, stress, and even roller skating. They usually arrive just around the time that *Publishers Weekly* announces the imminent publication of half a dozen books on each of these topics. Even though the marketplace can support several editions of certain classics (there are at least a dozen paperback editions of *Moby Dick*), or even 50 books on running, it is unlikely to be able to do so for most books. If you are planning a book in an area that is currently "hot," it has to be quite original.

## *Tips for Academics*

In the field of academic publishing, whether elementary, high school, or college textbooks, the writer has certain advantages and disadvantages.*

One advantage is that agents and "first readers" scarcely operate here, so that even though your proposal may be coming in over-the-transom, it will get more serious attention than will an over-the-transom submission at a trade publisher; the slush pile here is a more likely source of textbooks, and the editors usually specialize in a discipline and are more familiar with your field and hence the market for your book. You also have several other potential contacts not available to trade book authors: consulting editors (professors who read, evaluate, and recommend manuscripts), college travelers (textbook salesmen), academic conventions, and colleagues. Each or all of these can be a source for an editor's name, what kind of books publishers are currently pursuing, what areas they are lukewarm about, a possible formal or informal (by letter or phone call) introduction, and information on whether a publisher is expanding the list or cutting back. Pursue any or all of these potential contacts in preference to sending in an unsolicited proposal.

Incidentally, a scholarly convention is no place to peddle a book; don't walk around to every booth trying to hand an editor a proposal or manuscript. Either write the editor before the convention and try to set up an appointment, or merely make an editor's acquaintance and ask whether you may send in your proposal.

A current disadvantage for textbook authors is that many houses are cutting back their lists and concentrating strictly on comprehensive textbooks for basic courses. Trade paperbacks have become more and more popular as texts, and though this trend has only put a small dent in high school and college textbook sales, it has decreased the number of supplementary and corollary books that text publishers are signing up. You can take advantage of this by going directly to the publishers of quality paperback lines, many of whom are devoting some attention to the educational market, for instance, Penguin, Torch, Anchor, Delta, and Vintage (all are paperback lines for major houses, as are many quality paperback lines). Even here though, there has been some tightening of belts lately, and your book should have considerable trade appeal. If the book is strictly for classrooms, these publishers won't consider it. Anthologists should note that almost all trade and textbook publishers are

*For an informative, free ten-page booklet, *An Author's Guide to Academic Publishing*, write to: College Division, A.A.P., One Park Avenue, New York, N.Y. 10016.

*18*

now up to their necks in anthologies and are extremely selective about taking on any new ones.

Most teachers and professors are bombarded by catalogs, mailing pieces, and "exam" copies; this should make it easier to keep track of which publishers might be interested in your book.

## Professional and Reference Books

This genre actually consists of books in a wide variety of fields, though it sometimes falls under one or two umbrellas at large houses, such as McGraw-Hill and Prentice-Hall, or may exist as a separate division or be the sole output of a smaller house. "Professional" usually refers to books for specialists or academics in the fields of the humanities and the social sciences: Books in psychology, for instance, will be sold not only to professors, but also to clinicians, researchers, social workers, and others. Libraries are also a prime market for these books. "Professional" is also sometimes used to describe divisions or houses that publish books in architecture, law, business, medicine, real estate, and what have you. A sprinkling of these titles will also be suitable as graduate-level textbooks. "Sci-tech" refers to books primarily for professionals in the hard sciences, scientists, engineers, technicians, et alia.

The list price tags are high, and the first printings are usually low, but the rewards for the author can often be more generous than you might think. Handbooks, source books, or reference books in any of these fields may go into multiple editions over a period of five, ten, or twenty years—for instance, a television repair manual for servicemen. If the book lists for $39.95 and the discount averages 25 percent and the author gets a 15 percent-of-net royalty (that is, $4.50 a copy), then a modest sale of even 5,000 copies adds up to a royalty check of $22,500. Though the production and start-up costs for reference books are quite high, even small sales mean big profits for publishers. Consequently this is an area that is now booming, and many editors are clamoring for more titles in virtually any field. Editors here are not at all intimidated by a project that may run to 200,000 or even 400,000 words; in fact, the bigger the book, the higher the list price, and the happier the publisher.

Just as with trade books or textbooks, you should provide a detailed outline and sample. Editors will look more carefully at your credentials; you may have to qualify as a certified expert in the field in order to get a contract. Moreover, a slim sample, with an estimated manuscript size of 250,000 words and a completion date of three to four years, generally stands less of a chance than a book that is half-written and will be completed in one to two years.

## *Elementary and High School Texts*

Approximately two dozen el-hi publishers, many of which are divisions of larger houses, account for the bulk of the publishing and sales in this field. Many of the ideas for books originate "in house," with the editor approaching a teacher, soliciting an outline, and then carefully supervising the writing of the text at each stage. A further refinement of this process is the "managed" text (now becoming more common in college text publishing as well), in which the publisher hires a professional writer who either works with the teacher or transforms an extensive outline into a finished book. Incidentally, practically all of the editors in this field are former teachers.

Books are commonly coauthored by two, three, or even four teachers,* primarily to capitalize on the unique geographical marketing picture that el-hi houses face. Twenty-nine states now have blanket adoption policies: A committee chooses the text for a course or grade level for the entire district, county, or state. California or Texas, for example, may purchase as many as 100,000 to 300,000 copies of a high school text (and even more for elementary school readers). It is clear to see the potential advantage to the publisher of having at least one coauthor from one of these states if he is trying to secure the "adoption" (sale).

With the stakes so high, the start-up costs so great, and the minimum sales expectations so large—at least 25,000 copies a year, with a first printing of perhaps half that amount—the el-hi publishers are very cautious about their decisions and conservative in their editorial policies, and have recently come under some fire for the blandness of their texts.

To be successful, a high school text has to sell at least 100,000 copies over a five-year period, and for an elementary school text, upwards of 300,000. Net profit margins match the high stakes, however; they run to approximately 16 percent, which is more than double the margin for trade publishers.

Successful books are generally revised every five years, which is how frequently most committees choose a new text (and about the time it takes for students to demolish a book). As with college text publishers, "travelers" sell the books, and their efforts are supplemented by the mailing of brochures, advertising in appropriate journals and magazines, and appearances at the yearly regional and national el-hi teacher conventions.

---

*The Teacher-Writer*, a recent newsletter geared specifically to el-hi and college textbook writers, is worth looking at. Write for a sample issue, enclosing $2.50, to: *Teacher-Writer*, 177 White Plains Road, Tarrytown, N.Y. 10591.

Whereas you may approach an el-hi publisher with a proposal and sample, the decision to offer a contract, or to actually publish the book, may be postponed until a final manuscript is delivered.

## Children's Books

A major branch in many publishing houses, both large and small, is the juvenile or juvenile/young adult division, though there are houses which publish exclusively children's books. The audience, however, is fragmented. One informal and flexible breakdown, based on reading levels and supplied by the Children's Book Council,* suggests five general categories: babies and prenursery schoolers, nursery school and kindergarten (ages 3 to 5), early school years (6 to 8), older children (9 to 12), and teenagers or young adults. Presumably you will identify one or more of these age groups as your audience when conceiving, writing, and submitting a children's book.

Virtually all that has already been said about submissions applies equally to children's books. One distinction to keep in mind, particularly for heavily illustrated "picture books," is that the publisher normally chooses the illustrator and does so *after* a manuscript has been accepted (usually with the writer's advice and consent). If your forte is writing, control the urge to send in your own or your wife's or husband's sketches. You run a greater risk of rejection if the illustrations don't go over—they can always be brought up if you get a serious nibble or an offer.

If you haven't read any children's books since your own prepubescence, you are in for a surprise. There are scarcely any taboos left, and many books are candid and realistic about unmentionables as well as mentionables. A would-be author might innocently surmise that a children's book can be polished off in a long weekend; it isn't quite so simple. If you have had a vague urge to turn your hand in that direction, it might help to read one of the three books listed in the appendix which discuss the writing and publishing of children's books.

Children's books have been hard hit by inflation and recession: Rising production costs have joined with a declining birth rate and taxpayer revolts—such as Proposition 13 in California, which cut drastically into public and school library budgets, the major source for children's book sales—to force publishers to adopt some strict measures. According to

*Who will send you on request a free and informative small pamphlet: "Writing Children's Books." Write to: Children's Book Council, 67 Irving Place, New York, N.Y. 10003.

James Giblen, the publisher of Clarion Books, many houses will now use less color, use thinner paper, order smaller first print runs (which raises unit costs), let low-selling books go out of print, and cut back on both the staff and the number of titles published each season. To compensate for the shrinking market, publishers hope to increase "penetration" into the consumer market (libraries now account for over 80 percent of sales) via sales in supermarkets and variety stores, and by bringing out more pop-up books, game books, and tie-ins with TV programs and movies. In the near future, home television cassettes and filmstrips, both adapted from children's books, may boost revenues for publishers and authors alike.

## Poetry

In trade houses the reception to unrecognized serious poets—excluding humorous, sentimental, or "popular" versifiers—is more than dismal. Most houses will not even read a manuscript unless it comes highly touted by some distinguished literary figure or similar luminary. According to a survey undertaken by Poets and Writers, Inc., which traced the publication history in trade publishing of *first* novels and *first* books of poems during the years 1952–1977, an average of two books of poetry a year were published during this period (this figure excludes poets who had one book or more published by a small press). The figures they secured for the *total* number of books of poetry published during this time are not that much more heartening: an average of sixty books of poems per year. Bear in mind that there are at least 150 poets with national reputations who are taking up those sixty slots. Incidentally, there is no indication that these figures have improved since 1977, or that they will during the eighties.

Though one of the leading publishers of poetry, Atheneum, publishes six books of poems a year, rotating among eighteen recognized poets on their list, they are not considering any new manuscripts by unpublished poets. According to their poetry editor, one reason that so little poetry is published by trade houses is that very few editors have a serious enough interest in poetry, or are adequate judges of it, to take on or feel comfortable with such a responsibility. Publishers, many of whom do maintain an old-fashioned commitment to literature (and may feel a bit guilty because of current accusations of crass commercialism), would perhaps be willing to break even or take a small loss and publish poetry, but they are unable to find a suitable or willing editor within the house. Unlike decisions about other projects in a trade house, that for signing a book of poems generally rests exclusively with one editor; other decision makers are usually not interested in evaluating poetry or just don't know enough about it.

When collections of poems are published, they tend to average 64 to 72 pages in length, are published simultaneously in cloth and paper, and have a first print run of 2,500 to 5,000 copies (the latter only for a poet with a reputation and track record). Most of the sales are to libraries, college bookstores, and from readings by the poets (this latter generally separates the red from the black).

In fact, trade houses that choose their poets carefully and wisely don't usually lose money on poetry. With small first printings and high list prices, they will often sell out their stock in two to three years. One continuing source of revenue (and sometimes profit) is from second serial rights; that is, when poems are selected to be reprinted in anthologies, primarily for high school and college textbooks. These "permissions" fees can add up to a tidy sum for poet and publisher alike. Occasionally British rights are sold, but foreign translations are rare. Advances, when given, range from $250 to $500, but may go as low as $100 or as high as $1,000; royalties are conventional (see Chapter 3).

It seems clear that it is an exercise in futility for poets to attempt to break in with trade houses (or try to get an agent, for that matter: Poets such as Lowell, Berryman, Bishop, and Moore didn't have one, and times haven't changed). Most poetry in the U.S. is published by small and university presses, and those are the places to try.

## Fiction

The case for literary fiction and first novels is not quite so grim, but considering the large number of novels coming in over the transom and the small number of first novels published by trade houses each year, there is scant reason for a major in creative writing to conclude that he can support a family by writing novels. According to the aforementioned Poets and Writers survey, an average of 100 first novels were published each year from 1955 to 1972; since then the figure has declined to about 75 a year (this figure excludes category fiction—mysteries, westerns, science fiction—but does include some gothics and romances). A number of these first-novel writers may have already made a name for themselves in some other way, or published nonfiction, such as Jimmy Breslin, Erich Segal, or Peter Benchley. Of course there are some astounding first-novel successes—*Jonathan Livingston Seagull, Scruples, The Third World War, Watership Down, Hanta-Yo,* and others—but these are needles in haystacks. For better or worse, the best-seller lists, over the decades, generally contain repeated and familiar names: Wouk, Michener, Robbins, Hailey, Vonnegut, and others.

Figures for the total clothbound fiction published during this period are more reassuring, with an average of 1,000 novels a year (again, excluding category fiction but including gothics and romances), but it follows that nine out of ten were by previously published novelists. And most don't fare as well as you might think, since the fanfare about best-selling novels and huge paperback rights sales tends to skew the realities of the economics of publishing novels. Most novelists, even those who publish a book every two years or so and have five or more under their belts, fail to sell out their first printings (which only average 5,000 to 6,000 copies) and don't have their books picked up by paperback reprinters.

The big ones pay for the small ones: 10 percent of any trade house's fiction list pays for the other 90 percent. Novels, unlike nonfiction, have to be priced competitively. Even a long novel cannot carry the list price it should, in order to make a modest first printing pay for the book. Therefore some publishers calculate that in order just to break even, a clothbound novel has to sell 15,000 to 20,000 copies, which rarely happens. Yes, but what about subsidiary rights? In fact, a first novel has about one chance in five of being taken by a paperback house, even for a modest price, and the figures are not much better for repeat fiction. (Actually, almost the entire first print run of first novels is sold to library wholesalers; not only won't chain stores carry first novels, but most of the 9,000 standard book outlets won't either.)

Hitherto, trade houses could generally count on a small percentage of their novels selling to mass market reprinters for six figures or more (which the author and publisher split, usually 50/50). These few rights sales usually financed the balance of the novels on the list—as did a few books that sold very well in cloth or were selections for major book-clubs—and turned in a profit as well. In the sixties and seventies hardback publishers were often less than aggressive or thorough in promoting and marketing some of their novels, since they could count on those few big rights sales, frequently concluded before the book was actually published. But no more. The six-figure sales have ominously declined, and trade publishers will not only cut back somewhat on publishing novels, especially serious or literary ones, but they now realize the need for, and may concentrate on, giving more attention to, and better promoting, the novels they do publish.

The mass market houses have increased their own lists of paperback original fiction, not only category fiction and romances, but both commercial and literary fiction too. They have reduced the number of modest books, novels by unknown authors and six-figure blockbusters that they were buying, and prefer to concentrate on developing their own list of respectable and best-selling novels.

A little more bad news: Close to two-thirds of first novels don't sell over 2,500 copies, are ordered or sit on bookshelves for an average of six to eight weeks after publication, have heavy returns of almost one-third, and when remaindered, bring in to the originating publisher an average of 10¢ to 25¢ a copy (whereas remainders by best-selling authors are "auctioned" off, and can recoup as much as $1 or more for the publisher). The outlook for the eighties appears no better.

If I have painted a thoroughly bleak picture, take heart, it is not really that hopeless: Interest in commercial or popular fiction is still high— suspense thrillers, "faction" novels, and historical romances head the list. Secondly, there are the paperback houses; there, fiction outsells nonfiction by three to one (these figures are reversed for cloth), and, as I pointed out, these publishers are increasing their lists of original literary fiction, both in mass market and trade paperback formats. Moreover, the university presses continue to increase their own output of serious fiction, and this is even more encouraging for those writing short stories, which trade houses generally consider as precarious as poetry in the marketplace (even the sale of over 100,000 copies of Cheever's collected stories is unlikely to put a dent in the conventional wisdom about such collections). Several university presses now publish one or more collections a year (the universities of Illinois and Missouri now head the list), and the small presses, which are explored in detail in Chapter 8, are always looking for a good literary novel.

It seems clear, though, that the author of a literary first novel will have a very difficult time finding a hardcover trade publisher in spite of the fact that most editors are very interested themselves in good literary fiction, and more often than not came into publishing for that very reason. But the economics are brutal, the conglomerates totally unsympathetic to the notion of nurturing authors for their first few novels— the first two or three books by many successful authors, such as John Updike, sold modestly—and so the outlook remains pessimistic. If you do submit a literary first novel, nine out of ten houses will expect a completed manuscript, not sample chapters. Your chances of having your manuscript read and carefully considered—by an editor *or* an agent—are more than doubled if you had a story or a chapter from the work "in progress" printed in a national publication, or if you can secure a letter of enthusiastic recommendation from a known writer, distinguished mentor, or creative writing teacher.

But whether or not your novel will actually be given more than a perfunctory glance is questionable. Consider the following anecdote

reported by Douglas Peters, a professor of psychology, in an article from the September 1980 issue of *The Sciences:*

> In 1977, the publishing process of the literary world was tested in a unique way. Jerzy Kosinski, the Polish-born author of the 1969 award-winning novel *Steps*, allowed Chuck Ross, a Los Angeles free-lance writer, to resubmit a typed manuscript of *Steps* as though it were the work of an aspiring but unknown author. Ross changed the title and substituted a pseudonym for Kosinski's name. He sent the disguised manuscript to 14 major publishers requesting that they consider it for possible publication. What prompted this charade was concern about the difficulties that face unknown writers in getting their work published. It was strongly suggested that even if unknown authors were to write novels of the caliber of *Steps,* they would have difficulty finding a publisher because their names were not recognized in literary circles.
>
> Remarkably, the editorial consultants for the publishing houses failed to detect the deception. None realized that the manuscript which was sent to them for review was actually a verbatim copy of Kosinski's novel, which had won the National Book Award in 1969. What was even more surprising was that every publisher returned the manuscript with letters of rejection. The biggest shock of all, though, was that one of the publishers who rejected the manuscript, Random House, was actually the original publisher of *Steps*.

## Original Paperbacks: A New Market?

To help steer us through the maze of paperbacks, some general definitions are in order. A "mass market" or rack-sized paperback is 4¼ inches by 7 inches and will fit into those racks you find in drug stores and airport lounges. A "trade" or "quality" paperback is roughly in the 5½ inch by 8 inch format, give or take an inch either way. An "outsized" or "oversized" paperback ranges from 8½ inches by 11 inches upward. As of 1980, many hardcover houses have trade paperback lines, as do most of the mass market publishers. Either of them can, and will on occasion, put out an oversized paperback. Most of the mass market houses are now owned by, or are subdivisions of, hardcover houses (which in turn are owned by a conglomerate), and some have developed their own hardcover division, as have Warner Books and New American Library.

In the last ten years or so, mass market publishers such as Avon, Bantam, Dell, Warner, and Fawcett have increased their output of paperback originals (which ranges from 40 to 50 percent of their lists). For various reasons, such as the increasingly high prices of hardcover books (and consequently consumer reluctance to buy them), a decreasing resistance to reviewing paperbacks, the greater consumption of paperbacks as texts in high school and college, and the frequently high prices and occasionally extravagant auctions for paperback reprint rights—Bantam paid $3.2 million for Judith Krantz's *Princess Daisy*—paperback houses have stepped up their quotas of original titles.

Paperback executives now cite additional reasons for this phenomenon. Hardback houses traditionally "lease" the mass market rights for five to seven years, and then can demand a better deal (or new advance) if the book has become a successful backlist title, whereas an original remains with the house for the full copyright term, or at least so long as they keep the book in print. Also, some hardcover houses "take the money and run," failing to adequately promote and publicize the book they sold to the reprinter for a half million dollars, perhaps even before publication date, and the reprinter may have to devote an additional huge sum to this task. Or perhaps the book will fail to live up to expectations, garnering only mediocre or poor reviews and/or selling poorly in hardback, and will have these strikes against it when the paperback salesmen go out to sell stores the book.

The paperback houses realize they can just as successfully spend six figures to promote and advertise a paperback original, using money they didn't spend in an auction. And they have the option—now more frequently exercised—to make a "reverse" rights sale; that is, to lease hardcover rights and to withhold paperback publication for a season or a year, or even to publish the book simultaneously in both cloth and paper. In fact, several mass market houses have recently started their own hardcover lines in order to have the flexibility to market a book according to what they feel will be the ideal strategy. All of these factors have made it harder for trade cloth publishers to sell mass market paperback rights, even for books that have had good reviews and were written by authors whose first book(s) was successful.

This ongoing trend is good news for novelists, especially of "category" fiction (science fiction, mysteries, romances, etc.), since this is a major area of growth in originals. But it is true with both general fiction and nonfiction. If you feel your book has a potentially broad readership (most paperback houses won't sign a title unless they estimate sales of 50,000 to 75,000 copies in a period of twelve to eighteen months), you may be better off going directly to a mass market house. So far, agents and established authors still concentrate on getting published by hardcover houses first, so the competition from pro's and even over-the-transom is not quite as keen. In the long run, if your book is successful (goes back for another printing), you may earn more money for it, since you will not have to split your paperback royalties with the hardcover publisher (50/50 is the common arrangement). Recently, however, mass-market unit sales have slightly declined, probably because the median price for a paperback is close to $3.00, and with inflation, consumers are cutting back on impulse purchases. My optimism, then, has to be tempered by the realization that mass market houses are also concentrating their attention on the "leaders," that is, the big books.

Still, a paperback original is worth considering, provided your book potentially has a "mass" market, that is, a broad readership. Here again, you may be better off skipping the top seven or eight houses and approaching one or more of the dozen or so less glamorous paperback houses, such as Popular Library, Harlequin, or Ace. Many of the smaller paperback houses concentrate on certain areas, such as science fiction (or pornography—always doing well!), which you can ascertain by bookstore browsing or writing for a catalog. They have the same ground rules for proposals.

For over a decade the "outsized" paperback original has continued to sell well. Some mass market and hardcover publishers have published a number of these books, and since the sales have usually been good, this format will remain, even though it could no longer be designated a growth area. Probably the success of *The Whole Earth Catalog* (now in its sixteenth edition) is responsible for touching off this phenomenon. Incidentally, a completely new *Whole Earth Catalog*, compiled again by Steward Brand, has just appeared. Of course, your book has to lend itself to large-format presentation, either because it contains a lot of artwork (all graphic material, including photographs, charts, maps, illustrations, etc., is known as artwork), or because it is a catalog-type book, or for any reasons you can think of that justify that size book. A novel, for instance, is rarely suitable.

Finally, as I mentioned before, publishers with trade (quality) paper-back lines are increasing their number of originals. The watershed for the dramatic increase in the number of trade paperback originals, especially from mass market houses, began with Avon's successful remarketing of *The Flame and the Flower* in 1972, after it had already been a huge success in a mass market edition. The larger-format sale of an initial 30,000 copies proved there was a new market even after the book had been sold. Avon followed this experiment by publishing *Shanna* as a trade paperback original, but in "mass market style"; that is, via traditional mass market wholesalers and outlets. Its sale of over one million copies opened the floodgates for other mass market publishers to use this format and method to sell books in numbers hitherto reserved for mass market paperbacks. "It has become clear," said Peter Mayer, then head of Avon Books, "that a book doesn't have to be published in hardcover first to become an enormous success in paperback."

If a publisher of trade paperbacks can estimate a sale of 15,000 copies or more over an eighteen-month period, they will seriously consider your proposal. They will often simultaneously print a small number of clothbound copies, say 1,500 to 3,000, to catch some library, professional, and mail order sales, and for those people who are not happy unless they have a clothbound book (and also because the chances of getting reviewed are still considerably increased by having a clothbound edition). But most houses now feel that to warrant hardcover publication the book has to be able to sell over 5,000 copies.

## The Bottom Line

Intangibles like friendship, contacts, editors' idiosyncracies, parent corporation's interests or caprices, and acts of God can also have an effect on the acceptance or rejection of your proposal; ideally, they have a minimal impact. If you have a good idea and can execute it well, you should be able to find a publisher even if it takes a while. The unpublished author is often too quickly discouraged and gives up after receiving several rejections (although some authors *never* give up); the next submission might mean a contract. The number of proposals sent to publishers each year is huge, but the number of books that are published each year is even more astounding.

An unplanned or hasty or impulsive decision as to the choice of publishers is bound to increase the number of rejections you get. Correspondingly, a calculated effort to determine the "right" publisher can pay off in time saved and heartache—no one gets totally hardened to rejections, not even agents. The more subtle distinctions, such as which publishers will do a better job of promoting and selling your book, are very difficult for the unagented author to take into account in selecting a publisher.

Every editor or publisher is enthusiastic, encouraging, and often full of promises when signing up your book. Unfortunately, there's many a slip twixt cup and lip, and numerous authors become dissatisfied with the "handling" of their book, though often their complaints stem from unrealistic expectations. All I can offer is some suggestions for hedging your bets in the contract itself (in Chapter 3) and some suggestions in the chapter on marketing that can help you maximize your participation in the publisher's fulfillment of "adequate performance," that is, ideally fulfilling the role as producer and marketer of your book.


## Do You Need an Agent?*

There is no disputing that a good agent is not only worth his 10 percent commission—beware of any agent that charges more than that; this is the conventional fee for agents—since he can not only generally negotiate a more lucrative contract but can also, by virtue of his experience, contacts, and authority, help see to it that your book gets the treatment it deserves, and place it with the ideal editor and the ideal house for that particular book. But the ideal is not often achieved, and not every agent is a good one—nor are even good ones miracle workers. The variety of steps and factors involved between the submission of your proposal and the appearance of the book in a store are often governed by people and forces beyond the agent's circle or control, which may prevent him from being completely effective. If you have just had a best seller and are now working on your next book, then a good agent can virtually call the shots. A lot of money has been made on your book, and a battalion of other publishers—not to mention your own publisher—are eager and willing to be as cooperative and generous as you could possibly want. So your agent can then write the ideal contract. But how many of you have just had a best seller?

The Society of Authors' Representatives, organized by both literary and dramatic agents in 1928, contains approximately fifty members. It is a voluntary organization of agents whose individual members subscribe to certain ethical practices—such as not advertising their services—all of which are described in a small brochure "The Literary Agent," which you can obtain upon request.** Their description of an agent's functions includes: negotiating the sale or licensing of certain rights to publishers; retaining certain rights for later disposition, such as magazine or film rights;† examining contracts and negotiating modifications; recommending approval or rejection of a contract; examining royalty statements; checking on a publisher's handling of a book, such as advertising

---

*Literary Agents: A Complete Guide* will tell you everything you need to know and more. Send $3.95 to: Poets and Writers, Inc., 201 West 54th Street, New York, N.Y. 10019.

**Society of Authors' Representatives, 101 Park Avenue, New York, New York 10017

†British and foreign translation rights are handled by an agent's overseas agent, so the commission increases to 15 or, now more commonly, 20 percent. Virtually all publishers have a subsidiary rights department of their own to handle these additional markets for your book, in case you do not have an agent.

and publicity; and checking on copyright. In addition, a good agent will act as an editorial adviser both with the proposal and occasionally with your book, article, or short story, though agents tread lightly when it comes to substantive editing, since their recommendations may be in direct contrast to those of an editor—and it is the editor who buys the manuscript. Finally, the agent acts as a buffer between you and rejection slips, saves you the time and hassle of dealing with publishers, and acts as a dispassionate arbitrator in the event of problems—and they do occur. All in all, the advantages are sufficient to recommend getting an agent, *provided you can*, and provided he's a good one—there's the rub. Only about half of all agents belong to S.A.R.; there's no particular stigma in not being a member of that establishment or the newly formed Independent Literary Agents Association (now consisting of about fifty members). There is a complete list of agents in *LMP*.

There are approximately 250 agencies that represent writers, and though the procedure for approaching an agent is about the same as for a publisher, that is, a letter and a proposal, the odds of getting taken on as a client are six times as slim (remember: 1,500 trade publishers versus 250 agencies)! What decreases your chances even further is that agents in general want to represent "professional" writers, that is, people who either make a living as writers and thus can be counted upon to keep churning out publishable work, or writers who have proven through prior publication that their work is commercial and that it is worth an agent's time and efforts to handle it. (Selling your article to a specialized magazine at five cents a word is not what I mean, since an article that grosses $150 for you means a $15 fee for the agent.) Thus, agents concentrate on professional and previously published writers. Not that they don't occasionally take on new writers, but it doesn't occur with any more frequency than publishers take on new writers. As you can imagine then, agents have their own slush piles and send out a stream of rejection letters.* If you have a contact—a friend, relative, teacher, writer, etc.—who can or will pave the way for you, then it's worth a try. If not, why spend the time and effort soliciting the middleman when you can go directly to the source?

If you feel that you really do need an agent, since you expect to be quite active as a writer and not just a weekend scribe, then find a commercial publisher who wants your book (by *commercial* I mean a trade publisher who will pay an advance and a royalty), and then call or write an agent and present him with a *fait accompli*, asking him to negotiate the contract for you. Don't think this means he will necessarily

---

*One reason is that many agents do not handle all genres; most will not take on children's books, for example, and virtually none will consider poetry. I don't handle fiction, but half the queries I receive are about novels. See *LMP* or *Writer's Market* for agents' specialties.

grab the bait; it will just increase your chances, and with persistence you will probably get a nibble. But the agent will still want to see your work first, and it's no guarantee you will be hooking a good agent.

I can't tell you how to judge a good from a mediocre agent; it's like trying to judge a good shrink—you can't tell until you get your head shrunk a little. If at all possible, meet him or her and don't spare the questions. From the quality of the answers and your reliance on your own instincts, you should be able to make a judgment, and time will tell whether it was a good one. A good agent cannot always sell your writing, nor can he see to it that your book doesn't die on the shelves. He earns his commission because he cares and he tries.

There are one- and two-man (or woman) agencies, and then there are big ones that employ between five and twenty-five representatives, some of whom are specialists in selling certain rights: film rights, British rights, first serial rights to magazines, etc. These larger agencies often combine literary and dramatic agents under one roof. A disadvantage at a big agency for a writer who hasn't yet "made it" is the position of a small fish in a big pond. What is most important is finding someone who appears to believe in you and your writing and doesn't act as if he or she is doing you a favor.

Be cautious of the "agencies" who advertise in writing magazines and charge a fee for evaluating your manuscript. Both practices are frowned upon by established agents and editors. If you have to pay someone to help make your work saleable, it will probably never be saleable. It's an editor's job to help midwife a good manuscript into its best possible shape.

In sum, the answer to the question, do you need an agent? is no, you don't *need* one, though it would be useful to have one eventually. Once you have a book published by a recognized publisher, you will probably find agents are more receptive to your work. But by following the guidelines in this chapter for approaching a publisher and carefully reading through the chapter on contracts, you will know enough to represent and protect yourself adequately. Sure, you may not squeeze out that extra $1,000 in advances, but if your book sells, you will get it later anyway. Keep this in mind if you find the "small print" in Chapter 3 putting you to sleep.

# 2
# *How a Publisher Evaluates a Proposal or a Manuscript*

Your manuscript is both good and original; but the part that is good is not original, and the part that is original is not good.
                                                —Samuel Johnson

The procedure for reviewing and evaluating proposals and manuscripts differs considerably from house to house, as do the procedures for almost everything else in publishing.What follows is the "typical" procedure for the "average" publisher.

At most houses when a proposal or manuscript is first received it is numbered and logged in so that its arrival and location can be kept track of. At that point a short note or postcard may be sent to the author indicating the material has arrived and will be considered "shortly."

### *The First Reader*

For many trade houses the first step on the editorial ladder is an apprenticeship known as the first reader. The first reader's job is to go through the slush pile, reading the unsolicited proposals and manuscripts that arrive in order to separate the wheat from the chaff. Most of the submissions go immediately onto a rejection pile, either because they are poorly written or because they are obviously unsuitable for that house. For instance, that house never publishes cookbooks, mysteries, textbooks, or poetry. At some houses, particularly the larger ones, this initial review may be the sole or primary task of the first reader, who consequently deserves your sympathy—day in and day out he or she only reads proposals and manuscripts. At many houses the part-time first

33

readers are the secretaries, editorial assistants, or even mail room clerks, since first reader is one way of starting at the bottom of the editorial hierarchy. They may be attached to a particular editor, executive editor, or editor-in-chief, or they may not; whatever the house structure, it is often not the editor you write to who reads the manuscript or proposal first. Outside of trade and juvenile publishing—in textbook divisions, professional books, law, etc.—it is not the convention to have first readers; the editor usually goes through the slush pile personally.

The first reader may prepare a short memorandum, usually one page or less, which briefly describes the book, the market, the suitability for that house, as well as giving any other suggestion or information thought pertinent, and either recommends further consideration—advising the editor or another reader to look at it—or rejection.* If the reader is experienced and recommends a rejection, it may go no further than the out-box, though if it has been personally addressed to an editor or came in via an agent or some other "contact," the editor will usually at least read the covering letter and the outline, if not the sample. If the first reader's report is negative, the editor will either skim it and turn it back to the out-box or, more rarely, pass it on to another reader. Or perhaps something will catch his eye and he will read it carefully and decide the reader was mistaken in making a negative judgment.

Some houses circulate a weekly list of the manuscripts and proposals that have arrived in-house, so that any editor who may be interested in that topic (or author or agent) can request a photocopy of the proposal, though usually it must pass muster with the first reader before it gets on this list, if it is an unsolicited proposal.


## The Editor Bites

In any case, if the first reader recommends further consideration, then the editor will usually read the material carefully, deciding whether it is the kind of book that interests him, or whether it may perhaps be more suitable for a colleague who has a particular interest in that subject. The other considerations the editor keeps in mind while reading are: Is it well written, will it sell, is it suitable for the house, does he have enough time and does he want to spend it with this book (editors are usually at work on half a dozen or more manuscripts at any given time), is there sufficient material on which to make a decision, has the book commercial potential for subsidiary rights sales (especially paperback reprint and bookclub)? The income from these rights is often crucial for a trade house and may

---

*A sample reader's report is printed in the appendix.

mean the difference between profit and loss for the publisher, particularly when the overall list is considered. If the answers to most of these questions are positive, and the editor tentatively decides he is interested in going on to the next stage, he may—at some houses—photocopy the material and circulate it to one or more colleagues, both to enlist their support for the weekly editorial meeting (where the final decision is made), and to have the benefit of their opinions and advice: Perhaps they know that another house is already producing a similar book, or that a certain book club would probably take it, or that the author is ''difficult,'' or that the sales manager is dead-set against another cookbook for next year since they already have two under contract. More frequently now, people in marketing and promotion are consulted informally for their opinion at this stage, as well as later on at the editorial meeting; marketing input on acquisition decisions is a growing fact of life in publishing.

## *Editor's Checklist*

Most publishers have a form that editors must fill out for each book they wish to contract. It normally covers five basic areas of evaluation: marketing, costs, contractual, editorial, and price. This form can range from two to six pages, or it may just be a memo typed up by the editor. Whatever the name, size, or arrangement, it is an attempt thoroughly to analyze and estimate the potential costs and income for that book. In addition to these five areas, the editor will usually provide a fifty- to one hundred-word description of the book. This checklist, with or without the proposal, may be circulated to other editors, the editor-in-chief, the sales manager, the publicity director, and anyone else who either plays a role in the weekly editorial meeting or has a say in the determination of whether or not to sign up the book (at some houses the president must approve all new contracts).

**Marketing Evaluation.** This usually contains an analysis of the author's previous publications: date(s), title(s), number of copies sold and subsidiary rights sales, and any other marketing information provided by the author or secured from other sources (though most publishers are *very* reticent about releasing any kind of sales information). It estimates the prepublication sales, known as the salesmen's "advance,"* as well as the first year's sales, and sometimes the second and third, if it is the kind of book that will have a shelf life, for instance, a

---

*See Chapter 7 for a discussion of advance sales.

history of Canada. Many trade books have a shelf life of six months or so (although in the past few years some bookstores and chains are returning books as soon as two or three months after receiving them, if they are not "moving" from the shelves), while most successful texts, juveniles, reference, and technical books, have a life of three to five years. The sales estimate may project low, medium, and high figures. Subsidiary rights possibilities, particularly reprint and bookclub, are projected, as is the book's potential as a house quality paperback, provided the house has its own paperback line. Recommendations for advertising, publicity, and promotion may be suggested, both the type and budget, as well as any other pertinent marketing information, such as: The author would make a good appearance on radio or TV, the book should be brought out quickly because of its topicality or potential competition, the book is particularly suitable for mail-order sales, and so forth.

**Product Evaluation.** The chief element of this evaluation is an estimate of the costs involved in producing the first print run. Since the estimated typesetting and manufacturing costs, determination of print run, and list price are crucial and complicated factors, they deserve a separate section; let's hold off for those with a taste for figures until the end of this chapter.

The product evaluation also contains your estimate of the length of the manuscript as well as the editor's estimate of the number of printed pages, the suggested trim size of the book, and the special features, such as photos, maps, charts, index. Naturally, a complete manuscript permits a more accurate estimate of the final costs than a proposal. If there are to be any additional costs, such as permissions fees for extracts or complete units (for an anthology), translation fees, libel readings, index charge,* these will be listed. If the book is an import, usually from Great Britain, the cost of the books or the plates—actually negatives—the transportation costs, and individual unit-costs of each book will be calculated.

**Contractual and Editorial Evaluation.** Here the editor estimates how much of an advance and what royalty percentage may be needed to get the book. If there is an agent, the editor may already know how much is being asked, though of course this is negotiable. If he is dealing with the author directly, he may or may not have discussed terms, but until the editorial meeting and the determination to take on the book, all outside discussions are tentative. He may estimate that he can get the book for a $4,000 advance but suggest going to $7,500 if necessary, that is, if the

*In most cases, if you don't want to do the index yourself, a publisher will subcontract it to a free-lance expert, and deduct the cost from your first royalty check, or bill you for the cost.

author or agent holds out for more than is offered, or if the book is being considered at another publishing house and will have to be "bid" on. We will discuss this in greater detail in the next chapter.

Unusual features of the potential contract are listed, such as any deviation from standard contract terms, for example, the agent wants a 60/40 split on paperback reprint rights instead of the normal 50/50, or a British publisher might share the production costs, or the author will clear permissions for the anthology only for North America or the English language (cheaper than world rights). Anything the editor has learned about the author and his or her relations with other publishers and editors may be recounted here, since it's a small enough industry for information and gossip to be passed around either casually or sometimes upon request. Will there be any special problems in copyediting the manuscript, and approximately how much time will it take (scientific or mathematical symbols, for instance, are both more time-consuming to edit and more costly to typeset)? Finally, the competing books, if any, and the effect they could have on sales may be discussed. Here the editor may either rely on the author's discussion in his proposal and merely double-check the *Subject Guide to Books in Print,* or he may send an assistant to the library, or go personally, both to check the shelves and perhaps to scrutinize a few titles closely. He may call an authority in the relevant field and ask for advice or send that person the proposal or manuscript for a critique or a reading, which will not only compare the book to others in the field but will evaluate its general quality, coverage, etc. This is a very common procedure for textbooks, technical, reference, and scientific books, but is infrequent in trade publishing.

**Price Evaluation.** Based on the various costs, such as typesetting, paper, printing, binding, and the suggested number of copies for the first printing, a tentative list price for the book is given, which is calculated to recoup the publisher's investment after the sale of X number of copies, that is, after the "break-even" point, and earn a pretax profit on additional sales. The figures are broken down in various other ways: the book's potential contribution to the publisher's overhead (the "indirect costs"), the estimated gross income on the sale of the entire print run, etc. Other costs, such as royalties, are calculated to determine what may here loosely be called a profit-and-loss statement for that particular book.

Some of these estimates and calculations are, of course, based solely on an editor's past experience with other titles and hunch. Editors are handicappers, and a close examination of any editor's or publisher's list will show that they bat around .333 (if they are going to stay in business). Approximately one-third of their titles earn back more than they cost the publisher to secure, produce, and market. That helps explain why two-thirds of the authors you meet are disgruntled with their publishers.

The editor's checklist is, as you can see, a densely packed document, whose figures must add up properly *before* the book is formally presented to the house for consideration. No matter how exciting, delightful, and important the editor may think the book is, if the cost of producing your 900-page full-color illustrated study of the Ojibwa Indians means the house either has to price the book at $59.50 for a first printing of 5,000 copies or sell 35,000 copies at $14.95 just to break even, they probably won't do it. This is not to say that expensive books aren't often published and sometimes profitable, but rather that as the investment increases so does the publisher's sense of caution. His instincts about the first year's sales or ''guarantees'' (for example, a book club promise to take 5,000 copies) must be compatible with the realization that the bigger the wager, the better the odds must be. In the long run though, most publishing decisions are still gambles, and it's part of the excitement and anxiety that gives editors, salesmen, and publishers both a sense of adventure and an ulcer.

## The Editorial Meeting

Most houses hold a weekly or bimonthly editorial meeting in which, among other matters, the proposals or manuscripts that editors wish to sign up are evaluated, discussed, and then either rejected, held over, or approved. Provided your book has passed the first two hurdles, that is, the editor wants to sign it and the figures add up, it now faces its roughest critics. Attending this meeting may be: most of the editors and their superiors, the sales manager and his superior, the marketing manager, the subsidiary rights director, the publicity director, the managing editor, and perhaps even the art director, advertising manager, production director, and others; it varies from house to house. At some places the editors are *not* in attendance—only the upper echelon of executives casts ballots on the final decision.

Normally, most of the staff in attendance will have had a chance to look over the checklist and perhaps the proposal as well. As the editor has merely estimated one of the crucial figures, namely how many copies the book will sell in its first year, he may find that his own enthusiastic guess will be tempered by more sober or pessimistic predictions. Other questions are raised and other opinions may be aired with respect to the market, the audience, the competition, the subsidiary rights potential, the suitability of the book for the house, the cost and number of copies for the first print run, the amount of the advance to be paid, the list price, etc. As a consequence, some of the estimates the editor has made may be modified. Gradually, the drift of the discussion will move toward the pro or the con, and the final decision is usually a consensual one rather than a specific casting of votes, though it may come to that on occasion. The editor, of course, will defend his project. He has already convinced himself that the book should be signed, and may be able to sway less optimistic voices. Depending on his clout, that is, his age, experience, position in the hierarchy, and his track record, he may prevail in spite of a generally skeptical attitude toward the book; though of course he is sticking his neck out, and several failures with "unpopular" projects will tarnish his clout.

It is possible for a final decision to be withheld at this meeting, to be put off until certain questions are answered or certain options explored. Is it true, for instance, that Random House is already planning to bring out a book on games for pocket calculators on their spring list? Isn't there a book on the history of Indonesia that a British publisher has already promised us a first look at? Isn't that the same author who signed several contracts with some other publishers, yet never delivered the manuscripts? Perhaps we should wait to see a few more chapters before signing the book? Maybe we should get a reading from an expert in that field? Let's check out the bookclub or paperback reprint possibilities before we commit ourselves (either because the author or agent is asking for a high advance and the publisher wants to hedge his bet, or the book is very expensive to produce and only the assurance of a subsidiary rights sale can guarantee the recouping of the costs). These are just a few of the questions which may put your proposal on hold until satisfactory answers are found.

Presuming that there are no unanswered questions, however, a decision will be reached, though occasionally with some qualifications: We will only pay so much for an advance, the book will have to be shorter or longer, the maximum number of illustrations will have to be cut in half, etc. If the decision is a positive one, the editor will call or write to you and say those magic words, "We want to do the book." If the decision is negative, the editor will often let you know why, in contrast to the vague rejection you may receive if the book never got past the first reader.

The editorial meeting is by no means the sole method of arriving at a decision to sign up a book. In smaller houses with only a single editor or two the decision may be reached merely on the basis of a discussion between the editor and the editor-in-chief, who will, nevertheless, have reviewed the proposal and checklist. In other divisions, such as for textbooks, the custom is to send the material up the ladder, getting approval or not from the executives occupying higher rungs. The same would be true for most specialty types of publishing. In some houses, an executive such as the editor-in-chief, or even the vice-president, continues to keep his hand in by signing and editing a few books a year (somewhere between twelve and twenty is considered a normal load for an editor). Such executives usually sign up books of authors they have previously worked with or books for which the major question may not be whether to sign, but how much of an advance they are willing to pay. Their projects may not require the editorial meeting hurdle. Editors who specialize in certain types of books, such as mysteries or women's studies, or who edit series, such as travel books or ethnographies, may only have to get an O.K. from their superior. And again, some editors with clout or special arrangements may have virtual *carte blanche,* though in almost every case a superior must approve the advance if not the book. Don't forget a commitment to publish a book means a production investment of from $8,000 (which would just about pay for a pamphlet nowadays) to $50,000; and this figure does not take into account advances which can escalate to $250,000 for a ''hot'' project or author (Richard Nixon is purported to have received a $2 million guarantee for his memoirs).

There are some companies whose evaluation procedures do not fit into this bell curve. At one end of the scale is a major publisher whose decisions seem to be made rather capriciously. I will call the editor and explain the project over the phone to him in about two minutes. If he likes it, he tells me he will ''try it out'' at the editorial meeting. Tuesday afternoon, after the editorial meeting, he calls me and says, ''They love it; we'll take it. How much do you want?'' I send him the proposal then, and two weeks later I have a contract on my desk (not that he always operates that way). Mind you, the phone call is not for Norman Mailer's next novel, but for a midwestern professor's Marxist attack on the institution of marriage. Small and privately owned publishing houses still make snap judgments on occasion, but they make them less often now.

At the other extreme, sometimes the result of conglomerate takeovers, is the requirement of a five-year profit-and-loss statement, a complex and elaborate projection and analysis of the costs and sales over a five-year period, breaking down the figures so that each and every variable—even the six dollars for copyright—is worked over in a number of ways. This mountain of bureaucratic paperwork seems to soothe the corporate beast, as if the piles of papers themselves will insure the success of the project.

Finally, there are those deals concluded over lunches or on the telephone with an author or agent, in which the project seems so obviously a winner and the author's track record is so successful that any subsequent evaluation by the house is merely *pro forma*—that book is going to be signed.

Almost any financial commitment above the average, whether in production costs or advances, will almost certainly require the president's approval. One expensive failure can rock the foundation of a moderate-sized company; equally, one huge success can put a small company on the map, as B. Kliban's *CAT* (1975) did for Workman Publishing Company. The stakes are high in publishing, so most decisions are not made on impulse.

As you will have concluded by now, the decision to contract or reject a book is not a simple one, nor does it usually hinge on an individual editor's tastes or whims. It normally depends on a number of factors and a variety of people, so that when and if your book is rejected, you ought not to jump to hasty conclusions—especially since you may never have even considered some of the factors weighed—nor should you be overly discouraged. Your next submission, even if it is your fifteenth for that particular project, may result in a contract.

For those of you that have a taste for figures, the following section will analyze in greater detail the mathematics that publishers use to decide on their list price and print runs (first printings). Since these decisions are tentatively made during the period in which your proposal is being considered, this is as appropriate a place as any to discuss this process, even though it will go through a more complex and careful refinement when your completed manuscript arrives in house.

## Cost Estimates, Print Runs, and Pricing

From a publisher's point of view, there are three vital factors in the creation of a book over which he has a measure of control: the production costs, the number of copies on the first print run, and the list price. As the sales of most books do not warrant a second printing, the ideal juggling of these three variables is often the difference between profit and loss, so that the final decisions are made only after considerable caucusing and refinement of earlier estimates. The two basic stages at which these calculations are usually made are: before the editor presents the book for approval, and after the final manuscript is delivered. Two subsequent events can change the print run decision and sometimes even the price. The first is a subsidiary rights sale of folded and gathered sheets or bound copies to a book club or to a British or Canadian publisher, both of which are attempted before the book is "put on press." The second is a determination at the end of a sales conference (or even after the salesmen have made their first round of calls) that the original estimate of how many copies can be sold in the first six months or a year was too low or too high. So long as the plates are not yet on the press—and this usually doesn't occur until at least six months after your manuscript has been delivered—the number of copies to be run off can be increased or decreased.

**Plant and Manufacturing Costs.** A cost estimate is determined on the basis of two major expenses: the plant and manufacturing costs. Plant costs generally include the typography (normally called composition), the negatives and the plates, the jacket art and plates, any preparation and plate costs for illustrations, and for many publishers, the cost of copy-editing and proofreading, which is sometimes assigned to each book on the basis of hourly rates. Naturally the editorial charges are very rough estimates if they are made on the basis of your proposal, since the manuscript (and the editorial problems it may entail) is often a year or more away from delivery. The plant costs are a one-time charge, that is, regardless of whether the publisher decides to print ten or fifty thousand copies, or has to go back for ten successive reprintings, the plant costs are a single charge, and they only have to be written off one time.

The manufacturing costs, primarily the paper, printing, and binding costs of the text, the cases, and covers, are costs reincurred for each successive reprinting. Hence, any calculations of the "unit-cost"—the cost of a single book—for the first printing means adding the plant and manufacturing costs together and dividing by the number of copies to be run off on the first printing. On the other hand, a second printing unit-cost can be roughly calculated by dividing only the manufacturing costs by the number of copies reprinted. It is apparent, then, that the publisher's total costs for the second and successive printings are reduced, and not only does his profit increase, but this accounts in part for the normal escalation of royalty percentages for the author (typically 10 percent of list price for the first 5,000 copies, 12½ percent for the next 5,000 copies, and 15 percent thereafter). On the other hand, the cost of paper has been increasing so rapidly in the last few years that a delayed second printing can cost almost as much as the first printing, even though there are no plant costs.

In order to arrive at a preliminary estimate of the plant and manufacturing costs, the editor must supply the production department—whose job it is to make these calculations—with the following information: the approximate number of words in the final manuscript, the approximate amount of artwork, the suggested trim size (the actual length and width of the printed page), and the ideal number of printed pages. This latter number may seem immutably linked to the number of words, but there is some flexibility because of the possible variation in the size of the printed page, the size of the type used, and the amount of margin on the final printed page. The editor usually does not suggest details for other variables which influence the costs, such as: the quality and thickness of the paper, the cases, the jacket, the method of printing, the manner in which the signatures are bound together—sewn or glued—and several other minor details. These are normally left up to the designer and the production manager, who are working within certain parameters of their own, for instance, the house prefers certain trim sizes, designs, qualities of paper, and so forth.

But the crucial figure in determining costs is how many copies to print. For this number, the editor has both a guideline and some leeway. The guideline is that the "normal" first printing of an average book for that house is 5,000, 6,000, or 7,500 copies, and the leeway is that he can request a cost estimate for all three figures to see how they add up.

*Normal* is a rather elusive term here. On any trade publisher's spring or fall list, well over 50 percent of the books are expected to have a modest to moderate sale. For this category of books, most trade publishers will have a first printing minimum of 5,000 copies and a maximum of 10,000. Less than the minimum will make the publisher's cost per unit too high for a "reasonable" list price, and more than the maximum may be too optimistic and leave him with thousands of copies in the warehouse which will have to be remaindered at a fraction of their cost. So if we were to pick an "average" first printing for an "average" trade clothbound book, it would be 6,000 copies. For the sake of discussion, let's work with that figure, keeping in mind that first print runs can range from roughly 2,000 copies (for reference, technical, university press, and other specialized books) to 25,000 or more for books the publisher believes are going to "take off." (Mass market paperback first printings normally range from 50,000 to 150,000 copies, sometimes escalating to over a million for anticipated best sellers.)

The editor, then, supplies the production manager with those figures and suggestions and from a day to a week later receives what is often called a "preliminary cost estimate." This gives the estimated costs for plant and manufacturing, broken down into the individual costs of each item, such as for typography, plates, covers, and so forth, as well as the individual unit-cost for both plant charges and manufacturing charges for each single book.

Let's take an average trade book that contains, all told, approximately 75,000 words and will print to 212 pages. The plant cost will run to approximately $4,000, and the manufacturing cost for a first printing of 6,000 copies will be in the neighborhood of $6,000. The unit-cost for plant is thus $.67 per copy, and the unit manufacturing cost is $1.00 per copy—I just divided the 6,000 into each charge. The total unit-cost then of manufacturing and plant is $1.67. With this figure the editor can now extrapolate further.

**The List Price.** Publishers normally determine the list price of a book on the "cost of sales," that is, the direct costs of plant, manufacturing, and royalties. But in order to figure in the cost of royalties, you need a list price to take 10 percent of, which places the editor in a cart-before-the-horse situation. Even though the author will be paid an advance against royalties—let's say $4,000 on this book—it is the actual royalty percentage on 6,000 copies that is used for determining cost of sales. Since this average book will disperse approximately 300 copies for publicity, reviews, promotion, good will, and author's copies, we will calculate the royalties on 5,700 copies. (For textbook publishers free "examination" copies are a major expense in advertising and publicity, and may be figured in as a cost of sales.) To get this figure the editor will try out a list price that seems reasonable, based on the plant and manufacturing costs, to see how it adds up. Let's say he assigns a tentative $9.95 list price. The royalties add up to $5,843 based on 10 percent of list for the first 5,000 copies, and 12½ percent for the next 700 copies. This gives him an average unit-cost of $1.02 for royalties for each book. Thus, the unit-cost of sales is:

| | |
|---|---|
| Plant | .666 |
| Manufacturing | 1.00 |
| Royalty | 1.025 |
| Total | $2.691 |

That is, $2.69 per copy.

As a rule of thumb, most publishers use a formula that tells them to multiply this unit-cost by four, five, or six to arrive at a list price (that we have, in fact, tentatively calculated) that will not only pay for the direct cost and help contribute to his overhead, but will also earn for the publisher a pretax profit of roughly 15 percent, provided he actually sells most of that first printing. This formula has been partly derived by figuring out on a yearly basis the average total costs of his other expenses, namely the "indirect costs," and apportioning them amongst the books he publishes in any single year. These indirect or "operating" costs consist of the publisher's normal expenses: salaries, promotion, publicity, advertising, travel and entertainment, salesmen's commissions, order processing, shipping, warehousing, and general and administrative expenses—rent and so forth—but let's not belabor the bookkeeping. Suffice to say that in addition to the cost of sales of each book, the publisher must somehow figure in his operating expenses, and this is normally compensated for by using the formula approach. Thus our average book, with the $2.69 unit-cost of sales, and the tentative list price of $9.95, is about four times the unit-cost.

From these figures the editor can now deduce a number of other figures that he needs in order to complete his product evaluation on his checklist and to see whether the figures add up.

It will be easier to visualize if we lay it out in the form of a chart, but first a word about discounts. Discounts are what publishers give to booksellers, and the average discount for a trade publisher is 47 percent, that is, the publisher only averages a net receipt of 53 percent of the list price of each book he sells (the details of marketing will be examined in Chapter 7). For our book then, which tentatively lists for $9.95, the publisher will only receive $5.27 per copy.

FIGURE 1

*Prepublication Estimate of Profit and Loss*

| | | | Per Copy |
|---|---|---|---|
| Total Copies Printed | 6,000 | | |
| Total Copies Sold | | 5,700 | |
| Retail Price | $9.95 | | |
| Revenue per Copy at 47% discount | | $    5.27 | |
| Total Gross Revenue | | $30,039.00 | |
| | | | Per Copy |
| Plant Costs | | $ 4.000.00 | $ .666 |
| Paper, Printing & Binding | | $ 6.000.00 | $1.00 |
| Royalty | | $ 5,843.00 | $1.025 |
| Total Cost of Sales | | $15,843.00 | $2.691 |
| Break-even Copies | 3,006 | | |
| Gross Margin | | $14,196.00 | |
| Operating Expenses | | | |
| (roughly 45% of gross revenue) | | $13,517.00 | |
| Net Profit (before taxes) | | $    679.00 | |

Notice one additional new term on our chart, the *gross margin* which is, as you can see, the amount left over by subtracting the total cost of sales from the total gross revenue. Does it look pretty good? The publisher has to sell only 3,006 copies—only about half of his first printing—to break even. Even after allocating operating expenses there is still a small profit of over $675, if he sells 5,700 copies. Let's consider some problems. We haven't figured in returns (books returned for credit to the publisher by bookstores that have been unable to sell them), which average 15 to 20 percent throughout the industry. Even if we calculated the returns at 15 percent, that would force us to subtract over $4,500 from the gross revenue, giving us a net loss of over $3,500. Then, as we pointed out before, probably no more than a third of a publisher's list earns a profit, so it's a good guess that they will not sell out their first printing. What's the solution to this cul-de-sac?

First of all, the editor can increase his list price to $10.95; remember, he's sitting at his desk preparing a *preliminary* estimate and trying to make the figures add up—with the help of a pocket calculator probably—so he's free to change the list price. That will add an additional $3,021 to his gross revenue and put him almost back in the black. Also, we have not considered the subsidiary rights, particularly paperback reprint and bookclub sales.* Any kind of sale there is gravy and will immediately boost the potential income, but this contribution will not manifest itself until much later in the game, after the book has been set in galleys, so he can't fall back on it at this preliminary stage.

The solution, if you want to call it that, is this: While less than half of the publisher's list pays for itself, a certain percentage of titles will go back for reprinting and earn much more than a 15 percent pretax profit. Don't forget that on a reprinting of, say, 5,000 copies, the publisher pays only the royalty and the manufacturing costs on each copy; the plant costs have already been written off on the first printing. For our book, this would mean his unit-cost on the next 5,000 copies is about $2.02, though in reality the escalating royalty and the mounting cost of paper will increase his cost by at least 15 percent. Also, subsidiary rights income averages about 10 to 20 percent of net revenue overall for many trade publishers, and can add up to a crucial amount in the profit-and-loss columns. Most trade publishers are in the black only because of that extra 10 to 20 percent; without it, many would go under. Lastly, a certain number of books on the list become "back list titles," that is, continue to sell, even at a modest rate, for a number of years and earn their investment back more slowly, perhaps in two to three years.

But the reality is that in spite of the estimating that the editor does—and he must of necessity juggle the figures somewhat so that each book appears as if it will make a profit—he knows, and so does the rest of the staff, that fewer than half of the books are going to pay the way for the bulk of them, and he often does not know in advance which are which.

The kind of bookkeeping that is hypothesized here varies from company to company in so many different ways that it isn't useful mentioning some of the alternatives. Also, I have simplified some of the statistics and calculations—there's only so much a writer wishes to know about the figures. But in the main the above is a generally accurate portrait of

---

*A bookclub sale may, paradoxically, cause the publisher to boost the list price, since book clubs want a significantly lower discounted price for their members, which is most profitably achieved by raising the publisher's list price.

the figures, methods, and madness that go into determining the cost estimate, print run, and list price. Between the preliminary estimate the editor prepares for his checklist, which will be a major determinant in the decision to reject or approve the proposal, and the final list price and print run, many a minor change will be made. The cost of paper has been increasing at such a rapid rate that the manufacturing costs a year later will probably be higher, or the author's first novel may have caught on and a readership now exists so that the first printing for his new novel is upped to 12,500. In fact, however, the trend is now toward smaller print runs. Due to a recent I.R.S. decision which may prohibit publishers from writing off a percentage of their warehouse inventory, some publishers are now printing for as little as ninety days at a time. The result is a higher unit cost, a higher list price, and, ultimately, fewer sales.

Once the manuscript is delivered, all these figures, except the guess about how many copies will sell, can be refined so that the actual costs can be calculated, and the decision about the list price can be reviewed and changed, if need be. The importance of the decision of the first print run cannot be overestimated. The difference between 6,000 and 7,500 copies is often the difference between profit and loss (with 1,500 copies sitting in the warehouse as proof), and many an editor, editor-in-chief, and sales manager has learned to temper his optimism the hard way; there is always the temptation to print more copies, since the unit-costs go down as the print order goes up. But the real pro's are usually conservative; it's better to go back for a reprinting than to chance getting stuck with an over-printing. It's still guesswork, though, and there is no way in publishing to avoid this gamble.

Outside of trade publishing, that is, for textbooks, technical and scientific books, and juveniles, there are certain variables and factors that change some of the ground rules; for example, lower discounts (textbooks normally sell to bookstores at a 20 percent discount), lower first-print-run quantities (professional books may have a first print run of 2,000 to 3,000 copies), or a longer shelf life (juveniles are expected to sell over a number of years). Thus the figuring may be different in certain dimensions, but editors are still stuck with some of the same perennial gambles: How many should we print, and how many can we sell?

Many authors complain about the high list price of their book, often accusing the publisher—after the fact—of having priced their book off the market. Normally this just isn't so. Very careful planning supports some of these hunches, and the decisions are usually arrived at by a putting together of experienced heads: the editor, the editor-in-chief, the sales manager, and maybe others. Most publishers do, on occasion, consider "how much the market can bear" in figuring their list price, and the accusation that they are ripping off the public with outrageous

# 3

# *How to Understand and Negotiate a Book Contract*

Writing is the only profession where no one considers you
ridiculous if you earn no money.

—Jules Renard

Most authors, surprisingly enough, pay very little attention to their book
contracts. Having discussed an advance and a royalty with the editor
involved—which often means that the editor has told the author what the
terms are going to be—the author is normally content to sign the contract
after a perfunctory glance to see that his or her name is properly spelled.
Even considering the legalese in many contracts, this indifference does
not seem reasonable, and a casual attitude at this point can result in more
than the loss of money from sources obscure to most writers. There are
legal and long-term ramifications to many clauses, some with a potential
for causing headaches or grief. What may appear to be a minor issue now
may turn out to be a major one later. A writer who can spend from one to
five years finishing a manuscript can certainly spare a few hours to
scrutinize a contract—and then try to negotiate it to his or her best
advantage.

By and large, most publishers are not out to take advantage of your
naïveté, but they are running a business for profit, in addition to their
other motives, and your goods and services are the source of their profits.
As a "partner" in this phase of the business, you will get a fairer share of
these profits by making an effort to understand what the terms of the
proffered contract mean, and by attempting to negotiate some of those
provisions which are modifiable, since virtually all "standard" publishing contracts heavily favor the publisher.*

---

*Both the Society of Authors' Representatives and the Authors Guild issue recommended
contracts, but only one publisher I know of has adopted either on a regular basis, and agents can
substitute them for the publisher's contract only on infrequent occasions.

Just as horsetrading is one of an agent's skills, so do many editors develop this knack by virtue of the same capitalist commandment that governs any other business: Buy cheap and sell dear. As conglomerates continue to acquire publishing houses, this commandment's alter ego, "let's look at the bottom line," is taking precedence over any earlier publishing canons. The moral is that as the publisher is no longer a patron, the author is constrained to look after his own interests.

But in one chapter it would not be possible either to analyze a sample contract thoroughly or to make detailed recommendations for all the differing contingencies, clauses, and provisions that are found in the bewildering variety of publishing contracts in use today. I also realize that most authors have neither the will nor the desire to nitpick over every detail and that most professional writers expect an agent to provide this service. Therefore, I will only survey and interpret the most common and vital provisions in a contract.

I must stress that this chapter is a superficial view and interpretation of a contract. The Authors Guild 28,000-word pamphlet—available to members only—"Your Book Contract," finds more gopher holes in the average contract than are found in all of Kansas, and even their analysis is far from complete. While the S.A.R. and the A.G. are making inroads in changing conventions and "standard" clauses so that authors can more equitably share in the income from their books, almost every contract still contains so many covert twists and implications in it that a book would be needed to explicate the contract, analyze the pitfalls, and suggest the changes to request. Even if such a book existed, the un-agented author would be unable to take advantage of it: Unless you are a very successful author, or unless your book is virtually guaranteed to make it big, the publisher is sitting in the catbird seat and will not agree to the ideal contract, such as the one issued by the S.A.R. The only partial remedy is to write and publish a book and then join the Authors Guild and get an agent.

If an editor has been successful in getting your proposal or manuscript approved by the editorial board, you will receive a phone call, or sometimes a letter, in which you are not only told the good news, but are extended an offer. Since editors assume, and rightly so, that authors are generally innocent about contracts and terms, the offer will consist of an advance against royalties and a mumbled reference to "our standard royalties." An advance is a payment made, usually prior to publication, which has to be earned back by the sale of copies of your book before any additional royalty payments are made. As an example, if the royalty rate is 10 percent of the list price of the book—for convenience's sake, let's price it at $10.00—then the author will receive $1.00 for every copy sold. If the advance is $4,000, then the book has to sell more than 4,000 copies before earning additional money for its author. However, if the book sells less than 4,000 copies, the author does not have to repay the difference to the publisher; it's for keeps, provided the contract describes the advance as "guaranteed," "non-returnable" or "not repayable to the publisher," or unless the author defaults by not delivering the manuscript on time or breaks the contract in some other way. Most contracts make such a guarantee, and you should insist on this assurance.

As pleased as you may be by this phone call, you do not want indelibly to commit yourself to those terms or the unseen contract; you can express your delight and still ask for a chance to think it over. Meanwhile, you also want to ask for a blank copy of the contract or a rough draft with the terms pencilled in, and the opportunity to examine it at leisure. Don't accept any excuses, you have a perfect right to look it over. Negotiating a contract once it has already been signed or passed through executive hands is a much more awkward task, and an author is inclined to go along with it rather than request changes.

In the appendix you will find a representative contract printed in its entirety. Since some of the clauses are negligible or self-explanatory, I have omitted a discussion of them here. On the other hand, I have added some clauses here that do not appear in the contract in the appendix, since they are common enough possibly to appear in your contract. Though most contracts identify each clause by an abbreviated caption in the left-hand margin, they do not necessarily conform from house to house either in their order of presentation or in their designation; nor does my order here conform to the order of the clauses in the contract in the appendix. Nevertheless, you should have no trouble identifying each corresponding clause by comparing it with your own contract.

The least complicated contract that I have seen contained about fifteen clauses; the prize for long-windedness goes to a major publisher with a 108-clause contract. The last clause reads: "Captions or marginal notes, and the table of contents of this agreement are for convenience only, and are not to be deemed part of this agreement." Amen.

The contract we are using for a guide is a representative one; it contains the basic and vital elements found in virtually all trade contracts. However, bear in mind that it is a *trade* contract; there are a few elementary differences in contracts for textbooks, juveniles, professional books, and mass market paperbacks, which we will discuss later in this chapter.

If you read this chapter carefully, you may know as much about contracts, if not more, than many editors. Lawyers and agents pore over these documents, but some editors are surprisingly unacquainted with even their own firm's contract. One consequence may be that an author will come to an agreement with an editor over the phone and then find that the document does not seem to fulfill the verbal agreement, albeit for harmless reasons—perhaps the editor did not understand your request. Obviously, you can return the contract and request the changes. But to prevent this kind of misunderstanding, you, the author—once you have scrutinized the contract and noted the changes you want—should write a letter to your editor detailing your requests and asking the editor to call once he has assimilated them. This will give the editor a chance to consult his superior or the appropriate executive(s), who may approve or reject your demands. Most decisions in publishing, as I have already pointed out, are not made autonomously. Remember that the contract is legally binding, whereas verbal assurances are not. If you consider any demand vital to the success of your book, such as placement of a mail order ad in a journal of mycology for your book on mushrooms of the southwest, get it in writing, either as a clause in the contract or in a letter from your editor. So much time elapses between signing up a book and its appearance, and so many editors play musical chairs in publishing, that an author should not rely on a verbal assurance, however sincere the intentions of the editor.

Remember also that you are *negotiating* a contract. Be prepared to compromise, as you may not have all your requests honored. If you feel that you do not want to budge on a certain demand, such as the size of an advance, you are free to go elsewhere and try your luck. I submitted this book (actually a proposal and sample chapters) to a house that offered me a $2,000 advance; I explained that $4,500 was closer to the figure I had in mind. The house offered no compromise; I went to another publisher. On the other hand, be wary of an editor who insists that his house's standard contract permits no deviation, and rejects all your demands. It just isn't so. If a publisher wants a book, he should and usually will compromise—up to a point, anyway. If he won't, *caveat vendor*.

For certain clauses, especially those that relate specifically to finances, there are conventional boundaries on either side of which you or the editor are over the line. For instance, on an unagented book the author/publisher split for foreign translation rights generally ranges from 50/50 to 90/10 (you get the 90). Some provisions are stickier, such as the size of an advance. The boundaries are hazy, so how does an author decide what his book is worth? After we examine the clauses, I will suggest some guidelines for these stickier provisions, but do not expect definitive advice, as it's still a horse-trader's game. It is a good idea to keep a sense of proportion in coming to an agreement with a publisher. At most, 1,500 writers in the United States earn their living from writing books and articles; the rest of us, say 20,000, enjoy the supplementary income, but are unlikely to join the ranks of full-time professionals and try not to fantasize too much about striking it rich in print. If you write a best seller, or even a "successful" book, you will have no trouble getting yourself an agent for the next one who will negotiate a stiffer contract for you. The time and effort it normally takes to get an offer from a publisher usually discourages a writer from shopping around for a better deal. My suggestions in this chapter notwithstanding, to some extent you are still faced with playing it by ear. If the offer seems fair, and compromises are made, you should accept it.

## Conventional Publishing Contract Features

**Grant of Rights.** Virtually all contracts begin with this clause, which delineates the territory in which your publisher has the exclusive right to publish, sell, and license rights for the book (commonly referred to in contracts as "the work"). The primary territory for a book publisher in this country consists of the United States, its possessions—the Virgin Islands, Guam, etc.—the Philippines, and Canada. The secondary territories are the British Commonwealth—the British Isles, Australia, New Zealand, etc.*—and other foreign countries in which the book may be translated. Traditionally either your agent or the subsidiary rights department of your publisher licenses other publishers in these secondary territories to produce and market the work in their own countries, though this clause also grants your publisher the *nonexclusive* right to sell the English-language edition throughout the world, except for the British Commonwealth. In other words, your U.S. publisher and his British licensee may compete for sales in, say, Denmark. Later in the contract a major clause spells out the disposition and revenue share of these secondary territorial rights, along with other subsidiary rights. Sometimes this first clause grants "world rights" to the publisher but will (or should) specify the author's share of revenue from the secondary territories in a later clause.

If you do not have an agent, the publisher will retain world rights, and—in essence acting as your agent—will attempt to sell or license these other rights.

**Copyright.** Most authors will ask that the work be copyrighted in their own name rather than in the name of the publisher, and publishers generally grant the request. Though having the copyright in your name does not give you ideal protection of your rights, as you are either

---

*A recent court decision has split this up-to-now automatic division of the English-language market, which was said to be monopolistic.

licensing, giving, or selling them depending on the wording of your contract and what subsidiary rights are sold, it is a modicum of protection, and you should insist on it. Otherwise the contract should specify that the copyright is held in trust for the author and will be reconveyed upon request. It is most important to retain copyright or have it assigned upon publication if you publish an article, short story, or poem in a magazine. I will discuss the whys and wherefores in the last chapter.

This clause should also oblige the publisher to register the U.S. copyright and to see to it that copyright is registered in other countries where the book is licensed, sold, or translated. It obliges you to cooperate with the publisher in securing or signing any documents required to keep the copyright in force.

Incidentally, many authors display an irrational or excessive concern for protecting their unpublished work against plagiarization or piracy. While an idea or even an outline for a book may have dubious legal protection, a partial or complete manuscript is virtually safe by reason of "common-law copyright," which now asserts that all unpublished writings are protected from the moment of execution until fifty years after the author's death. There is no need or value to putting *copyright* on any page of the manuscript as some authors do.

**Manuscript.** This clause estimates the approximate number of words your final manuscript will contain, the number of copies you are required to deliver to the publisher—usually the original plus one copy—and the due date of your manuscript. A key phrase in this clause is "delivered in final form and content acceptable to the publisher." Almost every contract contains that phrase or words to that effect, and they are much more important than they seem. They give the editor or the publisher the right to reject the manuscript if for one reason or another it is deemed unacceptable. If you receive a contract on the basis of a complete manuscript, this won't apply unless you really botch up a suggested revision—the publisher knows what he is getting. But if the contract is issued on the basis of an outline or an outline plus sample chapters, and the editor decides that the execution of the project is severely wanting and beyond redemption (he doesn't think a revision can cure the problem or the requested revision is inadequate), then the publisher is customarily entitled to cancel the contract. If the issue is clear-cut, for instance, the final manuscript does not adequately coincide with the outline, the author is not in a strong position to argue with the publisher's decision or to sue. But rarely is the issue clear-cut. More frequently the reasons given are: poorly written, insufficient exploration of the topic, outmoded data, etc. These reasons are sometimes open to question, and a reasonable editor will listen to your arguments, or may suggest that an unbiased expert(s) read the manuscript and submit a report on it, or the publisher may do this before notifying you of his own dissatisfaction. (Reader's reports are conventional in textbook publishing whether or not there are problems with the manuscript.) Sometimes the publisher's rejection of the manuscript on the basis of quality masks more cogent "commercial" reasons, which are not generally valid legally: The market has changed, a competing book appears, the book is no longer timely, etc. Nevertheless, these can be persuasive reasons for reconsideration on *your* part.

Invoking the "acceptable manuscript" clause is an uncommon event, but it happens often enough to consider it here. If it happens, what recourse do you have? Authors have gone to arbitration or sued publishers over this issue. A number of years ago a major publisher contracted for what he knew would be a favorable biography of Richard Nixon and forked over an $83,000 advance on signing, with two additional equal payments respectively due on delivery of a partial and then completed manuscript. When the Watergate scandal arose, and with it Mr. Nixon's reputation declined, the author contended that the publisher's rejection of the partial manuscript on the basis of "quality" was actually disguising more commercial considerations. A financial compromise was reached between the author and publisher out of court, and the book was later published by another firm.

As of now, there is no definitive legal ruling in cases like this, and they are either settled out of court, through arbitration, or in a suit, though the author is usually left holding the bag. If you feel that the publisher's arguments are flimsy or capricious, hiring a lawyer and attempting to pressure the publisher to publish the book may succeed, but most authors feel that if a publisher does not want their book, he will treat it as an orphan (and he will), so that it falls "stillbourne, as it were, from the press," as David Hume reported of his first *Treatise*. If you feel the publisher is wrong but sincere, try to persuade him with your own arguments, and suggest outside readers. If this fails and you still believe the book is sound, you are going to have to go out and find another publisher (best to keep the brouhaha to yourself) or sue or both.

Conventionally, the publisher will insist on repayment of any money advanced only if and when you sell the book to another publisher. If he demands it immediately, write and inform him that you will repay the advance when you place the book with another house. If this doesn't work and you receive a letter that sounds like it means business, get a lawyer. Common publishing practice is on your side, and the publisher knows it, even though the outcome will depend on a legal interpretation of the contract.

But as I said, this is an uncommon event. If the publisher decides to cancel the contract for reasons independent of your book, such as changing the direction of his list, a general cutback in titles, or cancelling a whole series, you are not legally obliged to return the advance, and in fact are justified in demanding or suing for the balance of any advance due.

On the other hand, late delivery is a much more common problem, and publishers have become increasingly rigorous over this breach of contract, especially if the author has received a sizeable advance. I estimate that 50 to 75 percent of the manuscripts an editor signs up are delivered anywhere from two months to a year and a half late, while approximately 10 percent are complete no-shows. Up to about 1970, publishers were more casual and tolerant of late delivery, but they have since begun to take a harder line, meaning that they can and sometimes will cancel a contract if the author is more than, say, three months late, particularly if the topic is faddish (and the competition is mounting) or timely. Editors are quite conscious that writers have blocks and other problems that delay a book, so they are accustomed to granting extensions. If you think you will exceed the delivery date, you should write for an extension at least two to three months beforehand; do not wait until the last minute. Also, it is best not to accept a verbal grant of an extension; politely request it in writing. The kind of letter that shows evidence of the author's progress and provides legitimate reasons for being late will find a more sympathetic ear. Since the majority of manuscripts *are* late, a publisher is not on firm legal ground if he cancels your manuscript a week after it is due. While there is no definite legal ruling on this point, you are entitled to a reasonable amount of time within which to deliver (say two to four months). Some contracts further stipulate that "time is of the essence," in which case your right to a reasonable extension is more tenuous. Without a written extension, you are on shaky grounds after three months, even though you may not be called on it. A second extension is sometimes given on request, but any author passing this extension has put himself out on a limb and is subject to the mercy of the publisher. Incidentally, the house has the right to demand repayment of any advance if the contract is cancelled for lateness or nondelivery.

**Author's Guarantee (Warranty and Indemnity Clause).** In this clause you guarantee the publisher that you have the right to sell him the book: The contents are written by you (not plagiarized), and none of the material is used without permission if owned, copyrighted, or controlled by someone else or some other publisher. That is, for instance, if you are quoting original source material such as tapes, diaries, letters, or what have you for a biography, you will have to secure written permission to use each item from either the author or the author's estate. It also implies that you cannot sell the same book to another publisher (don't think it hasn't been done). It further warranties that the book contains "no scandalous, libelous or unlawful matter," and indemnifies the publisher against any suits arising from this contingency. This last provision is one of the most unfair and unreasonable items in a publishing contract.

The author is here certifying that in the event of a claim or lawsuit brought against either the author or the publisher, the author must bear the full brunt of any payment of money that such a defense involves, which may include attorneys' fees, court costs, and any amount from a sustained judgment. Even if the claim or suit is not upheld in court, the author may still be liable for payment for costs up to that point. Some contracts modify this clause to splitting expenses, and a few hold the author financially responsible only if the claim is upheld or the judgment sustained. But with most publishers one must call it a pernicious clause, if only for the following two reasons: Most authors could be financially ruined for years if they lost a suit and had to pay heavy damages, whereas most publishers could write the amount off as a business loss. Also, publishers not only retain their own literary lawyers who are supposed to know what is libelous, slanderous, or unlawful, but they are also supposed to try to nip it in the bud by reading the manuscript before publishing it, that is, by authorizing a "libel reading" if the author or editor has any doubts about the material. Furthermore, many publishers carry "errors and omissions" insurance to protect them against expensive suits but fail to include the author under the umbrella. Both the Authors Guild and the Society of Authors' Representatives have tried and are continuing to try to change or modify this antiquated albatross, but it still remains in most contracts.

The only preventative is to familiarize yourself with what constitutes libel, slander, and unlawful matter, and if you have any doubts at all about the work, I would suggest you have a lawyer examine this clause and advise you on what changes you should *ask* for and what changes you might want to *insist* on. Unfortunately, interpretations of libel, slander, and unlawful matter are so ambiguous that often it is only in a specific case that there is a decision on what they in fact mean. At the least, if you have doubts, insist that your publisher authorize a libel reading when the manuscript is finished, a not unconventional chore that he is likely to undertake anyway if *he* has any doubts. It probably would not hurt to get an outside libel reading from a lawyer on your own. You might also try to negotiate this clause to state that the publisher will at least share equally in the defense and costs of any claim or suit, if it doesn't already read that way, and that your warranty is limited to the future earnings for that book. As a last resort, you can purchase libel insurance, which is now available to authors from several insurance companies.

**Copyrighted Material.** The author must initially indicate his intention to use extracts of copyrighted material (this does not apply to short "fair use" quotations) and agrees to supply the publisher with the written consent of the copyright holder at the time of the delivery of the manuscript.

**Material Supplied by Author.** This clause details the author's responsibility to supply any matter other than the manuscript itself, such as charts, illustrations, or photographs—referred to as artwork—as well as the written permission to use them if they are not directly produced by the author. It is important for you to state clearly in your proposal what type and amount of artwork is to appear in the book and then to decide in a discussion with your editor whose responsibility it will be to supply it. Normally the author is expected to supply all the artwork, but a variety of other options are common. For instance, you may supply rough drafts of charts, diagrams, or drawings to your editor, who will turn them over to an in-house or free-lance artist to render "camera-ready" copy. The cost of this could be tacked onto your advance, that is, deducted from future royalty payments. Sometimes the editor or the art director is both more experienced and more conveniently located to secure illustrations, and the house will provide all or some of them for your book.

Securing artwork may involve two types of expenses: the cost of preparation or reproduction and the permissions cost. For the latter your editor may provide a budget or ceiling beyond which the house will not advance the money. The cost of supplying all of your artwork, as well as the method of paying for it—out of your pocket, out of the publisher's pocket, advanced by the publisher and deducted from royalties, or some combination of these three—is negotiable, whether the artwork or extracts are of minor importance or whether they constitute the bulk of the book. In most cases the publisher will pay outright for artwork it secures and pay all permissions costs upon publication, charging them to your future royalty account. But since each book is quite different when it comes to artwork and permissions, and since the arrangements are negotiable, it is quite important to discuss these details with the editor, to have decisions made prior to signing the contract, and to insert in the contract any modification or arrangement that deviates from the clause as it is written.

This clause also exonerates the publisher in the event that the manuscript or artwork is damaged, destroyed, or lost in the mails. Of course publishers exercise due caution, but be particularly careful with original or irreplaceable artwork. Send it first-class registered mail, or better still, deliver it in person. It may be worth the extra expense for you to have such items as old photographs reproduced locally, supplying the publisher with the new print and the negative. With respect to the manuscript, notify the editor that you want the original returned to you when the book is published, and see that you get it.

**Publisher's Determination.** In essence, the publisher has the right to determine the format of the book, the method of publication, and the manner in which the book is marketed, which includes the number of copies on the first printing, the list price, etc. In some contracts the publisher also has the right to alter the title—an unconventional provision—though no publisher is likely to force a title on an author. If the editor thinks the title is not catchy, informative, or suitable, he will ask the author to supply some possible alternatives, or he may supply some himself, and by mutual agreement a new title will be chosen.

Though most publishers are reluctant to permit the author a voice in the style or format of the book, he could ask for the following amendment to this clause, so that it reads (approximately): "Publisher will consult in advance with the author concerning the format and style of all trade editions, and concerning the text, graphic material, and style of the dust jacket." Some will agree to it; most will not. You will need compelling reasons for insisting if you encounter resistance. Usually, if pressed, the editor will agree to showing you the rough sketch of the dust jacket and the jacket copy. If you have recommendations for either, send them in with your final manuscript or author's questionnaire. Though you both have the same ultimate goal, the publisher's experience, his cost limitations, and the conventions of that particular house usually outweigh an author's request on matters of style and format.

On the other hand, you should know whether the house intends to publish the book in a cloth or paper edition or both. Perhaps you feel quite strongly that only a paperback will reach the prime audience for the book, and you wish the publisher to insert a phrase here which "guarantees" paperback publication within a year or two after the cloth edition (provided your publisher has a paperback line). Or maybe you feel that the publisher's paperback line doesn't get enough exposure in the places where your book is most likely to sell, college bookstores, for instance, and you want to make sure he attempts to sell paperback rights. These are negotiable issues, though the publisher's experience is generally a more reliable guide to follow for marketing strategy. Normally the publisher's desire for maximum sales and the author's desire for maximum dissemination of his work will not be in conflict, but they can be.

**Advance Payments.** Conventionally, one-half of an advance is paid upon signing a contract and the other half on delivery of the final or revised manuscript. Occasionally, when the work is a lengthy one or is not to be delivered within, roughly, eighteen months, or when the advance is large, the publisher may want to pay the advance in three installments: on signing, on delivery of half the manuscript, and on delivery of the completed manuscript. Payment of the final installment upon publication is an occasional alternative I recommend resisting unless the total amount of the advance is very high, say over $20,000. Since the writer fulfills his part of the agreement by delivering a final manuscript, why should he wait another year for the publisher to ante up?

This clause further stipulates that the publisher may deduct any "overpayment," which means that if your first royalty statement indicates that the book has both paid off the advance and earned additional royalties, and there is a check enclosed or appears to be forthcoming, the publisher can deduct from the following royalty statement six months later any amount he has overpaid you because of interim "returns." When bookstores first order your book, all that are shipped and billed are listed as sold on your first statement, even though they are actually sent with a provision for "full" return privileges for up to a year or more. But the bookstores may not sell every copy. In fact, on a yearly basis, returns throughout the industry average 20 to 25 percent, ergo your publisher may have overpaid you by that much. However, in anticipation of these returns, many publishers commonly withhold 15 to 25 percent of your royalties from the first, second, or even third statement, pending returns, and may have a provision in this or a later clause which states that they can do so. A publisher may do it even if there is no such provision in the contract, as it is a conventional industrywide practice.

This clause also permits the publisher to deduct any overpayment for this work from a previous one, if there was one and if royalties are still being earned. You would want to make sure this does not mean or pertain to an unearned advance for the present work, which should be guaranteed and non-returnable.

**Book Royalties.** Practically all publishers pay royalty rates for trade and juvenile books based on the list (cover) price, and an author should resist any deviation from this policy except for textbooks and professional books, which generally pay royalties based on the net receipts (we will come to that later in the chapter). For clothbound sales in the United States, the common industrywide rate is: 10 percent for the first 5,000 copies sold, 12½ percent on the next 5,000 copies sold, and 15 percent thereafter. This is so conventional that you should resist any change in the publisher's favor—and not expect any in yours. Quality paperback royalties are a bit more flexible: The average rate is 6 percent of list for the first 7,500 or 10,000 copies, 7½ percent thereafter, though some contracts start at 5 percent, and some offer a flat 7½ percent, which is what you want to ask for. Agents and established authors sometimes demand and get higher royalties or additional escalations. The quality paperback we are discussing is the one issued by *your* publisher. If the paperback rights are sold by the subsidiary rights department to another publisher or to a mass market house, you will generally receive 50 percent of the proceeds and your publisher will negotiate the royalty rate.

Royalties are normally reduced by 25 to 50 percent in the following circumstances: export sales, such as to Canada or overseas; direct sales to the consumer either by mail, radio, television or in coupon ads (the cost of fulfillment—individually processing and shipping single orders —is the rationale for reduction); and copies sold at a discount of from 48 percent to 50 percent or higher. Copies sold as "overstock" or remainders pay anywhere from 5 to 10 percent of net proceeds. Note that most publishers have a provision regarding future printings of approximately 2,500 copies or less, which stipulates that royalties are decreased if sales do not exceed a certain amount within a six- or twelve-month period. The rationale is that the higher unit-cost of a small reprinting, plus the continuing costs of warehousing and keeping a modest-selling book in print, reduce the publisher's ratio of net income to—let's say—the amount of expended effort for your book. This seems kind of flimsy reasoning, but it is a common clause in many contracts. I would advise protesting a reduced royalty if the book sells over 1,000 copies a year.

**Subsidiary Rights.** Virtually every publisher has either a department or individual actively engaged in attempts to license (sell) these rights: In other words, the publisher will act as the author's agent. If the author has an agent, he would normally retain 100 percent of the following rights for his client: first serialization (prepublication of part, all, or a condensation of the book in a magazine or newspaper); British Commonwealth and foreign translation rights; motion picture, dramatic, radio and television rights. The publisher retains and attempts to license the other remaining rights, normally sharing the proceeds equally with the author.

Considering the total number of books published every year, only a fraction will earn revenue from a single subsidiary rights sale. Though the yield is higher for trade books, the odds are still against your book being sold to a book club or a mass market reprinter, the two most important subsidiary rights for a publisher. Nevertheless, the revenue from these rights is vital to trade publishers and, as I pointed out before, may determine the difference between profit and loss in any given year. The small percentage of books that are successful can generate huge sums from subsidiary rights. *Princess Daisy*, for example, was sold by its publisher for a $3.2 million advance. However, the majority of paperback reprint sales pay advances that range from $2,500 to $10,000, so do not let your fantasies run away with you; ditto for bookclub sales.

Since the sale of subsidiary rights is a function of marketing, I will discuss the methods in Chapter 7. What an author can negotiate is for a greater share of the revenue from rights normally retained by an agent. If the film or television rights for a novel are sold, a difference of 10 to 30 percent in the split of these rights might pay for a down payment on a house on Cape Cod right next to Norman Mailer's place. A nonfiction book can also be adapted for other media, even if less frequently. Whereas from many publishers you might receive half the "net compensation" from these rights had you not raised the issue, you are justified in asking for an 80/20 split on British and foreign translation rights, and a 90/10 split on first serial, motion picture, radio, television, and dramatic rights. Even though your book may seem a thoroughly unlikely candidate for any of these rights, there is no reason to give away more than you have to, just in case. For this book, for instance, a British edition or a translation is highly unlikely, since it is primarily about U.S. publishing practices, and written for U.S. authors. But portions of it are suitable for writer's magazines and have already appeared in several of them.

**Other Subsidiary Rights.** A variety of minor sub-rights are either spelled out in this clause or lumped under one heading, such as recordings, pictorial reproductions, and commercial rights (for instance, using Raggedy Ann or Peanuts on tee-shirts, wallpaper, napkins, or as dolls and toys).Though these rights are rarely exercised, there is little justification from the publisher's side for retaining *any* part of these rights since there is generally no attempt made to exploit them. By custom, however, most authors still sign over 50 percent without even knowing what these rights are. Though you might not want to make a federal case out of it, you are justified in asking for a 90/10 split, especially if there's the slightest chance of their being exercised—a minor industry has grown from the exploitation of characters in Tolkien's trilogy, *Lord of the Rings*, for example.

**Payments.** Most publishers send out royalty statements twice a year (though a small percentage report annually) and will include a check if one is due.A statement is sent three to five months after the royalties are calculated for a given six-month period. That is, a statement received on April 1 will reflect sales from the preceding June through December, giving the publisher three extra months to prepare the paperwork and to deduct returns. Most statements are notoriously inefficient and difficult to read, even though the Authors Guild and the S.A.R. have labored for years—so far without much success—to reform common practice. Usually the deficiency is in the lumping together of sales that carry different rates or the failure to clearly identify the different items. Be prepared to puzzle over your statement for half an hour with a pocket calculator and then to call or write your editor for an explanation. As mentioned before, many publishers will withhold 15 to 25 percent of earned royalties for the first two or three periods to compensate for expected returns. If the royalty due is less than $10, you may not receive a statement or check until the following royalty period (though you will get both if you request them).

Many publishers have a provision within this clause that authorizes them to withhold royalties in excess of $5,000 (or some higher amount that you fill in), which are then carried over to the following year, or successive years if the book continues to earn in excess of $5,000 per year. There are tax advantages for some authors under this provision, since a windfall from a paperback reprint sale, for example, may swell your income so much that year as to put you in the higher tax brackets. This problem, if you want to call it that, is a remote possibility, but since the Internal Revenue Service permits "income-averaging" the bonanza over a four-year period, as well as allows some other tax breaks for writers, I am reluctant to advise authors either to delete the provision or to add it if it is not already in the contract. Also, there's always the possibility, however slim, that your publisher will go broke or bankrupt before you are completely paid off. If you are in doubt, discuss the issue with an accountant.

**Author's Changes.** These are usually called "A.A.'s," author's alterations. They refer to any changes the author makes in the galleys or page proofs that are sent to the author for correction after the manuscript has been set in type. Chapters 5 and 6 describe the actual bookmaking process from manuscript to bound books, so it is sufficient to note here that any rewriting, revising, or additions you make in the galleys will obviously generate additional expenses for the publisher, discounting correction of the typesetter's mistakes. Any changes the author makes that cost more than 10 percent of the typesetter's first bill will have to be paid by the author himself. He may be billed for them right away or have the cost of them deducted from his future royalties. Resist any deviation in your disfavor from this common 10 percent arrangement.

The author is responsible for the "completeness and accuracy" of corrections made in galleys, though someone at the house will simultaneously be reading and correcting galleys. But if the typesetter inadvertently leaves out a paragraph or an entire page and the proofreader fails to catch it, don't blame the publisher if the book appears with that omission; you probably didn't go over the galleys carefully enough.

**Editing by Publisher.** This clause refers to copyediting (see Chapter 5); it assures the author that the publisher will not materially change the work.

**Free Copies.** Most contracts stipulate that the publisher will furnish the author with from six to twelve free copies and will sell him additional copies at a 40 percent or less discount. As almost every author winds up buying many more copies for relatives and friends, he should insist on a 40 percent discount (which actually escalates to 50 percent or more, since he receives royalties on these copies, too). Less than 40 percent for a trade book would mean that a bookstore gets a better discount than the author.

**Revisions.** If the first edition of the book is successful, and if it is the kind of book that lends itself to a second edition, such as in updating a textbook, a travel guide, a how-to, or a contemporary history, then the publisher may ask the author to revise the book. Successful textbooks, for instance, are often revised every three to four years. If the author cannot or does not wish to revise it himself, he can negotiate with the publisher, at that time, the cost of having someone else do the work, since this clause is usually vague about the apportionment of costs. If not vague, the following arrangement is fair: The author (or his estate) should either suggest someone or be able to approve the publisher's choice and be prepared to have either a flat fee or an advance and share of future royalties deducted from the second edition. The royalty share ranges from 15 to 50 percent, depending on the amount of work involved in revising, but authors should resist signing away more than 20 to 33 percent of the future royalties. A small but negotiable advance to cover the cost of preparing a revised edition is commonly given, if requested, even though it is generally not negotiated into this clause in your original contract.

**Discontinuance of Manufacture.** This clause is sometimes designated as the ''out-of-print'' or ''termination'' or ''reversion of rights'' clause. Some of the provisions are antiquated but have now become embedded in many publishing contracts. For instance, one conventional provision reads: ''If at any time the book shall be out of print, and the author shall notify the publisher to this effect. . . .'' In other words, *you* are supposed to tell the publisher when the book is out of print in order to reclaim the rights! We can define *out of print* as ''when copies are not available or offered for sale in the United States through normal retail channels in an English-language hardcover or paperback edition, issued by the publisher or by another publisher licensed by the original publisher, and are not listed in either publisher's catalog.'' I am paraphrasing a provision from the Authors Guild recommended contract.

Until such time as this antique is generally effaced from many contracts, I can only urge you to make sure that there is a clear provision for reclaiming *all* the rights (not just publication rights) and suggest some ploys for determining whether the book is still in print, as some publishers are less than forthright in proclaiming the book's demise. In the event that a work goes out of print, the conventional clause instructs the author to write the publisher requesting either that the book be reprinted, or that the rights revert to the author six months after the date of the letter, provided the publisher does not indicate or follow through on his intention to reprint it, or license someone else to reprint it. Make sure that your clause has some *specific* teeth in it as this one does.

The rub is how to know when the work is out of print. A little gumshoeing will do it. If you no longer receive a royalty statement—which may be the first sign—check the most recent *Books in Print*, write for your publisher's current catalog or order list to see if it is listed, and ask a friend to order five copies by mail. If all three of these indicate that your book is not available, then write to the publisher and request the rights. If your friend's request for copies results in a T.O.S. letter or invoice (temporarily out of stock), you have to follow up with a letter to your editor (or the president, if your editor is no longer there) demanding to know when copies will be available. T.O.S. is sometimes a gambit to permit the publisher to hold on to the rights, even though he is not selling the book and has no immediate intention to reprint it. Why does he bother, and why should you bother to get the rights back?

Works are occasionally rediscovered or exhumed and go on to become best sellers: It happened to Henry Roth's *Call It Sleep*, which was published in the thirties and rediscovered in the sixties. It also happened to Faulkner, many of whose books had been out of print until the mid-forties, when Malcolm Cowley revived Faulkner's reputation. A more likely possibility is that a reprinter, a publisher who specializes in reprinting out-of-print books in expensive hardcover editions, may come seeking the rights anywhere from five to fifty years after the book has presumably been laid to rest. And the rights will be worth an advance and royalty once again. Since it is impossible to predict what might happen, the author should have the benefit of the doubt.

You are also normally offered in the discontinuance-of-manufacture clause the right to buy the negatives or plates, if they still exist, and either the bound or unbound copies remaining in the warehouse, before the publisher destroys the plates and remainders the overstock. You will have little need for the former, unless you have rustled up a reprinter on your own, but you may want to stock up on some more copies at bargain rates.

**Competing Work**. As you might suspect, an editor or publisher would not take it kindly if an author were to write a book for another publisher that directly competed with the original. In most cases, common sense will provide the answer to what constitutes competition: Writing another introductory textbook in psychology for a different publisher would probably stimulate a lawsuit, whereas writing a juvenile version of a biography of Thomas Jefferson (provided you don't copy whole passages) would not compete with the trade edition. Many authors mine the same fields for several books: One of my clients is writing his fourth book on pocket calculators, but each one is clearly not in direct competition with the other; one is for high school students, one for college students, one for the general reader, and one for scientists. If in doubt, discuss the issue with your original editor before signing a second book; if you aren't satisfied with the answer, consult a lawyer.

**Options**. The option clause, which grants the publisher the first crack at the author's next book, made more sense in the days when publishers nurtured novelists, hoping to be rewarded for their faith by the financial success of the second, third, or fourth novel. However, nurture is in short supply nowadays (equally matched by most authors' tenuous loyalty to their publishers), even though almost every first literary novel loses money: Publishing them is both a sign of commitment to literature and a realization that the next generation's novelists have to come from somewhere. Though I urge nonfiction writers to insist on deleting this clause, as the publisher's case for it is a weak one, there is real merit to the argument for retaining it in the case of a first novel, a collection of short stories, or a book of poems. However, the clause should not be linked with the publication date of the first book and should be contingent upon the publisher reaching a decision within sixty days of submission (for a nonfiction book, on the basis of an extensive outline or a sample chapter), and ''acceptable terms to be negotiated'' or words to that effect. This means that if you are not satisfied with the terms that are offered, you are free to go elsewhere, provided you do not accept an equal or lower offer.

**Understanding or Changes**. This clause protects both you and the publisher from any arbitrary deviations from the agreement, unless by mutual consent in writing. What should also be included or implied in this or another clause is ''no *assignment* without mutual consent,'' signifying that the publisher cannot sell the contract to another publisher without the author's consent. Royalty income, however, can be assigned by the author at any time to a relative, heir, mistress, charity, or what you will.

**Construction, Heirs**. The contract is interpreted according to the laws of the state in which the publisher is located, in the event of legal disputes, and its terms are binding upon your heirs or their heirs, so long as the contract and copyright are in force.

## Other Possible Contract Features

As I stated earlier, the number of clauses in a contract can range from 15 to 108, and it would be impossible—and tedious—to discuss in a single chapter the entire range and variation of individual clauses. Nevertheless, here are some additional common clauses or provisions you might wish to know about.

**Time of Publication**. Some contracts contain a provision in one of the first few clauses obliging the publisher to produce the book within a certain number of months after delivery. Though six to nine months is the normal gestation period from date of delivery to "bound books" (official publication date is always six to seven weeks later), postponements do occur, either beyond or within the publisher's control. Reasons can range from lack of cash to war to strikes and to dilatory typesetters in South Korea (some publishers shop around the world for the cheapest bid). Publishers work within a yearly budget, a certain portion of which is allocated for producing books. As costs for individual titles can only be estimated until production is underway, and as delivery of manuscripts from authors is erratic, some juggling always takes place on a publisher's production schedule. An unexpected manuscript, or perhaps a potential best seller, may be delivered or contracted for, which can result in bumping one or more other low-priority books for later publication. Therefore, it is important to have a provision that states a specific amount of time within which the publisher has to produce the book. (Textbook publishers are more commonly self-indulgent with schedules.) Twelve to eighteen months is a legitimate request.

If you cannot get this provision inserted, the best way to prod a procrastinating publisher is to remind him of your existence: Polite or aggrieved letters to your editor, followed up by phone calls, are more potent than most authors realize. If you are ignored, write to the editor's superior. One extremely silent and considerate author I knew had his low-priority book bumped for three successive years. It wouldn't have happened if he had kicked up some dust. Actually a contract implies, even if it does not explicitly state, that the publisher will fulfill his responsibilities within a *reasonable* amount of time. If an excessive delay seems to be stretching into an interminable one, an author can legally reclaim the rights to his book.

**Examination of Accounts.** Many contracts contain a clause permitting the author or his representative (an accountant) to examine the ''books'' once or twice a year for errors in computing the sales upon which the royalties are paid. Authors are sometimes shocked by low sales figures on a royalty statement, having concluded from certain indications—perhaps a number of excellent reviews in mass circulation magazines or newspapers—that the book is selling well (but note that these are not a sure-fire guarantee of sales). Textbook authors hear from friends and colleagues around the country that their book is being adopted at many colleges. This clause would permit an author's accountant to verify invoices to determine if mistakes in calculating the royalties have been made. The clause usually states that if the error is in excess of 5 percent to the author's disadvantage, the publisher will pay for the accounting. Inadvertent errors do occur, since the introduction of computerized accounting has often created as many mistakes as it has eliminated. Deliberate falsification is an occasional topic of conversation at cocktail parties, but the damage to a reputable publisher who might be found engaging in this would far outweigh the sums involved, so I would discount this possibility. High initial sales may sometimes be cancelled out by unusually high returns, though the author may only see the final figure in the royalty statement, as returns are not listed separately. Before taking any formal steps, call your editor for an explanation if you feel something is wrong with the figures.

**Advertising Budget.** Unless you are a ''brand name'' author, most publishers will reject a request for an advertising budget specifically allocated for your book. Instead, you will generally be told that it is obviously to the publisher's advantage to advertise your book, and when the time comes, etc., etc. This is one of those verbal assurances more practiced in the breach than in the observance. Yearly advertising budgets are theoretically apportioned among all the publisher's titles; in practice, 20 percent of the books commandeer 80 percent of the budget, so that many of the books get but a single ad or none at all (excluding general announcement ads, which usually include all the books for that season).

If you can clearly identify a specific and easily targeted audience, you can make a good case for insisting on a few ads and request that the assurance be put in writing, either in the contract or in a letter. A specific audience usually has several magazines or journals that cater to its interests: A book on wolves would appeal to readers of *Natural History*, a study of folksongs would appeal to readers of the *Journal of American Folklore*, and so on, *ad infinitum*.

In lieu of an ad, a flier or brochure sent to subscribers of particular magazines or to members of certain organizations may be more effective, especially as much more information can be packed into a flier than an ad. Books that are appropriate for specific college courses, whether they are trade books or textbooks, can often effectively increase their sales by offering free "examination" copies in a mailing piece, and it is a common form of promotion. So, rather than requesting a budget *per se*, you might have more luck with a request for several ads or a flier. It's worth a try.

**Index.** Most nonfiction books either do or should have an index. Your contract negotiation should include a discussion with your editor on whether an index is necessary or advisable, and if so, who should prepare it. Most houses give you the option of doing it yourself or having the publisher subcontract it to a freelance professional indexer. In the latter case the convention is for the publisher to lay out the fee (generally between $300 and $500) and to have it deducted from future royalties. If you do not elect to do it yourself, make sure that your contract spells out who pays and when.

**Grant in Aid.** In the boom years, prior to 1970, some publishers, particularly textbook houses, occasionally provided a flat fee in the $500 range for a final typing, or for special expenses such as travel, equipment, computer time, or compilation of data by the author or research assistants. Some publishers will still provide this grant on request, but you should not expect it.

**Special Licenses**. Storage and retrieval systems, whether computerized, mechanical, electronic, on video tapes or yet-to-be-invented, may soon play a greater role in publishing than they have to date. The University of Michigan, for instance, has a huge number of scientific monographs and dissertations on microfilm, copies of which can be ordered by anyone. But no one is yet sure exactly how the expanded use of these systems will affect the publisher or the author. Obviously the author is entitled to a share in these rights—at least 50/50, but it would be preferable to change that to "on terms to be negotiated," until it becomes clear what you are both going to share. This provision, often found in the subsidiary rights clause, may conclude by stating that any additional subsidiary right not explicitly listed or that may arise in the future is to be: a) reserved for the author, b) reserved for the publisher, or c) shared by author and publisher. Try for "a" and make sure it isn't "b."

**Subsidiary Licenses.** The ins and outs of subsidiary rights sales are too complex to explore in detail here, but with a little imagination one can see that if the publisher has total control over the disposition of these rights, there are situations in which arrangements that are most advantageous to the publisher might not coincide with the author's best interests. Hence, every author should attempt to insert the following provision:

> The publisher shall submit to the author for his prior approval (such approval not to be unreasonably withheld or delayed) the terms of any license for bookclub distribution, paperback reprint, cheap edition, or pre- or postpublication periodical rights. Copies of the contract shall be furnished by the publisher to the author upon request, and the author's share shall be paid within thirty days.

This paraphrase of an S.A.R.-recommended contract clause permits an author a chance to put in his two cents and perhaps modify, approve, or disapprove of an arrangement that is normally presented to him as a *fait accompli.* Several years ago, for example, a U.S. Senator was chagrined to learn that a portion of his book—quite a sober and serious book, incidentally—was appearing in a magazine devoted primarily to illustrations of unclad females. The Senator probably did not have this provision in his contract (he was able to sue and settle nonetheless). However, the value of this clause is that it permits you to evaluate the publisher's intention for a rights sale and decide whether the outside offer appears "reasonable" and is in your best interests. For instance, a client who had published a book before I met him called me and said that his publisher, a university press, was about to sell the paperback rights for a $500 advance, even though his book had received excellent reviews in a variety of newspapers and trade journals and had been chosen as a main selection for a major book club. His publisher apparently had a standing arrangement with a paperback reprinter to offer first crack at all the books, and since 99 percent of them had modest sales expectations, the normal advance that had always been offered was $500. Since many university presses are not particularly concerned with subsidiary rights advances, this one felt no obligation to rock the boat or go out of its way to secure a better offer. My client wrote a polite but firm letter and managed to make a better arrangement, but he could just as easily have found out about it months later, when it would have been too late to do anything about it.

A further value to this clause is that it insures prompt payment to the author for his share of the rights sale, since he might normally have to wait six to nine months until the following royalty statement appeared. Any unearned advance, however, would be deducted from the author's share of this rights sale.

**Anthology Permissions Budget.** In addition to the anthology editor's advance, a publisher normally allocates a permissions budget, laying out the cost upon publication and deducting it from future royalties. Though the anthology editor—or author, to avoid confusion—may not be expected to know how much the total permissions costs are going to run, his editor will feel more comfortable with an educated guess, though he himself may provide a more accurate estimate than the author. Most journals and magazine articles run roughly $10 to $15 a page, whereas poems, short stories, plays, and chapters from novels or published books vary considerably in cost, depending on the specific publisher or copyright holder, as well as on the current reputation or prestige of the author of that selection. An outrageous request, say $750 for a short story (and sometimes even a pro-rata share of the royalties), can often be negotiated for a lower fee. If not, a substitute is probably the best solution. It is very important for the anthologist to make sure that the house is going to lay out the permissions costs and that this is stated clearly in the contract. An author I know received an unexpected letter from his publisher on publication date, reminding him that he should now mail out the $1,450 in permissions costs. Naturally, the author was flabbergasted; he had *assumed* this was the publisher's responsibility, and he had already spent his own advance.

Sometimes the author can press the publisher to pay a percentage of the permissions costs outright, perhaps up to 50 percent or more, especially if the anthology is obviously a unique and potentially promising one or if the author has a good track record or a distinguished reputation in his field. It's worth a try.

## *Negotiating an Advance for a Trade Book*

Virtually every trade publisher pays an author an advance against royalties for his book, though here and there one finds some publishers offering flat fees for books, an arrangement more common prior to 1950. Occasionally a book is commissioned by a publisher such as Time-Life (or perhaps by a national manufacturer) for a special market or for mail order sales—for instance, a history of a company, a review book, workbook or study guide for the educational market, a puzzle or game book, or a small pamphlet for a very specific audience. Under these circumstances, a flat fee may be justified, especially for a book that will be given away rather than sold. But generally agents and authors frown on a flat fee arrangement. After all, if a book sells in excess of what it costs to produce, shouldn't the author have a share in the profits? Therefore, be wary of a flat fee offer. Even if one were to calculate the number of hours it would take to write a commissioned book, and charge a very generous hourly fee (or word rate), the chances are that it will take half again as much time to produce the final manuscript as the author imagined, and the rate might therefore not exceed the U.S. minimum hourly wage.

How does an author determine what to ask for or to accept as a fair advance? As a rule of thumb in publishing goes, estimate the potential royalties the book might pay in its first year, and then deduct 20 to 25 percent. In other words, if your book will tentatively list for $10, and the publisher expects to sell 5,000 copies in the first year, then he should be willing to pay up to $4,000 for an advance (you recall that even before an offer is made, the publisher has estimated a list price, a first printing quantity, and the first year's sales). Both publishers and agents tend to use this guideline in negotiating advances, though the bookclub and paperback reprint potential (which may even be checked out before an offer is made) can jack up the figure considerably. One might therefore ask an editor for his tentative list price and first year's sales estimate and do some rapid mathematics before discussing the advance. The mean advance for trade books is roughly $4,000 to $7,500, a range to keep in mind if this is your maiden voyage. Make allowances for the fact that my experience is mainly with the top 100 nationally known publishers, as advances will run somewhat lower with smaller publishers, say, roughly $3,000 to $4,000.

These figures are predicated on the assumption that you earn a living, or part of one, in some other fashion or field, and that your book does not require extensive travel or extraordinary expenses. A writer with national magazine or newspaper credits, for example, would command a higher advance even for a first book, as would a previously published author with a good track record, or a celebrity, politician, jet-setter, magnate, etc. Most would have an agent, though, but there are some successful writers who are savvy about publishing and contracts and just do not believe in having an agent, but may employ a lawyer instead.

First novels are a stickier problem; not only are so few published every year (about 100) that it is difficult to talk about an average—and many of them are agented—but the odds are that the publisher is going to lose money even without paying an advance, especially if it's a literary novel. An over-the-transom first novel accepted for publication by a trade publisher is a rare event, considering the number that are submitted, and most authors are content to accept whatever token a publisher is willing to offer. For a ''literary'' novel, I would consider $2,500 to $5,000 fair, whereas a genre or category novel, such as a mystery, science fiction novel, or a romance, can be considered an average trade book. A short-story collection—the true *rara avis* in publishing—or a book of poems garners the smallest, if any, advance; say from $250 to $1,000.

Another way to deal with advances is just to ask for $1,000 more than an editor offers. He is usually working with a negotiable figure and will probably make an offer at the lower end of the spectrum, which you may be able to boost merely by *confidently* asking for it.

Many authors believe that the amount of an advance has a crucial relationship to the amount of effort the publisher will expend in promoting a book. Thus a small advance will inevitably result in a negligible effort. It just isn't so, or rather it is not true for books that have an advance of less than $10,000, which means most books. Almost every trade book requires a direct investment of $10,000 to $15,000, not counting the advance. Because of this, virtually every publisher will attempt to recoup his expense by performing the task of promoting and selling the book with at least a minimum of zeal. Of course, big advances place a greater pressure on the publisher to go all out for a book, but then, he wouldn't have given a big advance in the first place unless he believed the book would sell well, and had the intention to promote it heavily. This is kind of a Catch-22 in that the early decisions and expectations frequently become self-fulfilling prophecies. The exceptions, however, are daily occurrences. L.B.J.'s *Memoirs*, for example, was sold for over a million dollar advance, but no amount of publishing hoopla was able to recoup the investment.

Finally, there are a few publishers who are just reluctant to pay advances—and even a few authors who feel they aren't really entitled to accept money unless the book sells well enough for them to ''earn'' it. ''If you don't actually need the money,'' an editor may say, ''since you don't intend to live off of it, why ask for it? You'll get it back anyway if and when the book sells. Why should we tie up our capital in loaning you interest-free money? Besides, we are already gambling (or showing our good faith) by spending $10,000 to produce your book.''

Well, the answer is twofold: Advances are a commonly accepted convention, and publishers are paying them to get an exclusive option on your book and its potential income. You will be tying up or have tied up your time and efforts to produce something from which they expect to gain, so the advance is compensation for these efforts, whether or not your book sells. One could compare it to buying the manufacturing rights for a newly patented invention. Of course, some publishers, particularly small ones, cannot afford a hefty or even average advance. They operate on a tight budget, and an author might just decide to forego it. Even so, my own feeling is that if a publisher can afford to produce your book, he can afford at least a token advance for the author.

In any case, remember that if one publisher wants your book, probably another one will, too. If you feel that either the financial terms or the small print are grossly unfair or too unconventional, consider shopping elsewhere while you are "thinking it over." Most writers are unjustifiably timid about rocking the boat with their first contract and are inclined to go along with whatever is offered. Contracts *are* negotiable, and negotiations about specifics are only limited by how badly the publisher wants your book and by how badly you want that specific publisher to take it. Having said this, you can always console yourself—when the task is done, and you think you gave in too easily on the list of demands in front of you—with the thought that on the next one, either you will have an agent, or you will drive a harder bargain.

## Other Divisions

Contracts with other divisions or types of publishers, such as mass market, college text, juvenile, and professional, differ in certain conventions, particularly with reference to advances and royalty rates. By and large, contracts are shorter and simpler and subsidiary rights play a minor role, but the basic elements of these contracts are indistinguishable from trade contracts.

**Mass Market.** As mentioned before, mass market publishers continue to increase their list of originals, partly to offset the huge sums of money they have to pay in advances for best sellers. The contract is basically the same as a trade contract, and while advances are also roughly competitive with trade books, the range is wider. For example, an advance for a literary novel can be as low as $500, whereas for a genre novel it can run as high as $5,000 to $15,000. The common royalty rate is 6 percent of list for the first 150,000 copies, 8 percent thereafter, though 6 percent to 8 percent to 10 percent (after 300,000 copies) or 8 percent to 10 percent is not out of line and definitely worth requesting.

An editor will not make an offer unless he can project a minimum sales of 50,000 copies for the first year. Returns, incidentally, run much higher than for trade books, currently averaging 35 percent a year.

In the last ten years, some of the leading independent mass market publishers have been acquired by trade houses: For example, Holt, Rinehart & Winston bought Fawcett; Grosset & Dunlap bought Ace; and Random House bought Ballantine. Other trade houses have had their own mass market division for a long time, such as G. P. Putnam's Sons (Berkley) and Simon and Schuster (Pocket Books). It is important for an author who signs up his book with a trade house that has one of these divisions to know in advance whether he is authorizing the publisher to retain volume rights, that is, the right to publish the mass market version themselves as well as the cloth edition. The advantage is that the author will receive full royalties. He will not have to split paperback royalties as he normally would. The disadvantage is that if the book takes off and is quite successful in a cloth edition, he may miss out on his half of a huge advance from a literary auction, which are often conducted by trade publishers for their clothbound titles. If the book has a strong potential for a long shelf life, such as a "how-to," the author may be better off in the long run to have the originating publisher issue the mass market or quality paperback edition. For a successful novel, an auction is generally the better gamble for the author. Most publishers are also interested in the bird-in-hand and generally decide it's in their own best interests to auction the book, with their own mass market division coming in as one of the bidders. If these arrangements are clear before signing the contract, of if you have a "right of approval" provision, you will at least have had a chance to put in your two cents.

For originals, the mass market publisher will sometimes also attempt to sell subsidiary rights and may try to license a trade publisher to issue a clothbound edition, postponing paperback publication until the cloth edition has been out for a year. In this instance, your split should range from 75/25 to 90/10 rather than the conventional 50/50. Royalties from export sales for mass market paperbacks, by the way, are generally not reduced as they are for trade books.

**Original Quality Paperbacks or Oversized Paperbacks.** With both of these paperback formats royalty rates and advances are still somewhat fluid. Quality paperbacks generally pay 6 percent of list for the first 7,500 to 15,000, escalating to 7½ percent or 8 percent thereafter, though a request for an additional escalation to 10 percent after 20,000 to 25,000 or even 50,000 copies is not out of line. Advances are generally somewhat lower than for clothbound trade books, say in the $3,000 to $5,000 range. Oversized paperbacks should command average clothbound advances, but royalty rates are up for grabs. Some publishers treat them as paperbacks, some as cloth books. Use 8 percent of list to 20,000 copies, 10 percent to 35,000 copies, and 12 percent thereafter as a rough quide.

**Juveniles.** Again, the contracts are virtually the same as trade contracts, but some conventions change. Advances are generally lower, averaging $3,000 to $4,000, which may have to be split 50/50 with an illustrator for picture books. The common royalty rate is 10 percent of list for the first 10,000 copies, 12½ percent thereafter, but many contracts do escalate to 15 percent after 20,000 to 25,000 copies, so you can ask for it. Rising production costs and shrinking markets are now beginning to be reflected in royalty rates; some publishers may offer lower royalties for the first printing. The "library edition" occasionally pays royalties based on *net* receipts. Try to delete this provision, since more than 80 percent of juvenile sales are to libraries. Royalty rates for young adult (YA) books are often set as for regular trade book royalties, and those rates should be requested (10 percent to 5,000, 12½ percent to 10,000, 15 percent thereafter). Reduction of royalties for subsequent small printings are conventional but should be resisted; no more than a 25 percent reduction of royalties (if semiannual sales do not exceed 500 copies) should be accepted, since juveniles generally sell in smaller quantities over a longer period of time.

As the shelf life for a juvenile averages five to twenty years, in contrast to the six-months to one-year shelf life of most trade books, you might have an annuity if your juvenile is successful.

**College Textbooks.** Subsidiary rights for textbooks are negligible, and a 50/50 split is taken for granted. The major difference is in royalty rates, which are usually paid on the *net* receipts, the amount the publisher receives from the college bookstore. As the standard textbook discount to the bookstore is 20 percent, the royalty rate is based on 80 percent of the list price. A few text publishers now offer discounts from 20 to 33 percent, partly as a result of legitimate gripes from college bookstore owners and managers, whose operating costs hover at 26 to 27 percent— that is, the bookstores often lose money selling textbooks. This lower discount, known as a "short discount" (as opposed to the "long discount" for trade books, which averages 47 percent) accounts for the absence of textbooks in regular bookstores. No bookstore owner feels he can afford to stock them, even though some of them would appeal to the general public.

The royalty rates and advances are more flexible than for trade books and are definitely negotiable. Because of the sparsity of agents in this field, the naïveté of academics about contracts, and the general feeling among them that publications are valuable primarily as a means of securing promotion or tenure—rather than as an important income-producing avocation—many authors accept whatever terms a textbook editor offers. Don't.

A clothbound textbook should command a 15 percent-of-net royalty, but many publishers will start at 10 percent and escalate in two stages to 15 percent. What an author should initially ask for is 15 percent of net escalating to 18 percent after the sale of 7,500 to 15,000 copies. This is particularly warranted for a basic text, that is, a book appropriate as the sole text for a standard undergraduate course. The author should negotiate in the 12 percent to 18 percent range and certainly accept no less than an escalation to 15 percent. Escalations can also be linked to sales in any given year: for instance, 15 percent of net receipts to 5,000 copies, 17½ percent thereafter for additional sales in that particular year, or 17½ percent in any given year that the book sells over 5,000 copies. Rates for paperback text originals run a bit lower, in the 10-percent-escalating-to-15-percent range, as do anthologies.

Advances vary, and textbook editors are more inclined to use the "what do you need it for" spiel, even though advances are as much a convention in texts as they are in trade. Again, a fair advance depends on the potential market for the book, so that a hefty basic textbook for an undergraduate course may be worthy of a $10,000 to $30,000 advance, whereas a supplementary book, a graduate-level text, or an upper-division anthology may warrant no more than a $2,000 to $4,000 advance.

Most textbooks have their peak sales in their second and third year, and some few go on to become one of those legendary perennials, like Samuelson's *Economics*, that reaches an eighth or ninth revised edition over a period of twenty-five to thirty years, providing the author with well over a million dollars in accumulated royalties.

**El-Hi Textbooks.** These contracts are similar to—if more elaborate than—those of college text publishers, and the terms and clauses are usually less flexible, i.e., there is less room for negotiation. Perhaps the reason is that there haven't been, nor do there seem to be, any agents operating in this genre. Advances, especially considering the huge sales potential, range from token to minimal. A high advance would generally not exceed $5,000.

Royalties, paid on net receipts, are equally modest, but the potential volume of sales can more than make up for this disparity. Elementary text royalties range from 4 to 6 percent, and can descend to as low as 1 to 2 percent for basal reader or math series (though sales here for a successful series can reach astronomical proportions). Junior high text royalties go up to about 7 percent, and high school text royalties are in the 8 to 10 percent range. Incidentally, royalty escalations for el-hi contracts are not conventional, but that doesn't mean you don't want to ask for them. These royalties are usually split two, three, or four ways, as multiple authorship is much more common than not.

Authors should attempt to negotiate an escalation of royalties: for example, from 5 percent to 6 percent after the sale of 50,000 copies for an elementary text, and correspondingly for high school texts. The revision clause is important here (and generally too restrictive in el-hi contracts). For a second edition you should attempt to write in a higher escalation, an additional advance, and try to make sure that you have the right to "approve" both the writing and financial arrangements in case you cannot or will not prepare it yourself. After all, a revision means that your book was successful and made a bundle for the publisher. You should therefore have some more clout with the second edition, but you will have to negotiate it into the initial contract.

**Professional, Technical, and Scientific Books.** As in college texts, subsidiary rights are negligible, except possibly for bookclub rights. Over a hundred small to medium-size book clubs cater to professional and special interest groups, from lawyers to coin collectors, and the 50/50 share of revenue may be surprisingly high, considering that these "markets" have a much smaller base. Royalty rates are also based on net receipts (15 percent of net is common), and bookstore discounts generally range from 25 percent to 33⅓ percent. More than 50 percent of the sales are from mail order, libraries, or overseas markets, and a reduction in royalty rates for these sales is common. Advances are generally low, ranging from nothing to $5,000, but they are nevertheless negotiable.

## A Word to Translators

Translators have traditionally occupied the bottom rung of the financial ladder in publishing, although rates in recent years are improving. It is still common for translators to be paid a flat fee for books; the current rate for literary works ranges from a modest $35.00 per 1,000 words, up to $55.00, which is scarcely a living wage even for rapid and proficient translators. Technical works, however, may command as much as $75.00 per 1,000 words, and upward to $150.00 for legal, scientific, and banking books.

Some translators are now asking for—and getting—a "royalty override"; that is, a small royalty, usually 1 percent of the list price for trade books. In this case the flat fee can be construed as an advance against royalties or, preferably, the royalty is paid in addition to the flat fee. Furthermore some translators are asking for—and receiving—a share of the subsidiary rights, especially book club, paperback reprint, and sometimes British rights. Here you may want to ask for 10 percent of the net receipts. If *you* approach the publisher with a project, you are in a much stronger position and can negotiate upward from these figures; moreover, if the work is in public domain (i.e., there is no royalty to be paid to an author), there is no reason for you not to ask for and get conventional author's royalties. Royalties and fees for translators are now so fluid that it is difficult to state the conventions; when in doubt, ask for more than you expect, since it's a lot easier to work downward than upward.

Also significant is the issue of billing, which you will want spelled out in your letter of agreement: Is your name to go on the jacket and/or the title pages, in the press release, and in advertising in which the author's name appears? (I would say yes to all of these.) And is the translation to be copyrighted in your name? (Yes again.) Reviewers and publishers have traditionally been notoriously deficient in giving adequate credit to translators—except perhaps for poetry and drama—but in recent years they have gradually been redressing this omission. Translators are well advised to write to the "Translation Center"* for a general description of its aims and services (and to consult R. R. Bowker's recent sourcebook, *Translation & Translators*—see the bibliography). This office was founded in 1972 with a grant from the N.E.A., and operates as a nonprofit clearinghouse between translators and publishers. Twice a year the Center publishes a combined magazine/newsletter that contains translations as well as articles and information. Prizes, awards, and fellowship competitions, in addition to notices of direct support for nonprofit presses, are listed in the magazine. It is useful to be listed with the Center as a translator, since you may get commissions that way, but in any case you may call them up for free informal advice on publisher/author relations as well as on fees, royalties, letters of agreement, and other matters that arise in working with book or magazine publishers.

### The Last Word

Obviously there is no last word on contracts and negotiations. We have only skimmed the surface here, but many editors, agents, and publishers will disagree with some of my suggestions, guidelines, and interpretations. Let me emphasize again that virtually all clauses are negotiable and that I have addressed myself primarily to unagented

---

*The Translation Center, Columbia University, 307A Mathematics Building, New York, N.Y. 10027.

authors who do not yet have a strong enough track record to make greater demands. An agent or professional writer will increase the ante and may insist on more deletions, insertions, and modification than have been discussed or suggested here.

Let me repeat also that a telephone call or a discussion in a restaurant is not the way to cement terms for a contract: There are too many details to consider, and it is too disconcerting a setting for a ruffled author in which to represent himself adequately or rationally. Get a blank contract, study it, make notes, and write your editor a letter.

The writer who has the inclination to know more about contracts and negotiations will find several additional references in the suggested further reading list, but the best piece of advice I have to offer, for a writer who has published a book, is to join the Authors Guild.* Not only will he have access to a number of specific publications about contracts, but the bi-monthly magazine, *The Authors Guild Bulletin*, is an invaluable source of up-to-date information on the industry, as well as on all the topics discussed in this book. It is, of course, the closest approximation to a union a writer has, and as publishing is no longer the province of the Maxwell Perkinses or T. S. Eliots of yore, writers are more than ever in need of professional organizations. I do not mean to disparage either the commitments or virtues of my colleagues, but merely to stress that publishing is big business, and that most of the key financial decisions have been taken over by executives who generally pay more attention to the bottom line than to the well-turned phrase.

---

*Write for details on joining to: The Authors Guild, 234 West 44 Street, New York, N.Y. 10036.

# 4

# *How to Prepare a Final Manuscript*

I have rewritten—often several times—every word I have
ever published. My pencils outlast their erasures.
—Vladimir Nabokov

The ashtray is filled with cigarette butts, the eighth cup of coffee is sour
in your mouth, your back is killing you from bending over the typewriter
for seven hours, but you feel like a tiger (or tigress); you've just finished
your book. Now you are ready to think about sending it off to a publisher
or an agent. Maybe you have a contract or a "nibble" from an editor
who—because of your previously sent proposal—has asked to see the
final version of the manuscript. Or maybe you just sat down and wrote
the book, deciding to worry about publication when it was finished.

The revised version was prepared after weeks or months of reading
chapters to your patient spouse or after getting feedback from friends or
colleagues. The manuscript is a mess: Pages are cut in half and pasted
together, coffee stains decorate several chapters, scribbles you can
barely decipher fill the margins, and the page numbers were fouled up
somewhere around chapter three. It's time for the final typing, and the
preparation of a professional-looking manuscript.

### *The Mechanical Basics*

First things first: Change your ribbon, brush off the typeface, and treat
yourself to some first-rate white bond paper (14-pound or higher is
best)—*do not* use corrasable bond or onionskin. If you have a contract,
you will want to make three copies: the original and a clear second copy

for the publisher (a photocopy or carbon on the same bond as the original is OK), and one for yourself. The publisher's second copy will be used for designing and cost estimating. Needless to say, you should *always* keep one copy for yourself in case the others are lost, either in the mails or by the publisher.

Type on one side of the paper only, leaving margins of 1½ inches all around, and use the same typewriter for the entire manuscript so a word count will be accurate. Double-space all material, including quotations, notes, bibliography, and captions, and at the beginning of the introduction and each chapter leave about the first third of the page blank.

## *Reference Shelf*

Many publishers, particularly the bigger houses, print their own style guide, which they will send you along with a contract. Obviously, unless you have a contract before you prepare your final revision, it won't help you. Most writers have a small collection of reference books—you can't get by without at least a good dictionary. I recommend adding a thesaurus and a handbook for the mechanics of grammar and usage. Many good ones are available; you may still have a copy of one from your high school or college days. My favorite is Strunk and White's *The Elements of Style* (second edition, New York: Macmillan Publishing Co., 1972), a classic because of its amusingly pithy tone and concise rules. But it's a bit short; you should have something more substantial.

For complete coverage, and to learn all the ground rules in manuscript preparation—from style to book production and printing—you might consider buying one of the standard style manuals. Four well-known and highly respected manuals are:

*A Manual of Style,* 12th edition, Chicago: University of Chicago Press, 1969.

*U.S. Government Printing Office Style Manual,* Washington, D.C.: U.S. Government Printing Office, 1973.

Lewis Jordan, *New York Times Manual of Style and Usage,* New York: Times Books, 1976.

Marjorie E. Skillin and Robert M. Gay, *Words Into Type,* 3rd edition, Englewood Cliffs, N.J.: Prentice-Hall, 1974.

The best concise paperback style guide I've found, which will carry you from a first draft through proofreading and the preparation of an index, is Margaret Nicholson's *A Practical Style Guide for Authors & Editors* (New York: Holt, Rinehart & Winston, 1970).

In any case, you are probably preparing the manuscript without the publisher's style guide, but since most of them adopt some slight variation of a standard stylebook practice, you are on safe ground if you follow any reasonable format. The copyeditor may ask you to change your footnote style or placement, for instance, to conform to house standards, but if the conversion is only a few hours' work, the editor will probably have it done for you.

## *The Basic Arrangement*

A manuscript is divided into three parts: the front matter (sometimes called preliminaries), the text proper, and the back matter (sometimes called end matter).

**Front Matter.** Your front matter will vary considerably, depending on the type of book, but can consist of any or all of the following:

Title page (with your name and address 3 inches below the title)
Table of contents
List of illustrations
List of tables
List of abbreviations
Dedication
Preface or foreword
Acknowledgments
Introduction

All of this front matter (except the introduction) should be numbered in lower-case roman numerals in the upper right-hand corner.

*Preface, foreword,* and *introduction* are terms sometimes mistakenly used interchangeably. The preface is the author's account of the scope and purpose of the book, how it came to be written, and often includes the acknowledgments unless they are extensive. The foreword, frequently written by someone other than the author, is a kind of send-off for the book, suggesting the contents in a general way (sometimes relating it to other books in the field) and, ideally, stimulating the reader to proceed further. The introduction is concerned specifically with the contents of the book. The preface and/or foreword may precede the contents page and the introduction follow, but this varies depending on the book and house style. Most of these minor decisions on positioning take place "in house" so let's not quibble about them.

**Text.** Begin numbering your text with arabic numerals on the first page of the introduction, numbering the pages consecutively in the upper right-hand corner, from beginning to end, *not* chapter by chapter. Chapter numbers should be placed in the upper center of the page in upper-case roman numerals. It's a good idea to type your last name, title (abbreviated to one or two words), and chapter number in the far upper left margin on *every page* of the text. (Pages have a mysterious way of floating into some other editor's office.) Chapter titles are typed on the first page of each new chapter, about one-third down the page; use upper *and* lower case—the designer will decide on the style for these and other titles, headings, and subheadings.

If you are writing nonfiction, you will probably have subheadings in each chapter. Subheads should not be underlined (ditto for chapter titles) and should be typed with "initial capitals" only, meaning that the first letter of each word is capitalized except for prepositions, articles, and coordinate conjunctions (do not number or alphabetize these subheads). If you have major and minor subheads in a chapter ("A" level and "B" level), center the major subhead on the page, and begin the minor subhead flush with the margin. If it begins a paragraph, put a period after it and skip two spaces. Skip five or six lines if your subhead begins a new section.

If you cross-reference to other pages in the text, type one, two, or three dashes (space for the final printed page numbers) and write the proper manuscript page number in the margin, *in pencil*, on all three copies (as with all other handwritten notations). Try to avoid cross-references as much as possible, particularly of the "as I mentioned before" variety; they are usually unnecessary if your reader is reading carefully (let's be optimistic) and they increase typesetting costs considerably.

**Back Matter.** After the text proper you may have one or more appendixes, footnotes by chapter (we'll get to notes later), a bibliography, a glossary of terms, and an index of titles or authors or both (the subject index is prepared after the manuscript goes into proof). The back matter is listed with page numbers on the contents page.

Appendixes are less popular than they used to be and should be used only if necessary—not to pad the book with odds and ends of research that do not fit into the text. Documents, laws, charts, tables, or maps that are either too extensive or do not illuminate the text usually belong in an appendix.

The reference notes—footnotes numbered in the text on a chapter by chapter basis—are now usually printed with the back matter, though they can be placed at the end of each chapter. When you submit your manuscript, type the footnotes for each chapter on separate pages, numbering them consecutively (by chapter), and place them at the end of the text proper or after the appendix, if you have one (we'll get to the complete story on footnotes later).

The bibliography will contain at least a listing of your footnote sources, this time alphabetically either by title or author. It may be broken down into subject divisions as well. If you wish to add further suggested readings or books on the subject not specifically documented in the text, it's better to discuss this with your editor before you go to the trouble of preparing it.

Glossaries are helpful in technical books or those with many foreign words in them. Words are arranged in alphabetical order, each on a separate line and followed by its definition.

Over 90 percent of the trade books published do not require more complex front or end matter than has already been mentioned. If your book falls into the minority category, it's time for you to go out and buy one of the major style manuals.

**Extracts.** Any quotation that is set off from the text is called an extract. A short quotation of up to two lines of poetry and up to ten lines of prose can remain incorporated into the text. Merely set off the prose and poetry with quotation marks; if you are quoting two lines of verse, separate them with a slash. Larger quotations are indented on both sides and triple-spaced from the preceding and following text. If you wish to delete part of a quotation, use three ellipsis dots (periods) in the middle of a sentence, or four at the end. Do not use quotation marks to begin or end an indented extract; if they appear in the quoted material, use a 'single' quotation mark. On prose extracts, draw a straight penciled line on the left-hand margin (this is to keep the typesetter happy, something to keep in mind at every point in your preparation of the final manuscript). With poetry, duplicate the appearance of the original as closely as possible. Then make sure you triple-check your version against the original (ditto when you receive proofs). If you are finicky about it, and you should be, don't take your quotation of poetry, for instance, from an anthology, but go to the collected works or some similar scholarly, original, or fastidious source. If you make any changes in the original—adding a comment or italicizing—either point it out in the preceding text, in brackets within the quote, in parentheses after the quotation, or in a footnote.

**Footnotes**. There are basically two kinds of footnotes: a discursive reference to something in the text, or a citation for a source. Conventionally, the former is placed at the bottom of the page, and the latter at the end of the chapter or the end of the book. The various styles and complexities of footnotes are so legion that you ought to consult a style guide if you make substantial use of them in your text. As the University of Chicago's *Manual of Style* (widely used in publishing) points out: "No one manual can hope to protect editor and author from every thorn encountered in the thicket of scholarly documentation." Amen. I personally find most superfluous footnotes annoying; most trade readers do. Try as much as possible to incorporate those discursive references into the text, or else drop them completely. The discursive reference is indicated by an asterisk and a second one on the same page by a dagger. (Use two asterisks in your manuscript since you don't have a dagger on your typewriter.) There are two additional symbols, but if you put three or four symbols on the page your reader may stop reading right there, so I will not tempt you by listing them. Put the note at the bottom of your manuscript page, triple-spaced from the preceding text. If it's a long one, type it on a separate page marked "23 A" (or whatever) in the upper right-hand corner, and title the page "Footnote for page 23"; place the page directly after page 23.

Numbered footnotes, usually citations for sources, are all placed on a separate page (or pages), preferably at the end of the manuscript. Use a new set of numberings for each chapter's footnotes, titling the first page "Footnotes to Chapter I," etc. The number in the text itself is placed a half space above the line on which it appears and outside the period, though it is sometimes more sensible to put the note in the middle of the sentence—common sense will usually serve you here. Avoid footnoting either chapter titles or subheads. If cited books, articles, and poems are to be included in a bibliography, then an abbreviated version in the footnote will suffice, e.g., A. B. Keith, *Indian Logic*, p. 24. This would appear in your bibliography as: "Keith, Arthur Berriedale. *Indian Logic and Atomism*. Oxford: Oxford University Press, 1921." I won't go into the matter of *ibid.* and *op. cit.* except to repeat that substantial footnoting is best left to scholarly and technical books, or textbooks. Of most importance for your manuscript is *consistency*; decide in advance which style of footnoting you will use, and stick to it throughout the manuscript. Use the fullest possible documentation in footnotes, so that whatever style the house employs, you may only have to delete matter later rather than add it—a much more time-consuming task. The same advice regarding consistency, by the way, holds true for spelling, punctuation, and capitalization.

**Tables and Illustrations.** Tables differ from illustrations: They are typeset rather than reproduced from artwork. Illustrations include many different kinds of material: charts, graphs, maps, photos, paintings, and line drawings. Let's examine them separately, since they are listed and arranged separately in your manuscript. Only one copy of these is necessary for the publisher.

Tables are typed or pasted on the same size paper as your manuscript. Regardless of size, each one should be pasted on a separate page and numbered consecutively throughout the book, e.g., Table 3, not chapter by chapter, if you have less than, say, six. For over six tables, I recommend incorporating chapter references, e.g., Table 6.1, 6.2, 6.3, and so on. Always refer to your table by number in the text. At the top of the page, directly beneath the table number, goes the title or caption, which should be extremely brief:

> *Not:* Amount of money earned per year by free-lance writers on a state-by-state basis.
> *But:* Yearly Free-lance Writer Income
> (By state)

Just facts, no description or comments. Tables should be placed in a separate envelope, along with a numbered listing of them. (Duplicate the copy from your front matter.)

The best method of indicating the placement of your table or illustration to the designer and copyeditor is to type or draw two horizontal lines across the page and place the instructions within it.

---

Table 6.2 about here

---

Since the margins are often filled with copyeditor's or designer's notes, your own instructions may be confusing or overlooked there. Avoid the following: "As we see in table 6.2:". It implies the appearance of your table or illustration directly following the colon. In all likelihood, only short extracts or formulae will follow directly after the colon. Artwork, because of layout and page makeup requirements, rarely appears exactly where you want it to. This is the reason for referring to your table or illustration by number in the text.

A complete one-page table on 8½″ x 11″ typing paper will just about reduce to the average book page size (approximately 6″ x 9″). The making of tables is a story in itself, for which I again refer you to one of the standard style manuals.

If you have more than one kind of illustration, such as charts, maps, and plates (photos or engravings), then your list of illustrations for the front matter should be broken down by category and a copy of this list enclosed in the separate envelope in which you place the illustrations. They should be numbered in the sequence in which they appear in the manuscript (keeping in mind that over six should be numbered by chapter, e.g., Map 6.1, 6.2, and 6.3), although they may go unnumbered in the book—as movie stills frequently are, for instance. At the top of the page, the caption or title of the illustration is typed in:

Map 10. The Battle of Waterloo

Underneath the illustration, you may type in the legend, the explanation, usually in the form of a sentence or two, which illustrates the point of what you are reproducing. In print, caption and legend may be run on together, or only one or the other used. This decision and other related problems, such as placement, manner of reproduction, and what size the final illustrations should be, are all determined in conference with your editor.

Don't write or type on photos or original artwork; keep a separate list of these (what? another list!), numbering them consecutively, and on the back of each piece of artwork identify it (lightly in pencil) by number and caption. All artwork from which the publisher will reproduce should be protected by cardboard when you send it, and not folded, spindled, or mutilated—do not hold them together with paper clips, pins, staples, or whatever, for obvious reasons. Use rubber bands.

Whether or not you secure permission for an illustration, a "credit line" (statement of the source) is either necessary or appropriate. There are a variety of possibilities as to where they will appear in the book. For your manuscript it is sufficient to identify the source on the list provided with the separate envelope of illustrations. Just as for tables, indicate with two horizontal lines and a note therein where you think the illustration should be placed.

## Permissions and Copyright

The purpose of copyright is to grant the publisher or the author the exclusive right to control the publication and reprinting of the author's work for a specific period of time. After more than twenty years of legislative efforts, Congress has finally passed the first major revision of copyright law since 1909. The provisions of the new bill—which went into effect January 1, 1978—are both complicated and lengthy and extend to a number of areas which do not directly affect authors, such as jukeboxes, cable television, and record royalties. We will confine our discussion to several features that are pertinent to authors.*

*Circular R1, "The Nuts and Bolts of Copyright," available free from the Copyright Office (Library of Congress, Washington, D.C. 20559) is thorough and lucid on matters concerning writers.

Of most importance is the extension of copyright protection to fifty years after the author's death, which now conforms with international copyright provisions. Formerly, copyright was extended for twenty-eight years after the date of publication and was then renewable for another twenty-eight years. In 1962, when works published after 1906 should have begun to fall into public domain, Congress suspended this feature of the copyright law, so that those works then continued to enjoy protection, pending a final legislative resolution. The new bill extended existing protection to those works in their renewal term to a total of seventy-five years from first publication date; copyrights in the original twenty-eight-year term must be renewed, but the renewal will be for a period of forty-seven years, hence, also extending protection to seventy-five years—but only provided the copyright is renewed. Publishers will assist authors in renewing copyright as a matter of course if the rights have not reverted to the author. In the latter event, authors can write to the U.S. Copyright Office in Washington, D.C., and request a form for renewal of copyright, which should be filed during the year just prior to the twenty-eighth anniversary of the date of first publication.

Another important feature of the bill concerns unpublished works. Hitherto, "common law" copyright protected unpublished works in perpetuity, so that unpublished letters of John Adams, for instance, were still protected by copyright. The new bill dates the beginning of copyright from the time an author finishes a manuscript, so that published and unpublished works will be protected under the same copyright provision.

In any case, you may quote any kind or amount of material published prior to 1906 (or from any U.S. Government Printing Office publication*) without securing permission. After 1906, the doctrine of "fair use" determines how much material you may quote without securing permission. Unfortunately, no provision officially determines what amount of material constitutes "fair use." The rule of thumb most publishers and writers work with is that up to 500 words can be used from a full-length book without securing permission, provided the extract is not a single complete unit. The amount is correspondingly less for shorter works, such as articles, essays, or short stories. A simple footnote will suffice as an acknowledgment. If in doubt, write for permission; your editor will advise you on this. For photos,** songs, more than two lines of verse, maps, and tables, you are obliged to write for permission. Write to the *original* publisher or the copyright holder who is listed on the copyright page of the book; do not write, for instance, to

---

*A very few works produced under government grants may be copyrighted and will contain such a notice.

**Some writers and publishers now consider a modest number of movie stills and film-clip blow-ups as being covered by the doctrine of fair use.

the paperback publisher who is reprinting the book. If you address your letter to the rights and permissions department of the original publisher, they will forward it to the author, his estate, or his agent if the publisher no longer controls the copyright. Be explicit about the material you wish to quote: title, passage, page number(s), and number of words. You probably won't have to pay for any incidental quotations or extracts, but will identify the source of the quotation on the acknowledgments page, having asked the copyright holders for their preferred wording.

If you are preparing an anthology or any kind of work that draws heavily on copyrighted material, whether it is written or illustrative matter, permissions fees will generally have to be paid. Your editor will discuss with you the extent of the rights you should secure, that is, both the territory requested and the manner of publication (paperback, cloth-bound, textbook, etc.), as the amount of the fee will depend on these variables. The editor will also indicate an approximate permissions budget. If the total permissions fees for your anthology considerably exceed the budget, you may have to renegotiate the fee with some of the copyright holders (many are flexible) or provide some substitute selections. If there are fees for the use of the material, the publisher will generally pay them upon publication and subtract the amount from your future royalties (unless you have negotiated otherwise). The author or, rather, the editor of the anthology should begin writing for permission as soon as he or she has a contract. Sometimes a copyright holder is difficult to track down, and many are tardy in responding to requests, which may require follow-up letters. The original copies of the letters or forms that grant permission should be turned in to the publisher with the final manuscript; the author should photocopy a set for his own files.

## *Preparing an Anthology*

Not every manuscript consists primarily of original typewritten pages. The anthology or collection of previously published material is common in trade, textbook, and el-hi publishing. Sometimes referred to as a cut-and-paste job, an anthology only *looks* like an easy way to make a book. In practice, it presents considerable permissions problems; and, if not assembled accurately and carefully, it can become far more difficult to copyedit and produce than the average manuscript.

In serving as the editor of other writers' materials, you assume the obligation to respect their messages and their rights. In addition, you face the task of gathering material from many disparate sources and making certain that it appears in clear, legible form in your finished manuscript. Permissions problems aside, then, the primary objective in putting together an anthology is to avoid the kinds of typographical errors that will invariably be introduced if you retype the material. Whenever possible you should use original tear sheets from your sources. If none can be obtained, then you must rely on photocopying or photography.

Let us assume that your anthology will contain articles selected from readily available mass magazines and journals or books. Purchase enough copies so that you will have two complete versions of each chapter or article. You need two copies, obviously, because in pasting up you lose the reverse page. Make photocopies or disassemble the magazines or journals and cut up the pages, then assemble the individual articles. Cut away all the advertising or extraneous matter; if an article appears two or three columns to the page, carefully separate these and keep them in sequence. Paste the resulting pages or columns on 8½″ x 11″ bond sheets, leaving ample margins at top and bottom; number these sheets lightly in pencil, per article, as you create them. If you don't have rubber cement, use "magic" cellophane tape that can be written on with a pencil. Do not, of course, use regular cellophane tape or staples.

If you're working with materials that are still in copyright but ten or twenty years old, or if you're taking selections from bound books, tear sheets may not be the answer. Instead, you must locate a photocopying machine. Try the Yellow Pages for a nearby firm specializing in such service; its rates are much lower than those of the machine in the library, although you may be forced to use the latter if you cannot check out the particular books or periodicals you need. Whether you operate the machine yourself or pay someone else to do it, make sure you'll be producing not legal-sized sheets but regular 8½″ x 11″ pages. Inspect each of these carefully, and be honest: If you can't make out every character or symbol, the copyeditor can't either, and the typesetter will refuse to look at such material. Try again, or try a different machine. Be especially careful in photocopying sections from large, thick books; in such reproduction, their inside edges tend to blur and fade out. If you're taking materials from rare or over-sized books, you may have to turn to someone who can use a 35mm camera and ask him to photograph the pages you need. The resulting prints should be inspected carefully for size and legibility.

When you've assembled the articles in series according to your proposed table of contents, go over each article carefully and edit it. That's your job; you're functioning not as author but as editor of other peoples' writings. You can't change what they say, but you can, if you wish, shorten the selections—if you do, mention this and include a copy when you write for permission. Use dots (ellipses) to indicate cuts of a sentence or less (four for a complete sentence, three for part of a sentence) and line breaks for deletions longer than a paragraph. You should also assume the responsibility of doing some mechanical editing. Cut off or cross out anything—advertisements, running heads, page numbers, display type—that appears in the original but should not appear in the anthology you're creating. If the articles you've chosen are taken from twenty different sources, chances are that the original authors will be listed in twenty different ways. In your book, you don't want a headnote that gives the complete details of Margaret Mead's academic career, followed by an article that says only "by Barry Commoner." If you want headnotes for both, you've got to provide one for Commoner. Far better to eliminate such biographical matter, or give it briefly at the front of the book on a "Contributors" page. Incidentally, it would be your responsibility to create and type up such material, not the copy-editor's. Similarly, in the front matter of your manuscript you should give the complete data concerning your acknowledgments and permissions.

Unless you and your editor have discussed the necessity of doing so, avoid making stylistic changes in the individual articles—changing British spelling and punctuation to American, for example. If your articles have footnotes in the originals, these will probably vary considerably in format. One may list city, publisher, and date in a bibliographic reference; another may list only city and date. Discuss with your editor whether to regularize and implement these or to let the discrepancies stand. And speaking of notes, remember that if you cut material that includes footnotes, you must go through the remainder of the articles and adjust both the numbers that appear in the text and their corresponding numbers at the foot of the page or end of the article. If, in your anthology, you annotate the material yourself, type up your notes on separate pages and interleave them with the mounted tear sheets, or place them at the end of each selection.

In a few rare instances you may be unable to produce a good, legible copy of a page or pages. Do not take the necessary retyping job casually. Even at the hands of the best typist the copy may shift slightly in a hundred minute ways. Any newly typed copy of previously published material should be proofread carefully, character for character, line for line, before you incorporate it in the main manuscript. When ready for submission in its finished form, the manuscript will, of course, contain some original, typewritten pages—the front matter, possibly your own introductions or headnotes for the individual pieces. Treat these in the manner described earlier in this chapter.

So far you've created only one copy of the anthology, yet you are going to need three: an original and a copy to forward to the publisher, and an editor's or author's copy for yourself. Back to the photocopying machine. Now the wisdom of avoiding staples becomes apparent. Pages containing them cannot be loaded into an automatic copier and must be fed into the machine by hand, a page at a time. When you get them back, or if you make the extra copies yourself, it's time for more honesty. Look at all the pages of your new copies. A photocopy of photocopied material can often be so light as to be illegible, though some machines have a "dark" button which improves its reproduction. If copies are too light or illegible, you must scare up more tear sheets or better photocopies and repeat the process just described for each of your additional manuscripts. Remember, if what you send to the publisher can't be read, it won't get worked on; similarly, if the copy you keep for yourself is illegible in places, you will have a hard time working with your editor and copy-editor when they send you their queries.

One last *caveat*: If the articles you select for your anthology contain *photographic* illustrations, do not bother to paste these into your manuscript except for reference. They may look great to you, but they are of no use at all to the publisher. If you want them to appear in your finished book, you will have to correspond with the original publisher or magazine and obtain glossy prints of the photographs you want to appear in your book. If there are black-and-white line drawings or diagrams in the original and you provide tear sheets, these will satisfy your editor; if the drawings you submit are photocopies, they cannot be used for producing the book. Either they must be redrawn, or, as with the photographs, you should contact the original publisher and inquire about obtaining photostats of the drawings. If your anthology is to include a large number of either drawings or photographs, bring this to your editor's attention while you're still in the selection and planning stages. He or she can provide suggestions that may save you considerable labor, expense, or both.

## Doing a Revision

Let's jump ahead for a moment and assume you've already published a book. It's nonfiction, and it's sold well because it contains the latest information on the subject. But in two or three years new developments in the field begin to make what you've written seem a bit dated. Sales have tapered off, too, while newer competing books on the same subject have begun to appear. It's still a promising market, so your editor suggests you revise the book. The kind of manuscript you're expected to produce will be similar to an anthology manuscript. It will contain new typewritten material interleaved with printed tear sheets from the first edition. The main technical problem in preparing a manuscript of this sort is knowing how and when to change anything in the old typeset material. And when not to.

The lines and paragraphs in a book are reusable. The publisher's strategy in proposing a second edition depends in part on his workers photographing this type and moving it around within the revised book. While you're negotiating the revision, find out if the company intends to reset the type of the entire book. This is rare, but it might be the case for a book with very little text but a great many illustrations—a children's book, for example. If the type is to be reset, you will have considerable freedom in rewriting and making changes. In most instances, however, the firm expects you to rewrite and revise only certain agreed-upon passages or subjects, leaving considerable blocs of type, or even entire chapters, untouched.

**Assembling the Manuscript for Revision.** You must convert the book pages back into manuscript form, with type on only one side of the page. To do this, obtain two copies of the latest printing of the book. If in doubt about the number of that printing, consult your editor. When you have the right books, use a razor-bladed knife to remove their covers. Cut or carefully tear the pages out of their bindings in order to produce two stacks of identical pages.

Paste or tape these pages on individual sheets of 14- or 20-pound 8½" x 11" bond paper, following the pagination of the book. Paste down page 1 from the first stack, page 2 from the second stack, and so on. If the pages of your book are 8½" x 11" to begin with, don't bother taping them to blank sheets. Simply use a pencil to cross out alternate sides until you have a complete set of pages in sequence on one side only. If your book pages are larger than 8½" x 11", you must cut columns of type from each page and mount these in proper sequence, one to a sheet.

Make sure each page you've just produced carries a clearly legible page number. Supply missing numbers when necessary, in the upper-right-hand corner. Try to stay with the book's page numbers and avoid giving the manuscript a new numbering system. If you have to cut up columns and put them on successive pages, number these with decimals—page 22.1, 22.3, and so on.

Special planning must go into the process just described if your book contains numerous tables or illustrations. Remember that when you created the manuscript for the first edition, you had to make stacks of different elements that were going into the book—figures, graphs, photographs, maps, tables—and indicate approximately where you wanted them to appear in the text. Now you're reversing that process. And you may find that the numbers you gave to your photographs the first time around were used for in-house reference only, and dropped from the actual book. This is a common practice for nontechnical works. Before you begin to cut and tape, look through both copies of the books you obtained, and make certain everything has a number. If it doesn't, whatever it is, give it one—in both copies.

If your book has a lot of photographs, and they appear on glossy paper, bunched up at intervals throughout the work, they're in *signature* form, and relatively easy to locate. Diagrams or drawings may appear virtually anywhere. In either case, if they lack numbers, assign them numbers by chapter: Figure 3.1, 3.2, and so on. As you go through your disassembled pages and encounter these figures or tables or other elements, tape them to sheets of white paper and make separate stacks of them off to one side. When complete, these should be placed at the end of the manuscript; they are an integral part of it, but they do not carry manuscript page numbers. (Such a series of taped-up, printed photographs, for example, will be for reference only, but it will prove invaluable to anyone working with the actual negatives.) Each time you extract a table or drawing, there will be a "hole" or sometimes even an entire blank page in the typeset material you're remounting. Don't skip over these. Where such holes appear, write "Figure 5.18 about here," with a line above and below it, just as you did when you were putting together the first-edition manuscript.

In preparing a revision, the object is not to lose or misplace anything you might want to keep. Take the renumbering business seriously. The ease with which you will shortly be adding new tables or taking out old diagrams depends on how accurately you can identify and alter such series of elements. Incidentally, when you're making separate stacks of artwork, remember that the captions go with the figures; they move together. When you've attended to all such matters, and you're satisfied that the two books have been converted to a single, coherent manuscript, the next step is to make a photocopy of what you've just assembled.

Take into account the various kinds of copiers available in your vicinity and select the one that will produce the best, clearest copies. During your first visit you'll need to make only one copy of the pasted-up material. When you get home, put that stack of original pages away for safekeeping. Do not write or mark on it, since you may discover a need for more clear copies of certain pages or passages later on.

**Revising the Manuscript.** If you've kept a corrections file for your book's latest printing, transfer to your photocopied set of pages all the notations you've been saving that ask for appropriate and necessary changes (use a pen with black ink; blue ink and blue pencil do not photocopy adequately). The process is very similar to that of correcting or changing proofs, and you are expected to use the same proofreader's symbols. (This process is explained more fully in Chapter 6.) Whatever you write on these pages, be sure to respect a margin of at least a quarter of an inch on all sides of the 8½" x 11" sheet. You do not want anything to appear faded or illegible when you photocopy these pages again after finishing with the revision.

Similarly, if you have been keeping a revision file, get it out and review its marked copy and its notes and enclosures before you turn to your typewriter. Rewriting and revision are creative processes and not within the province of this book. Here your own writing habits will guide you, along with whatever understanding you have developed with your editor about what is to be rewritten or changed.

When you identify a passage that should be deleted entirely, simply draw a line around it (that is, enclose it within a box) and an X through it. Draw an arrow from the last line of text you want to keep to the point where the text resumes. Continue the line of the arrow to the next page, if necessary. If you decide to rewrite a line or two, do it in the margin; the same goes for changing words or phrases.

**Minimizing Changes.** You have a right to mark typographical, grammatical, and factual errors, or anything else that will straighten out the sense of a scrambled or obscure passage. You do not have a right to change anything that catches your fancy. It might be tempting to rewrite or reword something you have decided doesn't suit you, even though you and your editor agreed to it in the first edition. Don't do it. Such requests will be overruled if they do not fall within the agreed-upon limits and needs of the revision.

**Adding New Material.** If you want to add three new paragraphs totaling a hundred words at a point in the middle of what is now book page 10, simply type these out on a separate sheet, label it 10A, and write "Insert 10A goes here" with an appropriate caret at that point on page 10. Additional pages become 10B, 10C, and so on. At the bottom of the last page in any such series, write "Go to page 11" or whatever page you decide should follow page 10 (11 may have been removed already).

When you're satisfied with the revision of the text proper, go through the manuscript a few more times to check and readjust all numerical sequences—such as those of footnotes, figures, or picture captions— that may have been interrupted by the changes just made. You may have new permissions to obtain (and thus new credit lines on the acknowl- edgments page), new diagrams to prepare, new definitions for the glossary or out-of-date titles to be removed from the bibliography. You may also have to provide a new preface to the second edition. Treat all such material as inserts, and don't renumber the entire manuscript. The original page numbers—as much as you have been able to preserve of them—will be useful guides to the production workers whose task it will be to salvage as much type from your original book as possible. When everything is finally the way you want it, put your last name and the book's short title on each page. Having a rubber stamp with your name on it would be helpful at this point.

On your second trip to the copying machine, make the two copies to send to the publisher. It's all right if the images of the existing type look a bit faded this time, since type will not be set directly from those pages. Everything else, though, should be clear and legible, especially your marginal changes.

## *Some Additional Tips*

If your manuscript contains uncommon foreign words (particularly those written in other than the Latin alphabet), mathematical symbols, unusual names, unorthodox spellings, chemical symbols, etc., then prepare a separate sheet of them to which you draw specific attention. The same is true if you purposely "mispell," misname, misquote, or have an unconventional preference in usage. Be consistent throughout the manuscript if you use certain words or names the spelling of which is open to question, e.g., Shakespeare, Shakspeare, Shakespere. Foreign words are always italicized by underscoring, except for those in common use.

Try to avoid word breaks on the right-hand margin (for the typesetter's sake), especially of foreign words or technical terms. When called for, use two hyphens for a dash, one for hyphenating words. Avoid capitalization of complete words (in titles, captions, or anywhere else); the book designer will make these decisions.

Any diacritical marks not on your typewriter should be written in ink, carefully and clearly; do not use the single quotation mark (') for a *grave* or *aigu* accent, for instance.

And do not forget to write ''The End'' three spaces below the last line of the last chapter.

## *You're Not Finished Yet*

When you've come this far with your manuscript, put it down for a few days and forget it. Then, before you send it off, give it another close reading. You are bound to find a few errors, a phrase to add, some punctuation to change or a missing sentence. It wouldn't hurt to compare the rough draft with this final version, page by page, to make sure you haven't left something out in transcribing.

Avoid using the margins for final corrections for reasons already mentioned. Be especially careful and clear with these corrections; do not change or erase a letter, cross out the whole word and print or type the corrected word above it. To add an additional word or short phrase, indicate by a caret ( ∧ ) where it should appear, and print or type it directly above the caret and between the lines. If you have to change or insert a paragraph, retype the page. If an additional page is necessary, title it "25A," insert a caret where the new material is to be placed, and in pencil in the margin write "insert 25A." Be sure you indicate whether it is a new paragraph or to be run in. If there's more than one page of new matter, write "25A follows" on the bottom of page 25, number the new pages 25A, 25B, etc., and on the bottom of the last page write "26 follows." If you drop a complete page, say page 26, print "27 follows" at the bottom of page 25. If you add or delete more than a few pages, you should renumber the entire manuscript.

If the manuscript is messy and rife with changes, corrections, and cut and pasted pages, you are going to have one disgruntled editor on your hands (if you have a contract) or you may turn off a prospective publisher or agent. You might even have the cost of retyping the manuscript charged to your royalty account, or get a bill for 10 percent extra on composition costs (which you may be requested to pay on receipt). Be as neat as possible.

### Sending the Manuscript

After all the effort you've put in, you will want to exercise some care in wrapping and sending the manuscript. Typing-paper boxes are excellent containers for mailing (paste a label on the box with your name, address and book title), provided you wrap and tie them well. Don't use staples or other bindings on the manuscript; keep it flat without pages or chapters fastened. Any artwork should be placed between cardboard in the separate envelopes previously mentioned, and secured with rubber bands.

Send your material first class and registered, or be a gambler and save some money—and lose a few days—by mailing it fourth class, special handling. Address it to a particular person in the company, or at least to the appropriate department or division (see my previous suggestions in Chapter 1). If you do send it unsolicited,* enclose a stamped and self-addressed envelope or sufficient postage to cover return mailing costs.

Now . . . mix yourself a martini, pour yourself a glass of sherry, or crack open a bottle of champagne . . . you've earned it.

*In which case I recommend sending a photocopy of the manuscript.

# 5

# *How a Manuscript Is Processed by a Publisher*

> A book must be done according to the writer's conception of it as nearly perfect as possible, and the publishing problems begin then. That is, the publisher must not try to get a writer to fit the book to the conditions of the trade. It must be the other way around.
>
> —Maxwell Perkins

You have delivered the goods. And you followed, as closely as possible, the guidelines for manuscript preparation described in the preceding chapter. Take that well-deserved rest while you can. For there is additional work to be done, on your part as well as on the part of many others, before your manuscript becomes a book. Familiarizing yourself with what goes on inside a typical publishing house will make your contribution easier, speed the book's progress, and help to reduce any anxiety you may experience during the ensuing months.

Why should you care about the publisher's responsibility in the agreement you have made? Publishers, like nearly everyone else, work with possible combinations of time and money, and you have a vital interest in helping your publisher strike the right combination. Editing and producing your work economically means a lower cost for the finished book; getting it out on time, in the right season, at a competitive price, can boost sales. Greater sales mean more money for both you and the publisher; they can also mean wider distribution and greater acknowledgment of your status as an author.

The opportunity to cooperate with various members of the publishing house, then, is one of those offers you really cannot afford to refuse. In addition to these short-term reasons, there are some long-term considerations to be kept in mind.

No one wants or expects to be a one-book author. What you learn about the publishing process while your first book is coming out may give you a critical edge when the time comes to determine if your second book, assuming you write one, will get a contract. Publishing is currently undergoing considerable changes in its technology; it is also experiencing a high rate of job turnover among its editors and production specialists. During such transitional times, the successful author is the one who knows, literally, at all times during the life of any of his books, what's going on.

## Why Does It Take So Long?

An old saw in the publishing business states that "it takes about as long to make a book as it does to make a baby." True enough, but not inherently so. Bookmaking is a succession of tasks, many of which can be performed simultaneously, some of which can be speeded up considerably, depending on the available manpower and money the publisher is willing to devote to the project.

In recent years mass market paperback houses, geared up for the imminent release of important information (such as the Watergate transcripts) or seeking to capitalize on the timeliness of events (such as the mass suicides at Jonestown) have managed to put books on the newsstands within weeks or even days after the events described occurred. (The current record is probably still held by *The Pope's Journey to the United States—The Historic Record*, which Bantam published in 1965. Bound books were available for distribution slightly less than three days after receipt of the manuscript of the first chapter.)

Seasonal needs can dictate a book's schedule, too, causing copyeditors and printers to work overtime, for example, to get an expensive new cookbook out in time for the Christmas buying season, or a textbook ready well in advance of the fall semester. At the other end of the spectrum, certain specialized art books, technical works, dictionaries, and encyclopedias may be years or even decades in the making.

In between comes the "average" book—the novel, the freshman reader, the collection of critical essays, the illustrated children's story. Depending on their length, complexity, and the house priority assigned to them, all will require from six to twelve or even fifteen months before the finished volumes reach the bookstore. There are three main reasons for this, and they are often overlooked by the novice or even the experienced author: other books, subcontracting, and house priorities.

**The House Workload.** A publishing house—its employees, facilities, and associated suppliers—is not infinitely elastic. Typically, the staff is working to produce not only your book but also ten, twenty, or a hundred additional books as well. In the course of a single day, many of these books compete with your book for the attention of the editorial and production staff. Invariably delays, changed priorities, distractions, and communication failures plague this process. This state of affairs is industry-wide and does not seem to be affected by the size of the publishing operation.

In the smaller houses, which publish anywhere from five to twenty titles a year, as few as two or three persons, each wearing a variety of bookmaking "hats," may handle the entire production workload. Middle- to large-sized houses employ considerably more persons, many of whose functions are very specialized, to perform the tasks necessary to get your book out; but the greater number of titles issued annually by the larger firms offsets such increases in manpower. Neither extreme is inherently better or faster than the other, since all publishers, large or small, produce books in essentially the same way.

**Going Outside.** Another old saying holds that all one needs to become a publisher is an office, a secretary with a typewriter, and a supply of Maalox. This is because a considerable amount of the effort put forth to publish a book is not expended on the premises of the publishing house. Virtually every task or function to be described in this chapter can be subcontracted to another individual or firm. This extensive brokerage of assignments gives considerable flexibility to the publishing operation. During periods of slack time, the house is not encumbered with a large payroll; yet when the occasion demands it the supervisors are able to call on a large, diversified work force of specialized professionals. Heavy reliance on outside editorial and production help is not without its hazards, however; it can dissipate control and contribute to the unevenness of the final product. Moreover, the success of this concatenation of tasks is sometimes dependent on the availability and schedules of the outside subcontractors. If a typesetter, for example, misestimates the time necessary to set a particular book, or if a free-lance indexer fails to produce an index when it is needed, the house staff may be unable to make up the lost time. The book may lose its turn at the printer's—or, worse, miss its optimal marketing time. In house and out, workers strive to reduce the intervals and avoid delays, but this in turn can require more time for consultation and paperwork. If all the tasks *could* be performed under one roof, the book would come out sooner, but that is hardly, if ever, the case.

**The House Priorities.** Editorial and production work continues on a year-round basis in most publishing houses, but it is scheduled in ways that will make books available for distribution and sale during one of two basic seasons. Early on, your manuscript will be designated to appear either on the "fall list" of new books or the "spring list." For trade books these two seasons reflect consumer buying patterns. The spring list runs approximately from February to July and culminates with the kinds of books that will appeal, it is hoped, to summer vacation readers. For the fall list, running from August to December, emphasis is placed on producing books that will do well during the important Christmas buying season. For textbooks the time spans are more narrow, since the publisher must schedule books to appear during the major "adoption" periods, which in the fall run from mid-October to mid-December, and in the spring from March to the end of April. These are the periods when most teachers, professors, and textbook selection committees put in their book orders for the following semester.

A medium-sized publishing house, planning to issue a total of forty titles for its spring and fall lists, still expects only a fraction of those titles—from three to ten—to do well financially and to bring in most of the year's revenue. These especially promising titles, then, will be given higher priority than the other books proposed for the lists. Should delays from any quarter threaten these priority titles, time and effort will be diverted from works of lesser importance to ensure that the important titles will appear on time. The lower priority works get "bumped" on the monthly production schedule for periods ranging anywhere from one to six months or even more. Alternatively, a new and unexpected manuscript may suddenly be delivered, and the publisher may decide that this potential best seller *must* come out during the following season; other books suffer accordingly. Aside from hoping that your book will be considered a potential best seller, too, there is little you can do about such in-house juggling of priorities.

Taking these three factors into account—the house workload, the widespread practice of subcontracting, and the differences in priorities—it is clear that, even though the actual hours of editorial and production time devoted to your book may add up to only a few weeks or months, the average book still has a gestation period somewhere between that of a human and an elephant.

## Editing

Publishing houses come in various sizes and shapes. While their daily work remains essentially the same, titles and procedures may vary from one firm to the next. Your manuscript may land in a large publishing house having a number of specialized departments, each with its own way of doing things and cast of official-sounding titles. In another house of equal size, all the work may be carried out by seemingly nameless assistants who work almost exclusively for the book's acquiring editor. Or, your book may be turned out by some courageous soul operating out of his basement or garage who does almost everything himself.

The assumption for this chapter and the next will be that you have delivered a manuscript to a medium-sized trade house issuing—say— eighty titles a year. This firm has departments, and within those departments there are individuals wearing more than one hat. Chief among such multi-talented individuals, for your purposes, is your editor, who has a number of functions to fulfill before transmitting your manuscript to the copyediting and production departments. We will take a closer look at the editor's responsibilities and at the kinds of discussions he might have with other staff members and department heads. (Your editor is as likely to be a woman as a man. *He* is used here in the indefinite sense, not to suggest that publishing is a bastion of male chauvinism, which it certainly isn't.)

**Substantive Editing.** The making of books, regrettably, does not always go like clockwork. No matter how knowledgeable the author or how optimistic the acquiring editor, a newly arrived manuscript can sometimes turn out to have things wrong with it—not minor things, such as a missing footnote or an uncleared permission, but something major. The third chapter simply makes no sense, or the last quarter of the work is written in embarrassingly purplish prose, to give but two examples. Such calamities, having to do with the substance or meaning of the work, are the province of the book's acquiring editor. If your manuscript is destined for the trade market, he is probably the person who offered you the contract. He may have been in touch with you all along as you worked on earlier drafts. He may even have gone over them with you, page by page, making suggestions for improvements, offering more honest and more specific criticisms than you are likely to get from well-meaning colleagues or friends. In other words, there is a good chance that he has already devoted considerable effort to make certain the manuscript arrives in good shape. But he must still double-check it to be sure your complete final manuscript *is* in good shape.

Books and novels have been written about great editors: They are a rare breed. Perhaps Maxwell Perkins is best known, but there are other editors, less celebrated, whose achievements have been as great. Precisely what they do for an author and his manuscript is sometimes difficult to say, since their responsibilities are so broadly defined. In his posthumously published *Words & Faces*, Hiram Haydn, one of the preeminent American book editors of the postwar period, described it in this way:

Editorial work includes the study of the text of a given manuscript; the attempt to grasp, with imaginative precision, the writer's over-all "intent" (including, sometimes, themes or counterpoint of which he is not consciously aware), and to establish where he has fallen short; and finally, the give-and-take of the process of revision . . . . The editor must walk a thin line between remaining firm on changes he considers crucial and "taking over" the book. . . . It is his function to act as catalyst and as sounding board. It is not his book; he is the reader and consultant, not the writer.

The foregoing is an ideal description of what every editor would like to be able to do. In reality, and like nearly everything else in publishing these days, editors have felt the effects of the inflationary crunch, and many of them are running as fast as they can simply in order to stay in one place. In a recent article investigating "The Decline of Editing," *Time* magazine reporters found that "The traditional view of publishing as a leisurely life, carried on in mahogany offices and posh restaurants, has been replaced by the harrowing vision of a rat race on a roulette table." One editor they interviewed said "if Maxwell Perkins were around today, he wouldn't have time to be Maxwell Perkins."

Translated, what this means is that the bigger the firm, the greater the chance that the person who signed up your book won't do any line-by-line editorial work on it. What *Time* called the "belly editor," the person who took you out to lunch at a nice restaurant while you signed the contract, may next turn the manuscript over to a "pencil editor" in the house or even a free-lance copyeditor outside the house. That the book make sense is still the acquiring editor's responsibility; but especially if the manuscript is messy or complex, making it make sense is often delegated to someone else.

**Readers' Reports.** If your work is a textbook, and even if it appears to be in good shape and reads well, whoever is doing the substantive editing will usually take the precaution of sending it out for critical readings by scholars who are qualified in the same field. To narrow it down, if your work is a sociological study of prison conditions and recidivism, he will probably have on tap or be able to locate two or three sociologists with reputations and published works in similar areas. For an honorarium of from $150 to $200 apiece, they will look through a photocopy of your manuscript and send back two or three pages of comments about its strengths and weaknesses. For larger sums, and as requested, they will undertake more thorough readings and return more extensive, detailed reports. With these at hand, the acquiring editor can work through the troublesome sections of your manuscript, pointing out those changes or revisions that seem advisable.

The process of soliciting, evaluating, and implementing changes recommended by outside readers can be extremely time-consuming. In trade publishing it is an option, in the textbook world a commonplace. For reference works, such as dictionaries or medical books, several pages are sometimes needed to list all the experts, consultants, and advisers who at one time or another gave their opinions about the substance of the work. If serious, qualified readers believe there is something wrong with your manuscript, your editor will let you know what should be done. Never mind where his expertise is coming from—the identity of outside readers is usually not disclosed. Instead, remember the clause in your contract obligating you to deliver an *acceptable* manuscript. Weigh your editor's arguments, work with him, and try to satisfy both him and yourself that the work forms a meaningful and coherent whole.

**Contracts, Rights, and Permissions.** Months earlier, in order to convince higher management of the rightness of offering you a contract, your acquiring editor prepared a written evaluation of your book proposal. In that report, his designation of the marketing area—trade juvenile, for example—and the rights to be obtained—perhaps U.S. and Canadian but not British—governed the subsequent agreements you made with other publishers or authors for permission to reprint copyrighted material. This rquirement of manuscript preparation, discussed in greater detail in the preceding chapters, now becomes crucial. In some houses the acquiring editor or an assistant will check every permissions document; in other houses, the responsibility may fall to a copyeditor. Most large houses have a contract department (not to be confused with the rights-and-permissions department) that specializes in poring over the fine print of such documents.

If you have included five maps of Outer Mongolia that appeared two years ago in the *New York Times*, and you carefully obtained permission agreements from the *Times* corresponding to the marketing area or areas stipulated in your contract, you have no problem. Someone in the house will routinely check the form from the *Times*—and, as previously mentioned, that individual and your editor will insist that you submit the *originals* of such forms, while advising you to keep photocopies for your own reference.

If you have failed to clear the necessary permissions to use copyrighted material of any sort, or if you secured what you thought were the correct agreements but they turn out to be for the incorrect rights (either too restrictive or too broad), you will be asked to obtain the correct, appropriate agreements. Since the contract usually states that permissions fees are to be paid out of the author's future royalty account, the company's reasons for reviewing the forms so closely are strictly legal, not financial. It is your money that is being spent, not the firm's. Therefore you have a personal interest in helping to clear up any discrepancies—especially since if authors err in this respect, it is usually by obtaining rights that are too broad rather than too narrow. You may have agreed to pay $100 for world rights to reproduce half a page of another writer's work; but, since your book is to be sold in the United States only, if the discrepancy is pointed out by someone in the house, you could probably renegotiate and save yourself half the original fee.

The state of your permissions file may have still another effect on your immediate finances. Most houses will not officially deem your manuscript contractually "complete and satisfactory" until these documents are in order, and will withhold payment of the final portion of your advance until you obtain the correct agreements. If necessary, and if your acquiring editor agrees, you can work on this problem while the manuscript is being copyedited and designed. Until you have turned them all in, however, the manuscript cannot be sent for typesetting. The reason is obvious: The company only loses money if material set in type must later be deleted from the galley or page proofs because it is discovered that proper permission to reprint copyrighted material simply cannot be obtained or proved to be exorbitantly expensive.

**Paperwork.** The acquiring editor or his assistants must fill out several specialized forms for your book. Some circulate only within the house—to obtain a product code number, for example, or a job number, or the International Standard Book number. Other forms will travel outside the house to obtain the Library of Congress number for your book or the Cataloging in Publication data. Forms will go out to enable your book to be listed in *Publishers Weekly* and *Books in Print*; still other forms may be typed up in advance in order to facilitate rapid payment of permissions fees as soon as your book is published. At this time, if you have not filled out an author's questionnaire, you will be asked to do so. Even after submitting it, you may be queried by members of the editorial or promotional staff for additional information. Whatever they want to know, try to provide it for them as quickly as possible.

**Transmittal.** As the substantive editing, checking of permissions, and filing of in-house forms near completion, the acquiring editor arranges to transfer copies of your manuscript to the copyediting and production departments. Such a turnover of responsibility is usually accomplished at a "transmittal meeting" convened by the acquiring or sponsoring editor; this may also be a regularly scheduled weekly or monthly get-together.

It should be understood that under the exigencies of modern publishing, unless your book is a blockbuster, the transmittal meeting will probably not be devoted to your book alone. Your editor may have more than one manuscript to turn over, and other editors may take turns transmitting manuscripts at the same meeting.

By the time it is held, your editor will have had occasion to go over the estimates and recommendations contained in his original evaluation of your proposal. That report treated not only marketing areas and rights but also proposed list price, type of discount, variety of binding, trim size (the width and height of the book page), print run (number of copies of the first printing), projected publication date, estimated costs, and probable profit margin. In the days or weeks since your manuscript arrived, the acquiring editor has been comparing the reality of what you delivered with the ideality of his earlier forecasts. His substantive editing may enlarge, reduce, or otherwise modify the manuscript. Conversely, new features of the manuscript may persuade him to adjust his initial estimates. If it is now apparent that the black-and-white drawings you both agreed upon earlier simply will not do, and that a dozen full-color photographs are absolutely essential to illustrate your points and to compete with existing books, the editor will obtain estimates of the added expense from the production department. In thinking about a publication date, he will also keep in mind the extra time that may be required to produce such full-color plates and to incorporate them in the book.

Having done his homework about the nature of the actual manuscript and about the kind of book he would like it turned into, the acquiring editor summons his colleagues to a transmittal meeting. With a representative of the copyediting department, usually a chief copyeditor or managing editor, he describes the kind of copyediting he believes the manuscript requires. It might be described as "heavy" or "light"; a considerable amount of rewrite may be in order, or very little. If he is aware of any special copyediting problems posed by the manuscript, he may provide samples of proposed solutions. Next, with the production supervisor, he will go over book design and format, trim size, typesetting, method of printing, type of paper, variety of binding, extra proofs, and other manufacturing aspects. His suggestions concerning the design of the book's dust jacket might also be discussed with the production supervisor; and, if the house is large enough to have one, with the art director. Both individuals might be consulted concerning the preparation of the aforementioned full-color illustrations and any other artwork intended to appear in the book. Also present at this meeting would be a marketing director or representative, who would be concerned in general with sales promotion and advance publicity, and in particular with the content of the dust jacket copy.

In order to prepare estimates for their particular responsibilities, each of these individuals may have examined copies or portions of the manuscript prior to the meeting. There may be additional meetings, too, depending on the complexity and importance of your manuscript. Out of the discussions of those attending come the various agreements, assurances, modifications, and counterproposals that will enable the acquiring editor, as management's representative, to develop a tentative notion of when bound books will be available and approximately how much they will cost. He himself may not make such estimates, however. Instead, once he has set the date at which the sales department expects to have bound books, a scheduling director may draw up the proposed sequence of tasks and the dates by which they are to be accomplished. Similarly, the production supervisor, working with his own estimates of the manuscript and those provided by others at the meeting, prepares a more accurate preliminary cost estimate for the entire project.

Once estimate and schedule are drawn up, discussed, and agreed to by the various supervisors and department heads, transmittal is complete and the manuscript is launched. The original copy of the manuscript goes to the copyediting department; the duplicate copy goes to the production department for preliminary design. Before we follow them there, however, it would be wise to take a closer look at the techniques of estimating costs and of scheduling editorial and production time.

## Planning to Publish

An earlier chapter in this book described the nature and purpose of the cost estimate. This form, usually prepared by someone from the production department, enables the acquiring editor to make further calculations involving price, profit, and the feasibility of issuing a contract. If the manuscript delivered is not much different from the manuscript proposed, the original or preliminary cost estimate drawn up when the contract is signed may be sufficient to see the work through all but the final stages of book production. A month or two prior to the bound book date, however, a second, more accurate cost estimate is made, which enables management to review actual expenses and to assign the book a final price. For the moment, let us consider the manner in which the production supervisor evaluates the manuscript in order to prepare a cost estimate.

**Breakdown and Page Estimate.** In order to project material and manufacturing costs, the production supervisor must have ways of assessing and measuring the manuscript mechanically. For very brief or very routine works he may, of course, count pages, or he may count words. For important, original manuscripts, however, in which the company intends to invest considerable sums of money, his measuring must be more accurate. He will therefore prepare a breakdown, or character count, of the entire manuscript. This involves making a careful estimate of the total number of typewritten letters, punctuation marks, and spaces in the different parts of the typescript: front matter, text, back matter, footnotes, and so on. Also included are estimates for space that will be needed in the finished book for ''display type'' (chapter openings, subheadings), artwork, photographs, tables, and ''white space.'' These estimates are made either on the basis of actual design specifications (if they are available at this time) or on the basis of the acquiring editor's and production supervisor's ''feel'' for what the book should be like. With these figures, the supervisor can estimate the total number of pages the finished book will contain. He may have instructions to ''pad out'' a brief manuscript or to fit an overly long one within a fixed number of pages. Whatever his guidelines, the ease with which he arrives at a reliable forecast of page length depends on the orderliness and internal coherence of your manuscript. If it is typed on different typewriters, set at various line lengths; if the number of lines per page varies considerably; if you have written in numerous corrections, or pasted on strips of copy, or deleted extensively—the whole thing may be sent for retyping, possibly at your expense, before the cost estimate can be completed. An orderly, clean manuscript is even more important for the copyediting and typesetting processes that are about to begin. The typesetter in particular may decide an especially sloppy manuscript is ''penalty copy'' and charge a proportionately higher rate to set it.

**Scheduling.** In the words of John P. Dessauer, in his recent volume, *Book Publishing*, ''it is a lot easier to prepare a schedule than to keep one.'' Nevertheless, the challenge of preparing and enforcing your book's schedule must be accepted by someone in the publishing house, and that person is usually designated as the scheduling director; in a different house, his title might be that of managing editor or even executive editor. He is assisted, of course, by the acquiring editor and by representatives from all the various departments involved in working on the manuscript.

If your work carries a normal priority and does not require an accelerated production schedule in order to reap maximum sales, the scheduling director will work out a series of projected dates, from manuscript to bound books, by which certain essential tasks must be completed. For example, what follows is a proposed publication schedule for an average book issued by a well-known New York trade house:

| Weeks necessary | Activity |
|---|---|
| 4 | Transmittal and copyediting |
| 2 | Manufacturing (cost) analysis and design |
| 4 | Typesetting |
| 2½ | Proofreading and revising of galley proofs |
| 2 | Typesetting the revisions and making up page proofs |
| 1 | Reading page proofs |
| 2 | Typesetting corrections for page proofs and preparing reproduction proofs |
| 1 | Checking and correcting reproduction proofs |
| 2½ | Preparing and checking blue-line proofs; preparing plates |
| 1½ | Printing |
| 2½ | Binding |
| 2 | Shipment to warehouse from bindery |
| 3 | Shipment to bookstores |
| 30 | Publication 7½ months after transmittal of manuscript |

Schedules of this sort are always ideal and more honored in the breach than the observance. An ordinary novel of 256 pages can often be produced from start to finish in six months, and another five weeks allowed to get the books to the reviewers and the bookstores, as in the preceding schedule, without undue strain to the staff of any modern publishing house. On the other hand, a biology textbook with the same number of pages, but with numerous photographs, tables, and diagrams, plus a second color of ink (in addition, usually, to black) on every page, could take twice or even three times as long.

When a work is still in manuscript form there is no foolproof formula for determining exactly how long it will take to convert it into a bound book. It must pass through several production and manufacturing stages, and it will require the attention of a host of individuals. Both conditions increase the chances that some unexpected development may sabotage the schedule. However, the typical scheduling director has been looking at raw manuscripts for years and has developed a feel for what is difficult to copyedit and set in type, what is easy, what will take months to accomplish, what can be done within a week or ten days. In other words, he relies on a combination of experience, mechanical reckoning, and guesswork to arrive at a final projected date.

The scheduler's biggest question mark is the time that will be required by the first stage—copyediting—and the intervals (including mailing time) necessary for the author to examine the proofs. The staff must "turn around" or exchange the manuscript and its subsequent incarnations in type not only with the typesetter but also with the author, and it is the house-to-author-to-house turnaround that holds the greatest potential for unanticipated delays. Here the scheduler's success in allowing for the unexpected depends in part on his familiarity with the assignment. If the author lives on the other side of the continent, the scheduler adds more mailing time; if he learns that the author has final exams to administer and grade at exactly the same time galley proofs are scheduled to arrive, he must either make allowance for the inevitable delay or attempt to tighten the schedule at some other point.

The scheduler's success also depends in part on his ability to reckon the intervals necessary for the mechanical and in-house tasks over which he has considerable control. In this respect, a competent editorial-production staff gives the scheduler confidence that minor delays can be compensated for and unexpected obstacles overcome. In addition, once a book is well along in production, as in reproduction proofs, the time remaining until bound books can be estimated with a fairly high degree of reliability. The later the stage, the more mechanical the function, and consequently the less chance for errors in scheduling.

**Abbreviating a Schedule.** If your book is a crash project—if it simply must be out in five months' time or it will miss the Christmas buying season—the scheduling director simply accepts the publication date of December 1 as inevitable and works backward to establish dates for all the production stages leading up to it. In one house, in order to make sure those intervening dates are met, he might ask the managing editor and production supervisor to double or triple the number of people they normally would have working on such a project. In another, to avoid the confusion that inevitably accompanies such doubling up, the supervisors may pay overtime to a staff member or a special bonus to a free-lancer for working extra-long hours. And in still another, the copyeditor or proofreader may be told to shelve whatever else he may be working on and concentrate full-time on your book. Someone else's work, then, gets bumped; but, as pointed out earlier, this can happen to your book, too. Finally, in order to abbreviate a schedule, typesetters, printers, and binders are often willing to work overtime or even around the clock, if the publishing house is willing to put up the extra money.

As author, you will initially be told of the season—fall or spring—in which your publisher plans to bring out your book. There is little point in asking about the month or week until your manuscript is completely edited and proofs have returned from the typesetter. At that time you may be told of the proposed publication date, but policies vary from house to house concerning whether or not you will be shown an actual schedule. Regardless of the point at which schedules are drawn up, they have a tendency to change, especially after they are underway. If editorial queries are sent to you, or if you receive a set of galley proofs with the request that you mark and return them within a certain amount of time, you should do everything within your power to return them by the deadline cited. If you are a week or a month late, either the publication date gets pushed back by that same amount, or the house staff starts working overtime or doubling up to compensate for your delay. In the first instance, the delay could cause the book to miss its selling season; in the second, it could add to the book's cost and eventual price. Either way, it can spell reduced royalties for you, the author.

## *Copyediting*

At this point it is assumed that, at least in terms of substance, your work is ready for publication. Having arrived in the editorial department, the manuscript is now assigned to a staff copyeditor, who may have attended the transmittal meeting and be familiar with the work already. Should all the in-house copyeditors be occupied with other projects, the managing editor or chief copyeditor may offer the assignment to a free-lance copyeditor. If the latter resides in the same city, he comes to the publishing house to pick up and return manuscripts that he works on elsewhere, usually at home. (Experienced free-lance copyeditors often work for firms in other cities, exchanging the work to be done by mail.)

The copyeditor's stated task is to check and bring into line the internal consistency of the work at a number of levels. Supposedly he is not concerned with content and will only set off in pursuit of that elusive quality called style. In practice, however, the good copyeditor attends not only to the minute but also to the broad features of the work, and often comes up with criticisms of or suggestions about content that must be acknowledged and dealt with by acquiring editor and author.

Of all the functions in a publishing house, that of the copyeditor is perhaps least understood and easiest to underrate. The copyeditor enforces mechanical conventions—of spelling, grammar, punctuation, capitalization, abbreviation, and a host of additional stylistic matters— while knowing full well that conventions are not absolute and that they must be reinvoked and occasionally modified for each particular manuscript. Invariably the copyeditor catches typographical errors, infelicities of style, errors of fact, and logical inconsistencies overlooked by all previous readers. He will normally correct as many of these as possible on his own. If he finds anything seriously troubling, he will bring it to the attention of the managing editor or acquiring editor. If they cannot resolve the matter, they may "query" you or ask the copyeditor to do so.

Editorial querying, like substantive editing, may be accomplished piecemeal, chapter by chapter, or *en masse*, after the copyeditor has gone through the entire work. Although exceptions are made occasionally, most managing editors instruct their copyeditors not to return all or even part of the original manuscript to the author after it has been copyedited. In too many instances when this has been done, overanxious authors with the best of intentions have failed to concentrate on the queries and instead have taken it upon themselves to change or even to erase the copyeditor's marks, to rewrite passages and to type new pages containing inconsistencies (relative to the uniform style the copyeditor has worked to establish), and to shift elements around to such a degree that the manuscript must undergo additional, and unnecessary, copyediting—adding significantly to the costs. To avoid this, the copyeditor usually makes photocopies of the relevant manuscript pages, with queries noted in the margins; or writes queries on gummed tags or "flags" and attaches these to the photocopied pages; or simply types the queries in letter form. They may also be read to the author over the telephone, if time is short and the budget permits.

The preceding paragraph should not be interpreted to mean that securing answers for specific queries is the only reason for returning all or parts of a manuscript to an author, or that the copyeditor's changes are sacrosanct. Rather, they are proposed changes, and if they are shown to you, it is to gain your approval or disapproval, not to embarrass you or show you up. Admittedly, it is not always an entirely pleasant experience to have an impartial mirror held up before one's grammar, spelling, and prose style. Nevertheless, the copyeditor's proposed substitutions and changes are intended to improve your book, not to detract from it. You owe it to yourself to take each editorial query seriously, to weigh it impartially, and to resolve it thoroughly. If, for whatever reason, the copyeditor has changed a word, for example, and you disagree with the proposed substitution, the time to object is *now*, while the work is still in manuscript, and not when you see the new word for the first time in proofs and decide it should be changed back to the original word. Careful reading of any copyedited manuscript pages sent to you can save a great deal of money in resetting type. If there are disagreements, these should be carefully noted and returned to the copyeditor with the answered queries. Your counterproposals to the copyeditor's changes will stand out clearly on a photocopied page. If they do not go against the style established for the rest of the book, the copyeditor will usually accept them and transfer all such final changes and answered queries to the original manuscript.

Part of the copyeditor's importance in relation to the quality and success of the book is that he is usually the last, and sometimes the only, person on the staff to read the work in its entirety. Modern bookmaking procedures sometimes involve such pressures and short timetables that the acquiring editor may never have the time to sit down and reason about each line or paragraph of your manuscript. This responsibility may justifiably be delegated, and the buck usually stops at the copyeditor's desk. If he does not catch the anachronism, the potentially libelous remark, or the circular argument, such features may appear in the finished book, to the embarrassment of some and the potential revenue loss of all. Others will look at the work in its subsequent typeset stages, and still others, such as the proofreader, may examine virtually every letter of every word; but the copyeditor is often the last to read it with an intelligent, critical eye. His importance in this respect cannot be over-estimated.

Another of the copyeditor's duties is to mark the manuscript in such a way that the text will require a minimum of alterations after it is set in type. The disparity between the cost of a well-placed flick of his pencil on the manuscript page and the typesetter's charge for altering a single line of type after the work is in typeset form is astronomical. By thinking of everything, or almost everything, and resolving it in manuscript, the copyeditor performs an invaluable service in holding down costs. In many houses the copyeditor also keys (by marking with alphabetical symbols) the various headings and elements of the manuscript so that they can be readily identified and worked with by the book designer. In short, the copyeditor has a Janus-like role, looking back over what author and acquiring editor have done and ahead to what book designer and typesetter must still do.

## Designing the Book

While the copyediting continues and author and acquiring editor deal with any queries raised by the copyeditor, work may also proceed on three distinct but related aspects of bookmaking: interior design, preparation of camera-ready artwork, and exterior or cover design. If the work is simple—a novel, for example, divided into chapters and having no illustrations or footnotes—such design tasks can often be carried out concurrently with the copyediting. The production supervisor has already received the extra copy of the manuscript you provided; in addition, he may make photocopies of the original. With these, he can assign different design tasks to the appropriate departments or individuals.

A large house will have a separate design and production department and probably an art department, too. The smaller house may not have such clear-cut departments and, in fact, may free-lance some or all of the design tasks to be performed. The policies of the particular house, rather than the nature of the book, usually determine the sequence or degree of overlap in the execution of design functions. In some houses a manuscript must be copyedited and keyed before interior design can begin; in others the design is created first, and preparation of the interior artwork begins at the same time as the copyediting. A sketch for the cover artwork might be commissioned while the work is being copyedited; but in another house such a task might wait until the work is in pages. Remembering that these functions may be performed serially or all at once and that their sequence can vary, let's consider each in greater detail.

**Interior Design.** The designer is responsible for the technical specifications of the book: a set of practical, coherent, aesthetically pleasing dimensions and relations between figure (the printed text) and ground (the book page) that will guide typesetter, printer, binder, and cover artist. The second edition of Marshall Lee's *Bookmaking: The Illustrated Guide to Design/Production/Editing* (New York: R. R. Bowker Co., 1979) is probably the best single-volume work available on the subject. If you are starting out to create a profusely illustrated or typographically complex book, it would be wise to examine this work and to read the chapters on composition, typography, and illustration.

If the house is large enough, the designer may be a member of the staff. On the other hand, he may work for a firm to whom the design is jobbed out; or, he may be a free-lancer, either working for himself or moonlighting while holding down a position elsewhere in the industry. Regardless, the production supervisor sends the designer a copy of the manuscript or a sampling of its pages, originals or copies of the rough artwork and proposed photographs, and memos concerning the technical features already decided on at this point (such as trim size, type of binding, desired page length). The manuscript itself, if properly keyed, will call his attention to levels of subheadings, indented quotes or extracts, lists, special type, formulae, and tables. All this will be accompanied by additional memos from or conversations with the production supervisor concerning the general effect desired for the book: whether the design is to be conservative, modern, whimsical, hearts-and-flowers, and so on. Some designers specialize in one or the other, some are good with technical material, some have a touch for certain historical periods or intended audiences. An edited collection of essays about Matthew Arnold's views on industrialism, for example, would be likely to receive a conservative treatment. A similar collection about Ken Kesey's views might require a more radical design approach.

In a week or two the designer sends back the manuscript marked with type specifications, a composition order (a typed list of such specifications), and half a dozen or more two-page layouts, which are drawings to actual size, on artist's tracing paper, of typical and special pages in the book. Thus the width and height of the page area within which the type is to be reproduced, the size and variety of all the type to be set, the space between the lines of type (called "leading") and surrounding the display type (called "white space"), and possibly a hundred more technical choices and details are repeated in whole or in part in two or even three forms: marked manuscript, composition order, and layouts. Any one of these can be followed by knowledgeable typesetters and makeup men who are about to create the page images in type.

If the manuscript is to become part of an ongoing series, it may not be designed in the manner just described. Instead, it may simply be marked up in the house according to a standing composition order. The design of an existing book can be copied or modified, too, and applied to your manuscript by an experienced production worker. In fact, the designer may not do the complete mark-up, which may be delegated to someone in the house when the design specifications are returned.

**Sample Pages.** A special situation worth mentioning here is the decision to ask the typesetter for sample pages. If your book is long and complicated, and if the publisher has a lot riding on it, time may be allotted to test the proposed design by having only a few pages—usually between three and twelve—set by the typesetter and returned for further study. If faced with a future composition bill that could run above, say, $10,000 (three times the cost for an average novel), the production supervisor will usually take the precaution of asking for sample pages, which cost only a couple of hundred dollars. With a booklet of sample pages at hand, editors and designer can, if necessary, make further adjustments and refinements in the design before committing themselves to the major typesetting investment. Whether or not sample pages are ordered, if the design is sound and the copyediting completed, the original manuscript is ready to be sent to the typesetter. Work continues, however, on other elements that will appear as part of the finished book.

**Preparation of Artwork.** Bookworkers call everything that is not set in type art, whether it is a diagram of a petroleum pump, a photograph of Suzanne Somers, or a special diacritical mark over the *C* in Karel Čapek. Each of these is identified not so much by content as by the technique with which it is reproduced. Thus black-and-white photographs become "halftones" and diagrams become "line art." There are further refinements involving screens, second colors, and overlays, but these need not concern us here. If there are illustrations of any kind in your book and you have followed the suggestions in this book for preparing them, the artists and graphics specialists will handle the technicalities.

The exact location of these artists is not important. They may be attached to the production department; or, in a larger house, they may have a department of their own. The latter may also contain art editors, photo researchers, illustrators, photographers, and other graphics technicians, all of whom have the responsibility of ensuring that the art appears "right" in the finished book. In the smaller house, an experienced copyeditor may coordinate most of these tasks, sending to an outside firm or free-lancer the work requiring photo processing, keyline-and-paste-up, draftsmanship, or color separations.

Whatever the arrangement, your roughs (pencil sketches or diagrams you have created or borrowed), glossy photographs, and illustrations taken from other printed sources will be examined, classified, sometimes redrawn, and eventually rendered in camera-ready form. An important part of this process is the "sizing" of art: reducing, cropping, or otherwise rearranging the dimensions of your figure so that it will fit attractively within the confines of the prescribed page area. Also important is the setting, placement, and checking for accuracy of the captions or legends that appear above or below the diagrams or photographs, and the similar checking of "call-outs"—the labels, letters, and numbers that appear within the figure proper. Such checking may be the task of a production assistant, artist, copyeditor, or all three in concert.

**Exterior or Cover Design.** In the months preceding publication, perhaps no other physical part of the book receives as much attention from the promotion staff—and possibly the author—as the cover design. Whether the book is to be a paperback only or a clothbound edition with a dust jacket, its exterior is what the prospective buyer sees first. And every author is concerned, rightfully, about having an attractive cover on his book. Unfortunately this is an area where author and staff can come to considerable disagreement, if in fact the house even allows the author to see a proposed cover design. Most publishers have a standing policy against this, experience having taught them that the creation of such an important feature is something best left to the experts—in other words, the publisher's staff. The author, whose photograph may appear on the back of the cover or back flap, whose career may be described briefly in a "bio blurb," and whose life's work may be summed up in a paragraph or two on the flaps, rarely accepts his editor's assurances and sometimes tries to get in on the act by sending in sketches, copy, ideas, and ultimatums that he have the final say-so about the cover. Such altercations merely slow down the book and contribute to everyone's ulcer, author's included. The ideal arrangement, as far as the house is concerned, is that the author simply provide, as accurately and completely as possible, everything the staff requests in the way of autobiographical information or responses to questionnaires, report any changes or updatings in this material, and reply to his copyeditor's queries. However, a few previously published, successful authors insist on the right—often written into the contract—to examine, criticize, pass judgment on, and even veto the proposed jacket design and flap copy.

To begin the work on the book's exterior, the production supervisor or art director delegates someone to provide sketches for a proposed cover. Obviously, if the book is illustrated for children, a piece of the interior art may be adapted for the cover, or the featured artist may provide a sketch or sketches. Some houses do this for textbooks, too. For other books, the assignment falls either to an artist on the staff or to a free-lance artist, photographer, or book designer who specializes in jackets and covers. Whether inside the house or out, the individual accepting the assignment will be given some general guidelines—the trim size, copy to appear on the front cover, and other material describing what the book is about— and will return, within a few days or weeks, two or three hand-lettered sketches of his proposal for the cover. These are passed around the house and examined by practically everyone, and copies may even be flashed at the book salesmen if it is sales conference time.The various suggestions, criticisms, and counterproposals are bureaucratically funneled back to the artist, who may further refine the most favored sketch or produce new ones if none of the first batch proved satisfactory.

If the sketch has been requested and approved far enough in advance, the artist next waits until someone on the staff sends him ''bulk specs''— a set of specifications giving not only the cover or jacket trim size and other dimensions, but also the all-important width, in inches or fractions thereof, of the book's spine (also referred to as the shelfback). Normally spine width is not known exactly until the work has been entirely paged and no additional material (such as index) is still to come. If there is little time in which to prepare the cover or jacket, however, an experienced production worker can calculate and provide bulk specs in advance.

Type must also be set for the jacket or cover, sometimes under the staff's direction, sometimes under the supervision of the artist. With bulk specs and exterior type at hand, the artist can prepare and deliver a cover or jacket mechanical (also known as a mock-up or paste-up elsewhere in the graphics industry). This is an assemblage of type and artwork pasted in place on a piece of large, flat cardboard. Attached to it may be two or three acetate overlays—''flips.'' Although photographed individually, the images on the cardboard and the flips are superimposed in the final printing process to create the finished, multi-colored jacket or cover.

The cover or jacket is printed separately from the sheets that will make up the book—on thicker, heavier paper, on a different kind of press, perhaps even by a different company. The time at which it is finished depends on the house policy and on the type and importance of the book. When possible, trade houses like to have extra (dummy) jackets printed and available for distribution anywhere from three to four months before publication. These may lack flap copy—the descriptive and biographical lines immediately visible when you open the book's jacketed cover from either side—but at least they indicate how the front of the jacket will look. Book salesmen and publicity people use actual jackets or dummy jackets to promote advance sales of the book. For a title of lesser priority, the availability of finished jackets or covers may edge to within a month or two of the bound book date. In trade publishing, of course, that date may be six or eight weeks before the official publication date.

The development and execution of the exterior design, then, is concurrent with that of the text. While the exterior may be the work of hands outside the production department, usually the acquiring editor—and occasionally even the editor-in-chief or his assistants—keep close watch on the effect achieved. The involvement of copyeditor, designer, and artist will continue during the stages of typesetting, proofreading, printing, and binding to be described in the next chapter. As each successive task is completed, its results are sent back to the individual responsible for ordering it. This system of review and approval is followed during the remainder of the production and manufacturing processes.

# 6

# *How a Manuscript Is Turned into a Finished Book*

> There are men that will make you books and turn 'em loose
> into the world with as much dispatch as they would do a dish
> of fritters.
>
> —Miguel De Cervantes

Your work has moved along in the weeks since you delivered the manuscript. Management and staff have made key decisions concerning the physical aspects of the book and even about its advance promotion (to be discussed in greater detail in the next chapter).

You have answered the copyeditor's queries, the interior design is finished, and a design sketch for the cover is on order. Momentarily the original, copyedited version of the manuscript rests in the production offices, where, if this task has not been accomplished already, it is marked up with the designer's specifications, preparatory to sending it to a typesetter.

## *Setting the Text in Type*

In discussions with their editors, authors often ask "When are you going to send it [the copyedited manuscript] to the printer?" Few stop to realize that the work must first go to a typesetter and that typesetting and printing are two very different operations. We will discuss printing later in this chapter. For now, we must stress the important fact that for almost every publishing house in the United States and Canada, excepting a very few one-man presses, typesetting is done by an outside firm with priorities, schedules, and problems of its own. That firm is also, at the present time and for the next ten or fifteen years, in a considerable state of upheaval due to recent technological innovations and advancements in the art, the craft, and the business of typesetting. But out of the hundreds of commercial typesetting firms available, which one will get your manuscript?

It will depend, first of all, on which one submits the lowest bid. The production supervisor will normally contact two or three firms, submitting samples of the marked-up manuscript. He may not always accept the lowest bid, however, since he is also concerned with the quality the house is aiming for with your manuscript, and he has time factors to take into account. Having worked with typesetters for many years, the production supervisor knows their shortcomings and their particular areas of expertise. He must consider the delivery date the typesetter proposes, and he must weigh this against his own knowledge of the typesetter's past performance and reliability in meeting deadlines. Precisely who does get the job can affect not only the schedule but also the quality of the book, the remaining editorial tasks, and the manufacturing.

**Hot Metal or Film?** At the present time, for the kind of book one might buy at Brentano's or at the college bookstore, the production supervisor must choose from among three fundamental methods of typesetting: strike-on (direct impression), hot metal, or film (photocomposition).

Strike-on or direct impression methods of typesetting are the simplest and least costly of all. Simplest among these is merely typing the copy with a quality typewriter. The resulting page image is photographed and printing plates are made from the negatives. This method is most often used for low-budget books with a limited circulation. For more attractive, professional-looking books, more sophisticated kinds of typewriters are available: machines capable of setting copy in a variety of typefaces and with justified (vertically aligned) right-hand margins.

Hot metal is another name for Linotype or Monotype composition—systems named for machines that, operated by skilled craftsmen, cast the characters of your text in molten lead either singly (*Mono*type) or in lines (*Lino*type). From such castings, ink impressions can be made on paper (these are called reproduction proofs), which are then photographed in order to make the plates for offset printing. Linotype and Monotype were both invented in the late nineteenth century. As the first "keyboardable" means of setting type to gain widespread acceptance, they soon supplanted handset composition and became the dominant method of setting texts for books, newspapers, and magazines. Linotype was more typically used for straightforward bookwork; Monotype, considerably the more expensive of the two, was most often used for more complex typesetting, as in scientific or mathematical copy.

Both of these systems exist today, and both are in use. But there is a tendency among bookworkers to speak of them in the past tense, since the hot-metal era is coming to a close, and a new age of typesetting—that of film, or photocomposition—began in the seventies. There are many photocomposition devices, but almost all of them share a common operating principle. Characters are typeset when a high-intensity light source is directed through a matrix, or grid, that contains film negative images of all the alphanumeric characters and other commonly used symbols. When the light passes through the film negative grid, it exposes the appropriate succession of characters onto either film or photosensitive paper, which is then developed much the same as film from any camera.

Any of these three major categories of composition, or sub-categories thereof, may be superior to any of the others on the basis of the combination of economy, quality, speed, and flexibility required for a given project. It will be up to the house production and manufacturing specialists to decide which method of composition is best for your book. (The type you are now reading, for example, is 11/12 x 26 Times Roman; it was set by photocomposition on a Mergenthaler High Speed Linoterm.)

**Effects of the New Technology on Bookmaking.** The last few years have brought about some extremely sophisticated variations in photocomposition, many of them having to do with computer-assisted systems. Marshall Lee provides a good overview of such systems and their capabilities in Chapter 5 of the second edition of *Bookmaking*. Since the state of the art is changing rapidly, the average author need not be concerned with the details and intricacies of particular machines. He should be aware of the fact, however, that a technological revolution is still in progress, and that the bookmaking procedures to be described during the remainder of this chapter are themselves subject to considerable change under the influence of this technology. Like computers, typesetting and printing devices in the modern era will continue to breed new generations of machines. Undoubtedly these devices will invite departures from the basic editing and proofreading methods described in this book. Having a grasp of these methods, then, will make such departures easier to understand and to accept if and when they are proposed.

The electronic revolution in typesetting and printing has been mostly "good news," but it has not been without its occasional "bad news." Let us look briefly at some of the developments during this transitional period, and consider their effects on the author and his manuscript.

One result of the rapid proliferation of photocomposition machines during the last decade has been to hold down typesetting costs. Relative to increases in the costs of paper, binding, and skilled labor, typesetting has actually resisted inflation, and a page of type costs little more today than it did in 1975 when this book was first written. This is because of the fierce competition among new suppliers of film type who sprang up in the late seventies. All had just purchased the latest typesetting hardware, and all were eager to underbid each other and keep their own machines busy. For the author, this competitiveness means that books are still not as expensive as they might have been had not all the new gadgets come into play; and thus they remain more within the price range of the typical consumer.

On the debit side, the new machines have not meant greater speed in getting books through the publishing houses and out into the market. Most of the systems now in use were initially developed for newspaper work, where speed is of the essence, and where page formats are simple and type styles limited. The application of these systems in the world of bookmaking has not gone smoothly. Books can be far more complicated, with changes in type and format from page to page. Often it simply does not pay to try to generate such pages with the latest electronic equipment. Poetry, to take only one example, is still easier to set in hot metal. Anything set in film usually has to be positioned and pasted up in page form with a great deal of care, and the time and expense of doing this sometimes offsets economies in speed gained by the new machines.

One kind of book has shown great affinity for the new computer-assisted editing and typesetting systems. Catalogs, directories, and technical reference works or lists of spare parts are frequently updated, sometimes on an annual or even a quarterly basis. This reprinting process becomes considerably less expensive when the entire contents of each successive printing is keyboarded onto magnetic disks. A single disk is capable of containing not one but several entire books; the smaller, more portable "floppy" disk, about the size of a 45-rpm record, can still receive and store huge amounts of information in digitized form. This data can be called up for correction a column or a page at a time on the viewing screen of an electronic editing terminal. With no paste-up, then, one can very quickly change nomenclature in particular lines—addresses, say, or stock numbers—while leaving the remainder of the book virtually untouched.

Yet such rewards have not been without their drawbacks. On another level, the proliferation of electronic machinery has created a "Tower of Babel" situation, with dozens of machines and devices on the market, and very few of them able to "talk" to each other by exchanging tapes or disks across manufacturers' lines. In other words, they do not interface well, not even in terms of the various "codes" written on manuscripts prior to their being keyboarded. No electronic Linotype has emerged, then, one in which both buyers and suppliers of type could put their faith and trust for the next eighty or one hundred years. And none is likely to emerge. As one bookworker observed, "It's not the hardware that keeps going haywire. It's the software." In other words, the knowledge of the people using the machines.

A generation of bookworkers who are at home with the new electronic systems is now in the making, but until that generation matures and begins gaining access to upper levels of corporate management, there will continue to be a certain amount of confusion in the publishing business about the best way to utilize the new technology. The late seventies saw considerable interest in "in-house composition," whereby the publisher would have on his own premises the equipment to generate tapes and disks carrying coded information to drive the computer typesetting systems offered by the suppliers. This proved unsuccessful because of the interfacing problem just mentioned—the publisher willing to invest in such equipment found himself locked in to a limited number of suppliers; and all the equipment turned out to be outmoded in a few years anyway. In the eighties one frequently hears of allegedly sophisticated terminals, keyboards, scanners, and other promising devices purchased in the seventies now relegated to the basement. "Oh we have editing devices like that, with viewing screens," one bookworker reported, "only they're in the billing department."

This is not to say that such ventures are doomed to fail; they are being attempted regularly, in spite of the problems involved, and eventually some will succeed. But the rate at which such innovations become industry-wide is clearly not as rapid as was first imagined or hoped. A case in point is the development of in-house editing systems.

Equipment now on the market consists of a console or terminal with a keyboard and viewing screen whereon the skilled operator can edit, design, copyfit, make up, and issue a tape or disk for the typesetting of finished, camera-ready pages of a manuscript. Suppliers have been working on the integration of such systems for years. And some publishers have been willing to set up such equipment on an experimental basis, for use by authors working on special crash projects.

In one such experiment reported by *Publishers Weekly*, a husband-and-wife team wrote, edited, typeset, and paged their own profusely illustrated book, requiring just nine weeks from first manuscript page to the last camera-ready mechanical. According to *PW*, the book consisted of "75,000 words of main text, 35,000 words of special data panels, and 5,000 words of captions . . . 444 full-color illustrations, and 15 maps." The two were assisted by a number of editors and technicians, but their accomplishment in that short amount of time is astounding, and the savings gained were considerable. Why don't all publishers offer such facilities to their authors? Because while authors are expected to know how to write, not all of them can type well, and few know anything about book design or page makeup. The key word is ''skilled.'' The husband-and-wife team already knew editing and bookmaking; the average author does not. At the present time, then, the author's main contribution to electronic bookmaking will be to produce a clean, accessible manuscript on which the editors, designers, and type suppliers can add their many symbols and codes.

Small computers designed for use in the home are becoming increasingly available. It is almost inevitable, given another ten or twenty years, that software will be developed enabling such machines to be linked with commercial photocomposition devices. Even this will not be a smooth transition, however, as computers themselves will continue to go through new generations. With the era of voice-command computers just around the corner, it is difficult to predict the effect such machines will have on traditional bookmaking procedures.

**Reading the Proofs.** Once the contents of your manuscript are set in type, the resulting lines are proofread, or checked, character for character, space for space, to ensure that they follow the original copy. The first stage in which this is usually done is in galley proofs—long sheets of paper each of which contains the typeset material for about three book pages. The galleys are customarily proofread by one of the typesetter's proofreaders, corrections made, and the new, revised galleys sent to the publishing house. There another proofreader (either a member of the staff or a free-lancer) reads the master set of galleys (the set designated by the typesetter to be returned with all the requested changes clearly marked) against the manuscript. In some houses, and for some specialized books, such as law statutes or medical textbooks, proofreading is accomplished by two individuals working together—a copyreader, who reads aloud from the typeset galley, and a copyholder, who follows the manuscript and calls out when there are variances. Although this more traditional method of proofreading is rare in contemporary trade and textbook houses, largely because it is more expensive than single-person proofreading, it nevertheless has the virtue of being not only a much more accurate but also a much faster method.

Two duplicate sets of galley proofs are normally sent to the author with a request for his suggested corrections and a deadline—two or three weeks, unless the book is exceptionally long—by which he is to return one set. The other is his to keep, to be compared with page proofs, when they are available. When you receive your galleys, remember that they are being sent to you both for your approval of their appearance and their contents. You are not expected to proofread them yourself character for character, nor should you consider hiring your own professional proof-reader to go through them. The proofreaders already provided by type-setter and publishing house are more than adequate to catch whatever typographical errors the galleys may contain.

As you look over your proofs, it is important to realize that not all the elements contained in the manuscript may be present. The artwork you submitted in the form of roughs will be shown to you separately, in the form of photocopies of the camera-ready versions. The display type (chapter heads, ornaments, occasionally even subheads) may not show on the galley proofs; they may not show on page proofs, either, in which case they will be joined to the page image at a later stage, that of repro proofs, which you will not see. Captions and call-outs may also be sent to you on separate proofs. All such material deserves your closest attention: not to criticize and change unnecessarily, but to check for accuracy and to confirm.

While you are examining your galleys, additional sets are being looked at by the acquiring editor, managing editor, production super-visor, book designer, jacket designer, and promotional writers. The publicity department may order extra sets, which will be cut up by hand into approximate page lengths and bound individually with cardboard covers, or sent to a firm that provides such a service. The purpose of these extra sets of ''bound galleys'' will be discussed in the next chapter.

Galley proofs supplied by a hot-metal typesetter are ink impressions of the metal type; galleys from a strike-on or photocomposition typesetter may be Xeroxes, ozalids, or similar types of photocopy. In addition, galleys produced by a computerized method of photocomposition are sometimes called the first pass. The set type on these photocopies is broken up into page lengths, but in first-pass form such pages will still lack running heads, folios (page numbers), and some or all of the display type. Regardless of the manner in which your galley proofs are pro-duced, they all serve the common purpose of allowing typographical errors and substantive discrepancies to be noted and changed. The intent of all persons involved at this stage, however, should be to make as few changes in the proofs as possible, due to the high cost of changing lines already set in type.

**Marking the Proofs.** Whether you receive traditional, hot-metal galley proofs or photocopied sheets from a film typesetter, and whether you are shown galleys or pages or both, the necessary changes or corrections should be marked in the same manner. And it is important to remember that they should *not* be marked in the way you made correc-tions on your manuscript. A change in the latter, if it is properly double-spaced, is made directly on or over the affected word or letter, preferably in ink, spelled out, with no symbols or abbreviations. Corrections for typeset material, in contrast, are always made in the margins, never within the lines of type. Instead, a small caret ( ∧ ) at the affected point is sufficient to let the copyeditor know where your marginal change applies.

Even if your proofs require only a few corrections, it is a good idea to glance over a list of proofreader's marks, as contained in almost any style manual or in the back matter of most good dictionaries. You are not expected to master all of these symbols, but it will help if you familiarize yourself with them and study an example of typeset material with corrections marked and made, as in *Webster's New Collegiate Dictionary*.

Some additional points concerning marking proofs are well worth keeping in mind. First, always write in the margins and, if possible, in one margin rather than both. Second, always write horizontally, never vertically or up the sides of the proofs. Third, use a plain, medium-lead pencil, never ink. Fourth, do not write in script, but print, in capital and small letters, any changes you desire. Fifth, for corrections of a paragraph or longer, double-space them on a separate piece of paper; affix this "Insert A" (or "B" or "C") to the point on the proof where you also print "Insert A goes here." Draw arrows, if necessary, in order to be very specific about where Insert A begins. Sixth, to fasten a piece of paper to a galley sheet, do not use tape but paper clips or staples.

**A Dollar a Line.** As you begin to read through your proofs you will encounter three kinds of errors—printer's errors, house errors, and author's errors or alterations—distinguished on the basis of the individual responsible for making them. These categories have no significance for you now, and you should only concern yourself with making the changes you believe to be in order. When the copyeditor transfers your proposed changes to the master set of galleys, however, he will add abbreviations—*pe, ee,* and *aa*, or a similar system—so that he can clearly distinguish who is responsible for what. If the typesetter has garbled a word that was spelled correctly in the manuscript, the typesetter pays for correcting that line. If author and editor allow a misspelled word to stand in the manuscript and the typesetter dutifully sets it in its incorrect form, that is a house error, and the publisher pays for it. And if you, the author, decide to change something that was correct in the manuscript but is not to your liking now, that is an author's alteration. Let us consider how much it might cost to make these changes.

Compositors charge for changes in type not in terms of individual lines but on the basis of the materials, equipment, time, and skilled labor necessary to make them. Nevertheless, when the bill arrives, if an editor counts the lines reset he can easily calculate how much it cost to change an average line. At the present time, that cost ranges from seventy-five cents to a dollar. That may not sound like very much, but if you were to change three words on each of a set of eighty galleys (equivalent to about 244 book pages), the costs could run as high as $240. Moreover, if you were to add words, phrases, or sentences at places where they do not fit, without deleting material of equal length, the costs could double or triple. By adding a word to one line, you in effect push a word or syllable of equal length at the end of that line onto the next line, and so on. This "bumping" of type only ends when the compositor has reset lines until the excess words run into a blank line space or the space at the end of the paragraph. Sometimes, by narrowing the spacing between words, he can add the author's extra word and control the bumping effect within three or four lines. But, to restate the case for holding changes in typeset material to a minimum, if you were to insert the one-letter article "a" in the first line of a tightly set, ten-line paragraph, this could conceivably require resetting all ten lines, at a cost of from $7.50 to $10.

Everyone working on your galley proofs hopes that everything will be in order, that typos are few, and that you will not decide to rewrite or add new material. Some minor changes will invariably be made. However, if you insist on wholesale changes—rewriting portions that call for the substitution of several lines and even paragraphs or sections—the work will be slowed down (by the time it takes the typesetter to implement and proof such changes), it will cost more (in editorial and production time, plus the typesetter's charges), and as a result the price of the book may have to be increased, making it less competitive in the marketplace. This in turn can mean fewer sales and diminished royalties.

For protection against this unhappy but all-too-familiar turn of events, most publishing contracts stipulate that the author may be billed for changes he or she introduces into proofs above 10 percent of the original cost of composition. In plain terms, if it costs $5,000 to set your book in type, and if in galleys, pages, or both you change lines so that the resulting bill from the typesetter shoots up to $6,000, and if the copy-editor can demonstrate on the basis of the master set that there were few house errors, then the publisher, unless he is extremely tender-hearted or dares not antagonize you because of your reputation and sales record for previous books, may arrange to have $500 of that extra $1,000 taken off the top of your royalties. Such a state of affairs—delaying the book and losing money out of your own pocket—need never come about if you submit a truly finished manuscript in the first place and cooperate with your acquiring editor and copyeditor in the second.

**Turning the Proofs Around.** Depending on the nature of your book, its complexity, the success with which the schedule has been adhered to, and the imminence of the desired publication date, you may or may not see additional proofs after you have returned your marked set of galleys. For trade books, even those with lavish illustrations, the author may see only galleys. For scholarly or technical books, he will usually be sent page proofs, again to mark for errors and return by a certain time. An extremely important text, such as that of a classic American author issued by a university press, may go through five or six consecutive proofreadings (not to mention the Hinman collator, an elaborate and expensive mechanical comparer of printed texts) before receiving the seal of approval from the Center for Editions of American Authors.

When turning around page proofs, it is more important than ever that you make as few changes as possible, and then only word or line substitutions that will fit within the same spaces as the elements removed. The author who, having received page proofs, still attempts to rewrite and add new material, is only asking for further delay and unnecessary expense. If the changes proposed require refolioing (renumbering) the pages, the setback could be considerable.

**Skipping Galleys.** If pressed for time, a scheduling director may sometimes instruct the production supervisor to "go directly to pages." After the typesetter receives the marked manuscript, the next thing the house sees are not galley proofs but proofs of made-up pages. Unless expense is of no consequence, these cannot be changed or corrected to the degree that galley proofs can, but they have the virtue of eliminating the time necessary for proofreading and turning around galleys. Skipping galleys saves time for the publishing house, but it does not appreciably decrease the typesetter's costs nor his composition and makeup time. Usually the scheduling director resorts to this option only when he knows the manuscript presents so few typographical problems that it can go directly to pages without creating headaches farther down the line. If the space requirements for the art have not been carefully determined down to the last pica, or if the manuscript is so poorly written that many corrections are likely to be proposed by author and acquiring editor after the type has been set, then skipping galleys is not a good idea. Regardless, if you are told that the rush to get your book out is so great that galleys are being skipped, take that as a sign that page proofs—if you even get to see them—are almost sacrosanct.

**Making an Index.** Whether or not your book is to have an index is something that will have been decided months ago, perhaps even at the time the contract was signed. If your work is nonfiction, it probably should have an index—or even indexes. Before you reach the production stage of page proofs—the earliest practicable point at which an index can be made—there are three important decisions for you and your acquiring editor to make.

First, what kind of index does your book require? For a study of Pentagon spending policy, perhaps an index of persons, places, things, and key concepts would be sufficient. For a collection of critical essays on South American literature, you might also want the index to include the titles of literary works referred to, or even the first lines of poems quoted in translation. A gourmet's guide to the Far East might offer an index listing not only the names of the significant oriental restaurants and markets but also the exotic dishes and foodstuffs for which they are famous. With the use of italics and small capital letters it is possible to combine two or three indexes in one; this may not always be the wisest course, however. If you have written a book about science-fiction movies, the reader might find it helpful to have an index of film titles referred to; another index of directors, actors, and actresses; and a third, more general, index of the information—places, events, concepts—contained in the main body of your text. Remember that the index will be for the anonymous reader's use, not your own. If you cannot form a clear notion of what the index should do for the reader, discuss the nature of the index with your editor.

Second, what *form* should the index take? Basically, you have two choices, the indented style:

Tornados, 16, 26, 278–80, 303–12
   effects of, 27–28, 93–94
   formation of, 17, 27, 304
      in northern hemisphere, 304–5
      in southern hemisphere, 305–6
   and hailstones, 17, 27, 279
   prediction of, 28, 304–6
Waterspouts, 19, 31–33, 265–68

And the more compact, space-saving run-in style:

Music, relationship to Dionysus, 144
Myrtle, associated with the dead, 158; favorite of
   Dionysus, 158; used as a surrogate for semele, 158
Myth, aetiological in nature, 17; Greek, the nature of,
   23, 120; origins of, 17, 22–23; as poetry, 13–16; as a
   product of cult practices, 17

The kind of index may dictate the form. If you plan to employ italics, small capital letters, or boldface type to integrate two or more kinds of entries, the indented style may work better. For a highly detailed scholarly work, these features may still be incorporated to better advantage in a run-in style index. Here again, discussions with your editor are in order, and also with your typist, if you plan to prepare the index yourself.

Third, who will do the index? It is important to remember that most publishing contracts assign the responsibility for providing the index to the author. It is, in other words, an inherent part of the original manuscript, although not immediately deliverable. In practical terms, you as author can prepare the index yourself, you can hire an indexer of your own choosing, or you can ask the publishing house to do it for you. In either of the latter two instances, you will still pay. The house can have the index made, but the cost will be taken out of your royalties. Since it is coming out of your own pocket or your own time and energies in any event, the decision might well rest on other factors—do you have the time to do it yourself? the inclination? the know-how? If you answer affirmatively, the editor will provide guidelines for making the index, and there are a number of small, economical pamphlets on the market that will see you through such a project. Sina Spiker's *Indexing Your Book: A Practical Guide for Authors* (Madison: University of Wisconsin Press, 1954) is one of the best. The University of Chicago Press's *A Manual of Style* devotes an informative chapter to the techniques of making an index; the chapter is also available separately in pamphlet form.

The argument against an author making the index for his own book parallels that of the attorney traditionally advised against defending himself in court. By the time your work reaches page proofs, you may find that you have temporarily lost all objectivity about what it says. Furthermore, although you may be able to create an acceptable index for your own book, a professional indexer can usually do a better job, in less time, and in a form more convenient for the copyeditor. In fact, some houses are currently retreating from their former insistence that the author either prepare or pay for the index, and are including the cost of an in-house index as part of the total production costs.

But if you do decide to do the index, for whatever reason, what will it cost you to have someone else prepare it? Figure on about $100 per hundred book pages. If your book is technical or loaded with proper names, increase that to $150 per hundred pages. Professional indexers work by the hour and make around $6 or $7 an hour. They use all the shortcuts available, and for the average nonfiction book seldom turn in a bill over $500 or $600. If you decide to let the house arrange for making the index, ask your editor for a written estimate of how much it will cost. And to help him make an accurate estimate, be as specific as possible about the kind, the form, and the purpose of the index your book should have.

**Repro Proofs.** Set in type and circulated in proof form, your work has been checked by your own eyes and by those of the acquiring editor, proofreaders, artist, designer, and indexer. When all of these readings are finished, pages have been made up, and requests for any last-minute changes have been noted in the margins of the master set of page proofs, that set goes to the typesetter for what hopefully will be a final time. If there are many changes to be made, the typesetter may send back revised pages for yet another check by someone in the house, usually the copyeditor. When these go back, the typesetter is now ready to prepare "repros" (reproduction proofs). These are camera-ready proofs from which the printer's negatives for making the printing plates will be made. A hot-metal compositor will send back repro proofs in the form of high-quality ink impressions on dull-coated white paper; a photocompositor may go a step farther and supply film negatives.

Corrections can be made in repro proofs by "patching" (pasting over) an offending word or letter with a replacement cut from a duplicate set of repros, but with luck, very few such patches will be necessary. Positive prints of sized, camera-ready line drawings or graphs may be pasted down in the blank spaces already provided for; special marks or accents may also be drawn in over letters or at other necessary places. Prints of continuous-tone photographs will be available separately for checking against the spacing provided, but the actual "screened" negatives of the photos will not be incorporated into the text until the next step in the process, when film negatives are made for the entire book.

The production staff still has a bit of work to do at this stage, but the work of the editorial staff is virtually finished. Similarly, the author will normally have nothing to do with the remaining manufacturing steps of preparing the plates, selecting the paper, printing the sheets, binding the signatures, and warehousing the finished book. Nevertheless, the well-informed author should have a layman's knowledge of these steps, if for no other reason than to calm his fears during the eight- or ten-week interval it will require to accomplish them.

## *Preparing the Plates*

The firm selected weeks or months ago to print your book may have one, two, or a number of presses of different sizes and capabilities at its disposal. The dimensions of these machines affect the range of possible trim sizes originally contemplated for your book. Standard sizes throughout the industry—4⅛" x 6⅞" (mass market paperback), 5⅜" x 8", 5½" x 8¼", 6" x 9", 7½" x 9¼", 7" x 10", and 8½" x 11"—achieve the maximum efficiency of press time and leave the smallest amounts of waste trimmed away from the standard-sized sheets or rolls of paper. In addition to trim size, the printer and his various estimators and schedulers also must think in terms of signatures: sequences of eight, sixteen, or thirty-two pages formed by folding large rectangles of paper printed on both sides and trimmed open at three edges.

Signatures in turn, when collated into sequence, form the book proper, with pages running consecutively from 1 to the end. If one counts the front matter and the blank pages that may be present at the end, the total number of pages is usually a number divisible by eight, the smallest practicable signature for most modern printers. So that sheets or continuous rolls of paper may be printed, cut, folded, gathered, collated, and eventually bound together to form a book with all pages in proper sequence, either the individual repro proof pages or the film pages must be positioned accurately in relation to one another before printing plates are made. Grouping them together is called stripping and the resulting pattern, called an imposition, is predetermined by the number and size of the pages relative to the size capabilities of the press.

**Camera Work and Stripping.** Let us return momentarily to your book as it exists in the form of individual repro proof pages. After they have been checked and sent to the printer, they go to a camera room, which might be the printer's own or which might belong to a supplier several hundred miles away. Here the pages are photographed (shot), several at a time, with a large, high-quality industrial camera. After developing, the negatives go to a stripping room, where the screened negatives for the halftones are stripped—cut into and taped to the larger text negatives arranged in their proper positions. Imperfections in the text negatives are painted out with opaquing fluid. Elements of type or art may still be shifted slightly at this point, but the restripping process is expensive and time-consuming. (In general, the later changes are made in the sequence of manufacturing steps, the more expensive they become.)

The negatives of the individual pages, the negatives of the art, and the negatives of the halftones, then, are stripped together in a predetermined pattern of imposition to create the larger negatives—each containing from eight to twelve pages per side—from which the printing plates will be made. But before platemaking, these large negatives are put through a machine that produces positive contact prints known as blue lines, silver prints, or van dykes. These final proofs can be folded, cut by hand, and assembled in sequence, so that they resemble very closely the finished book in unbound form.

The blue lines are returned to the production department for approval and may possibly wend their way back to the editorial department. Authors rarely, if ever, see them. Except for the coloring, blue lines show the book pages and every element, every line of type, every illustration or accent mark as they will appear in the finished work. They are checked for overall appearance and for the accuracy with which they match the book's technical specifications: Are the gutter margins correct? Are the folios in proper sequence, the running heads correct right and left, the illustrations right-side up? If everyone has done his work, they are. House approval of blue lines gives the printer authorization to print. He may have directed the making of negatives and blue lines in his own shop, or he may now receive the negatives from a firm specializing in such camera and stripping work. He sends the negatives to his platemaking department, where, with arc-light exposures and carefully controlled chemical baths, the image of each large "flat" of page negatives is burned onto a specially prepared aluminum plate.

## Selecting the Paper

Except for very small runs, printers do not normally provide the paper on which your book is to be printed. Instead, someone in the production or purchasing department of your publishing house orders the necessary quantity of paper from a paper distributor and makes sure that it reaches the printer's plant sufficiently in advance of press time. Estimating paper needs and placing orders is a complicated business; it is also an extremely important process, since paper costs have skyrocketed in recent years and certain kinds of book paper are difficult to obtain.

If your book is to be a paperback (softbound) edition, the purchasing agent must order the paper for the text pages and the thicker, heavier paper for the cover. If your book is to be a hardback (casebound) edition, he must order paper for the text and possibly paper for the dust jacket. Unless the publishing house has its own bindery, the bindery that is contracted for the work typically supplies most of the additional materials necessary to create casebound books. The purchasing agent provides the bindery with specifications concerning the cloth, vinyl, or paper material that will constitute the case, the boards enclosed by such material to give rigidity to the case, the headbands, and the stamping die with which title and author's name are stamped on the front and spine of the case. Of all these, what probably concerns you most, as author, is the paper on which your text is to be printed. Its selection, like most other things in publishing, is determined by a variety of factors.

To begin, the purchaser must know if the book is to be printed by sheet-fed or web offset press, or by letterpress (these will be explained shortly), and he must know the exact dimensions of such presses. He must know the kinds of images that are to be printed (for example, halftones, four-color illustrations, or a second color of ink). He must know how the sheets will be folded after they emerge from the press. And he must know whether the house plan calls for the book to be beefed up (by the use of thick, bulky paper) or slimmed down (by the use of thin, low-bulking paper). Finally, he must know the number of copies to be printed. After some mechanical reckoning based on these figures, the purchaser can draw up his order and begin shopping for a supplier.

Your role as author in this paper-selection process is minimal. If you do have a suggestion or special requirement, be sure to communicate it to your acquiring editor. For example, if you have written a manual for beginning typists, such books are often printed on tinted paper, such as light green or blue, to reduce glare from overhead lights in the class-room. The point is certainly worth bringing up in preliminary discussions about your book. But be prepared, too, for the possibility that cost limitations may modify some of your original plans or hopes. You may have envisaged color photographs scattered throughout each chapter, near their references in the text. Your editor might decide, however, that if these are slightly re-edited and grouped on glossy (coated-stock) signatures of four or eight pages, the rest of the text may be printed on more economical, lower-bulking paper. Lend an ear, then, if your editor comes up with a suggestion that could result in savings for both you and the publisher.

### Printing the Sheets

The printing presses involved in bookmaking are so complex and the workers operating them so highly skilled that press time is not only expensive, it is also rigorously scheduled. The printing firm's management makes every effort to insure that its presses are continually busy, sometimes around the clock. This in turn means that their sales representatives must work closely with production and manufacturing people in the publishing houses. When both sides agree that folded signatures will be ready to ship from the printing firm's warehouse dock by November 10, they are also agreeing implicitly to a succession of camera, stripping, platemaking, and printing dates that will make that final shipping date possible. If the plates are not ready when the job is scheduled to go on the press, the printer may have a stand-by job ready. But if the plates are not ready because the publisher's representatives have been derelict in delivering camera-ready copy, or if the paper is not delivered as promised, the printing firm faces potential revenue loss due to the unexpected idling of its equipment—and the publisher may lose his press time. The book may have to wait days or weeks until suitable time is available again on an acceptable press, or the printing plan may have to be modified for a different press. In other words, procedures and schedules in contemporary commercial printing plants are virtually inexorable. The huge capital investment in the machines calls the tune, and everyone associated with the enterprise dances accordingly.

**Letterpress vs. Offset**. Long before the actual printing occurs, and possibly even before your manuscript arrives at the publishing house, the acquiring editor and production supervisor probably know which process will be used to print your book: letterpress or photo-offset. For very short runs of from 500 to 1,000 copies, some university presses and small private presses still rely on letterpress. With this method, after the type has been set in hot metal and proofed, and after engravings of line illustrations or halftones have been physically locked in with the pages of type, which are already in imposition, a relief plastic molding is made of the printing surface of each grouping of pages. Each mold in turn is used to cast a metal or plastic printing plate, the raised surface of which will receive ink and transfer or press it directly to the surface of the paper passing through the press. The camera has no part in the preparation for letterpress printing; the process involves no repro proofs, stripping, negatives, or blue lines. Except for very specialized printing firms, however, this traditional method is simply too expensive and inefficient for contemporary commercial usage. In 99 cases out of 100, the production supervisor knows the book will be printed by photo-offset.

There are two kinds of photo-offset presses: sheet-fed and continuous or web. Each has its advantages, each its drawbacks. Books printed in two or more colors of ink or containing full-color illustrations are more likely to be printed on sheet-fed presses for runs of 10,000 or under. In some such presses, each sheet of paper must be run through the press one time to print one color of ink on one side of the sheet. More sophisticated sheet-fed presses are able to print two colors consecutively in one pass of the sheet through the press. Some machines, called perfector presses, can print on both sides of the sheet during one pass. Multiple-color jobs call for multiple negatives and plates—one set for each color of ink used. Aligning (registering) these plates with each other is a complex, time-consuming job, especially for four- or five-color offset printing, which yields illustrations in "full" color. In the larger printing establishments, web presses can be set up to run two or more colors, but in the main they are used for the straight printing of one color only.

The web photo-offset press derives its name from the fact that the paper issues continuously from a large, man-sized roll, feeds through the printing surfaces at high speeds, and is chopped and folded into sheets as it emerges from the opposite end of the press. For runs above 5,000, it is superior to the sheet-fed method. For much larger runs—up to 100,000, for example—new rolls of paper can be spliced to the ends of previous rolls without shutting down the machine.

With both sheet-fed and web photo-offset presses, the printing plates do not come into direct contact with the paper. Instead, after the plates are inked, the image is "set off" in reverse (or mirror-image) form, onto a matching rubber-coated roller called a blanket cylinder, which transfers a right-reading image onto the paper passing through the press at high speeds. This offsetting method has the effect of reducing wear on the metal plates and extending the quality and life of the run.

**Gravure Printing**. In that hundredth instance mentioned a few paragraphs earlier, a third type of printing—sheet-fed or web-fed photogravure—might be used if your work is to be a large, expensive book containing high-quality photographic illustrations or reproductions of fine artworks. Photogravure is more complicated and more expensive than the other two methods, since its intaglio printing plates are difficult to prepare. It is seldom used in bookmaking, yet the familiar illustrated Sunday newspaper supplement in color is typically printed by photogravure; the process works well on inexpensive, uncoated paper and is no more expensive than offset printing for large runs (200,000 or more). If this method is chosen to print some or all of the pages of your book, be prepared for a lengthened production schedule. Although quality gravure printing is obtainable in this country, a considerable amount of it is done in Europe and Japan. Exchanging negatives and sheets with foreign suppliers can add to your book's schedule, but the greater quality achieved in illustrations is well worth the extra time.

**Ink-Jet Printing**. One new method of printing deserves mention here, since it has the potential for bringing about still additional changes in the typesetting and printing of books. The bed of an ink-jet press consists of thousands of tiny dots, each of which squirts out a controlled quantity of ink on command from a typesetting computer activated by a tape or disk. Imagine the huge light screen in any of several major-league ball parks reduced to page size, and emitting ink instead of light to create its patterns. This process has great attractiveness since it eliminates the need for both camerawork and platemaking.

Finally, one other printing method should be acknowledged here, since it is probably the one with which the average writer in the 1980s is most familiar—photocopying. This process is still far too expensive and inexact for commercial publishers, but for extremely short runs of one or two hundred copies—the range of the do-it-yourself publisher, the small press, or the PTA program committee—it may be competitive. The better copiers can now reproduce on both sides of a single sheet and on colored paper. They also show very few paste-up lines. Such machines became efficient and widely available in the 1970s; they promise to become more sophisticated in the 1980s. Ink-jet copiers have appeared and now compete with existing electrostatic models; further innovations are to be expected.

## Binding the Signatures

After the sheets of your book are printed, they must be taken to other locations and fed through a series of mechanical folders, gatherers (collators), and trimmers before all of the pages appear in proper order and correct trim size. Printed separately and in advance, special picture inserts of from four to eight pieces of glossy paper may be introduced mechanically during the gathering process, or they may be laboriously glued in place (tipped in) by hand. The largest complete book manufacturing firms may offer all the necessary printing, folding, gathering, and binding equipment under one roof. Smaller plants may have to ship the printed sheets to another location or even to another firm to be bound. This shipping time, of course, is "dead" time that adds to the overall time necessary to produce the book.

**Cloth or Paper?** The intended market for your book will determine the kind of binding it will get, whether clothbound or paperback (or both), and this will sometimes be spelled out in the contract. Beyond that, you will have little to do with the details and the mechanics of binding. The signatures of a clothbound book are usually sewn together (with thread, but sometimes with wire staples, too) and the case applied with adhesives. Small paperbacks or pamphlets are most often wire saddle-stitched—stapled in the center of the fold, like a comic book—while larger ones (over 128 pages) are almost always perfect bound. Only the very rare publisher—Dover Publications is an admirable example—issues sewn paperbacks.

In perfect binding the assembled signatures are held tightly while rotating knives slice away about an eighth of an inch of their spines. Next, a durable adhesive is applied to the spine and the cover is wrapped around and joined to the spine with the same glue. Rather than signatures of sixteen or thirty-two pages, which could conceivably be sewn together again should the binding fail, the book now consists of, say, 128 separate pieces of paper held together only by the glue along one edge. Bend back the pages of almost any paperback published ten or fifteen years ago, and chances are that at least some of the pages will fall out. Sadly, there is no way of putting them back. Recent improvements in the quality and durability of the hot-melt glue used in perfect binding, however, have drastically reduced this problem, although not completely eliminated it.

No one really expects paperbacks to last very long; it was the developing of perfect-binding that made them low in cost in the first place. The practice of perfect-binding paperbacks is industrywide and not likely to change. A more reprehensible practice, followed by some publishers, is to perfect-bind the signatures of a book and wrap them in a cloth case. The result gives the appearance of a traditional, sewn, casebound book but really is not. When authors have complained about this practice, publishers have attempted to justify it by pointing to the increased costs of binding in particular and book manufacturing in general. Observers of the debate have noted, with justification, that the question is largely academic, since almost any type of binding used in publishing today will suffice for the life of the paper used in the average book.

Contemporary book paper, made from wood pulp, is high in acid content, due to the nature of its manufacture; accordingly, its life span is predictably short. Diderot's *Dictionary*, printed in the eighteenth century on quality rag paper and carefully sewn and bound, will still be in good shape centuries hence, when the book you are holding in your hands has long since turned to dust. In fairness, however, few could afford to buy Diderot's volumes then, and today's new novel, nonfiction work, or college textbook is within the price range of every interested reader.

As with paper selection, if you believe your book needs a special binding, speak up. That typing manual, for example, may outsell the competition if it is bound with a wire or plastic spiral (comb bound) at the top. Let your editor know. And be prepared, again, for the possibility that binding requirements or cost limitations may dictate changes in your proposed format. Such a change might also be based on an innovative technique developed in the brief interval since you submitted your manuscript. Publishers and their associated manufacturers are constantly seeking new ways to combine methods and machines in order to save steps, cut costs, and speed production. The so-called mass market paperback available at your corner drugstore or supermarket, for example, most probably was printed and bound by processes extremely different from many of the methods described in this chapter.

The Cameron belt press, to cite one recent innovation, combines flexible-plate letterpress techniques with the latest folding and perfect-binding machinery to print, fold, and bind books in one continuous operation. The greatest assets of this complete book manufacturing operation are speed and economy. The Cameron process does not lend itself to high-quality reproduction of halftones, however, and it cannot print in more than one color.

## To the Warehouse

Your finished book, with or without jacket, is stacked in cardboard cartons designed to hold the maximum number of units of that particular trim size. An expensive law or medical textbook might first be shrink-wrapped in clear plastic to keep out the dust, or it might be inserted into a slipcover. The full cartons are stacked on a pallet for fork-lift handling, and the pallets are consigned to the warehouse, which can be located anywhere, including at the bindery. Remember, too, that although 5,000 copies of your book may have been printed, perhaps only 3,000 were bound. The sheets with which the additional 2,000 can be made up may be stored elsewhere, until needed.

From among the first few finished copies available the bindery supervisor will skim off a dozen or so books and send them back to the publishing house. There they will be distributed to key personnel, with a couple of copies going to you, the author, as soon as possible. Additional author's copies—from three to twelve, depending on your contract—will arrive a few days later. You will also be allowed to purchase more copies, if you need them, at a considerable discount ranging from 25 to 40 percent.

When that first package arrives, and you begin to leaf through your book, remember that no one is perfect—not you, not the people who work at the publishing house. If "they" have misspelled the name of a friend or colleague in the acknowledgments, or left an atom off the spiral of a particular DNA molecule in one of the illustrations, such minor errata can easily be fixed if and when the book reprints. For now, some congratulations are in order: You are a published author. By means of a wide range of techniques and procedures, some of which date from Gutenberg's day, some of which are products of the latest computer technology, your manuscript has been turned into a book. The process did not, after all, turn you into a nervous wreck; and it just might, with a bit of luck, pay for your trip to Europe next year. Like everything else in publishing, it all depends. Congratulations anyway.

# 7

# *How a Publisher Markets a Book*

What can I tell the buyers? I often think how shocked authors would be if they listened to the salesmen selling their books. They've worked a year on their book—two years, three years, maybe longer. And there it is. A word or two and a decision is made.
      —Bruce Bliven quoting book salesman George Scheer

Of all the major industries in the United States, surely book publishing is the most primitive, the most disorganized, and the most haphazard. Consider the following: What other industry would launch a national campaign for an untested product whose life span is usually less than a year and whose chances of recouping its investment are worse than one in three? What other industry would manufacture so many competing products with only the barest notion of which of them might succeed in the marketplace? What other industry would sink a hefty percentage of its capital into a variety of mechanisms designed to stimulate sales, knowing full well that the most effective method—that elusive "word of mouth"—is totally beyond its control? In many ways, a publisher acts like a Hopi shaman praying for rain: They both execute a number of rituals designed to convince themselves and their followers that they can control uncontrollable events, and then go home and cross their fingers. If rain doesn't fall, they blame themselves or their acolytes for not adequately performing some of the rituals, thereby angering the gods and spoiling the magic. "Go out and get some really smooth stones this time," they say, "and let's try again."

The limit of most authors' interest in the sales, distribution, publicity, advertising, and promotion of their books seems to boil down to two questions: Why haven't they advertised my book in the *New York Times,* and why can't I find my book in any #*!?# bookstore? Both legitimate questions have two sets of answers, one simple, one complex. The publisher's simple answers are: The advertising budget allocated for your book (provided there is one) can be more effectively spent in other media, since a full page in the "Book Review" section costs $6,450, and the reason your book isn't in the bookstore is that the store's book buyer didn't think he could sell your book in his store. Presuming that your curiosity is not satisfied by these answers, an exploration of the various methods employed in both stimulating interest in your book and providing the opportunity for someone to buy it will help to answer these questions in a more complex fashion. Nevertheless, an air of mystery and uncertainty will still remain for some vital questions, such as, what makes a best seller? After all, a successful book isn't quite like a better mouse trap. Would you have predicted, for instance, that a story about a Zen-spouting seagull would have flown to the top of the best-seller list?

Marketing a book consists of the following basic functions: publicity, that is, getting the word out (call it free advertising); sales, whether overseas, directly to the consumer, or to libraries, wholesalers or retailers; distribution, how a book gets from a publisher to a bookstore, newsstand, or library; advertising, either to the trade or to the consumer; and sales promotion, that is, helping the retailer to sell the book. Each function overlaps and reinforces the others, and most are performed simultaneously, so that it would not matter with which we began our discussion. In fact, the marketing of a book commences long before the book is off press; it begins with the delivery of your final manuscript to the publisher.

## *Author's Questionnaire*

As authors generally feel helpless about doing something to facilitate the sales of their book once they have delivered the manuscript, they may find solace in filling out the author's questionnaire. At least it is something to do. The questionnaire is in part designed to provide the publisher with biographical background material on the author. The data will be used to provide copy for the dust jacket, the publisher's catalog, ads, and even for copyright forms. Some of it will be used to help salesmen promote and sell the book, and it may also alert the sales or publicity department to other potential markets or audiences in which to promote the book or the author. The author's web of professional, vocational, and personal associations are all possible sources for publicity or sales.

Even more important than the author's background are his or her suggestions to help publicize and sell the book, and equally important, the author's own efforts to promote and sell the book. Too many authors prepare these questionnaires hastily, not fully realizing that the information only they can provide can help determine whether the book will be a success or a failure. Nor do they realize that once the final manuscript has been delivered, it is no longer the editor who is the key figure in nurturing the book, but the publicity director or someone else in the publicity department. (Consider it a transition from the obstetrician to the pediatrician.) Therefore, it is important to establish a relationship with someone in this department, preferably in person, but at least by mail or phone.

The form should request the names of people you know (or don't know) whose opinion would carry some weight in helping to publicize or sell the book, that is, people who might provide an endorsement or testimonial that praises the book. These remarks are generally called blurbs, and it is acknowledged that they can and do influence the reception of the book. While your editor will know some ideal people to query, you should be the source of the best leads.

These endorsements may be used on the dust jacket, in trade and consumer ads, in the press release, in the publisher's catalog, and in fliers or brochures. Their influence, however, extends to wholesalers, bookstore owners, reviewers, and bookclub and paperback reprint editors in addition to the consumer. While few of these people will admit to being seriously influenced by blurbs, there is little doubt that they operate as a signal and can draw attention to a book struggling for recognition among thousands of competitors. The inner circle, those 1,000 or so writers with national reputations, are usually going to have their books, reviewed and ordered by bookstores, with or without blurbs. The same will hold true for books by or about celebrities. But another 10,000 writers and their books will struggle for recognition, and endorsements by either noted authorities in relevant fields or by persons whose names or opinions have national clout may just provide the added nudge for the reviewer or book buyer to at least take a closer look at the book.

Therefore, in supplying names for possible blurbs, try to estimate carefully the potential impact of the endorser's statement: Will it really help draw attention to the book? You may have to be callous about dredging up tenuous relationships with people whom you might normally not dream of "bothering." After all, the fact that they will be asked for a blurb doesn't mean they have to or will respond. Besides, if they do like your book, and find the time to look at it, they will probably be glad to help—many "notables" deem this kind of request a professional responsibility, and successful authors in particular are aware that they did (and sometimes still do) need this kind of publicity. Don't be disappointed if less than half respond; some luminaries are inundated by requests. Preferably, this list will be a mix, comprised of people directly in the field or on the periphery of it, and just plain VIP's. The intended audience for your book will suggest the range of endorsements that can help: The broader the potential appeal of the book, the further you can range outside of its specific intended audience. For a novel, for instance, just about anyone with a ''name'' will do.

The publisher will generally pull anywhere from five to twenty-five extra sets of galleys for testimonials, which the publicity department will send out, generally accompanied by a letter. If you think a personal letter from you will make a difference, don't hesitate to have it sent with the galleys.

Beyond this prime list, the writer should supply the names of from twenty-five to fifty people whose opinion of the book will influence that elusive word-of-mouth campaign. Not just specialists, but anyone who would read the book and is in a position to spread the word, from the local president of the Rotary Club to your college alumni director. These people will be sent bound copies of the book as soon as it is off press.

Two more lists are needed: the names of publications that might review the book, and the names of ideal media in which to advertise the book. The publicity department has its own extensive file of review media, not only a basic list, but a whole series of special-interest lists as well, such as periodicals for sports fans, history buffs, and animal fanciers. But there are always a considerable number of specialized or particularly regional media that only the author might ferret out. You may sell more copies of your book from a review (or an ad) in a local newsletter with a circulation of 2,500 than from a review in the *New York Times*.

As the author cannot generally expect a national advertising campaign for the book, a list of carefully selected media catering to those readers who constitute the most clearly identifiable market for the book may sway the publisher to place more than the token ad(s) most books generally get. Preferable to a mere list is a letter to your editor or contact in publicity, stressing both the potential value and the reasons for suggesting ads in those particular places. In addition to an ad, perhaps a brochure or flier sent to members of an organization or subscribers to a journal can also be justified. If you belong to or have a connection with an appropriate organization or association, you will want to inform and assist your editor with a potential ''special sale.'' A book for consumers on furs, for example, might be purchased in quantity by a large fur manufacturer as a give-away for the annual fur convention. Special sales have increasing interest for trade houses during these inflationary times, and it may be only through your connection that such a sale is even considered or pursued.

Generally, the publicity department's knowledge and experience will carry the ball in deciding the most effective means and methods of promoting your book, but a letter from you accompanying your author's questionnaire, with a variety of *specific* and intelligent suggestions for promoting your book, can sometimes make the difference between success and failure. With a nonfiction book, the chances are that no one knows the book's audience or market better than the author; not to exploit this knowledge as carefully and as thoroughly as possible is a mistake many writers make, assuming that the publisher is the expert and knows exactly what to do. One word of caution, though: Don't overdo it. Incessant letters or phone calls will have a negative effect.

## *Publicity*

The number of people in the publicity department can range from a single department manager and combined secretary-assistant, to eight to ten members, some of whom may specialize, such as in radio and television promotion, or author's tours. The role of the publicity department in affecting the ultimate success or failure of a book cannot be overestimated. All other considerations aside, a crucial problem for a trade book is to gain the attention of the consumer as well as the appropriate people within the media and the publishing industry. Though over 20,000 trade books a year are clamoring for this attention, only upwards of 5,000 or so will get enough to make a difference in sales. Just as an example, the *New York Times Book Review* receives about 35 books a day, or 12,000 a year, out of which they review roughly 2,000. This discrepancy between the number of books published and the amount of space available—whether on bookstore shelves, in libraries, in review media,* on interview shows, etc.—is the essential marketing problem for every publisher, and the effective coordination and efforts of the various departments is the means of tackling it. Even if one accepts the truism that word of mouth is what sells books, it is rarely fruitful unless the groundwork is supplied by the publisher. In recent years the publicity department's problem has increased due to the shrinkage of review and first-serial media: A number of large-circulation magazines have vanished, such as *Life* (now reborn, but with a considerably smaller circulation), *Look,* and *Colliers,* and the increased cost of newsprint and paper has cut down on newspaper reviewing, particularly in Sunday supplements. Compensating somewhat for this trend is a growth in

---

*According to A.A.P. statistics, fewer than 15 percent of published books get reviewed; conventional publishing wisdom has it that bad news, i.e., poor reviews, is better than no reviews at all.

smaller-circulation special-interest magazines: For example, half a dozen futurology magazines, such as *Omni,* have cropped up in the past few years. Nevertheless the publication of roughly 20,000 new trade books each year sustains the squeeze for space and attention.

**Blurbs.** As pointed out, the first step in publicity is to help secure blurbs, relying on leads from both the author and the editor—or in fact from anyone in the house who may know someone whose testimonial might have a beneficial influence.

**Early Review Copies.** As soon as the galleys are ready, one set is cut up into approximate book-page size, and then photocopied sets are made. A number of these are sent out for blurbs, but more importantly, the bound galleys represent the first set of review copies to be mailed out.

A number are sent well in advance of publication date to trade publications such as *Publishers Weekly, Library Journal,* and *The Kirkus Reviews* (the top three), which are read by librarians, reviewers, bookstore and wholesale book buyers, and mass market and bookclub editors. Not only are these reviews the first indication of the critical reception of the book, but the select audience that reads them has a significant impact on the fate of the book. An enthusiastic review in *Publishers Weekly* will usually result in a greater number of consumer reviews, more nibbles for potential rights sales, and higher prepublication bookstore orders. A good review for a middling book in *Library Journal,* for instance, will usually insure the publisher of a library sale of 750 to 1,500 copies, provided the book is not too specialized, and a rave review can boost this figure to 3,000 or 4,000 copies. Early trade reviews or sub-rights sales can influence the publisher himself, both in the decision on the quantity of the first or second printing (sometimes ordered even prior to publication date) and on the advertising budget for the book. And, of course, these reviews, if favorable, can provide good copy for the first or second set of ads for the book. Poor advance reviews, on the other hand, have a negative psychological effect on the publicity department as well as on salesmen and others in the house. It can short-circuit the kind of enthusiasm necessary for the whole house to push the book. Just as the number of titles in the marketplace competes for the consumer's attention, the number of titles each firm publishes every season competes for the attention of everyone in the firm.

A number of sets of the bound galleys—anywhere from just a few to over a hundred sets are pulled, depending on the publisher's expectations for that particular book—are sent to consumer review media. Some of the major daily newspapers, such as the *New York Times,* the *Chicago Tribune,* the *Wall Street Journal,* as well as the syndicated book reviewers, need copies well in advance of publication. (Bound galleys are generally ready about four months before publication date.) Some of them will also be sent to Sunday supplements and national magazines such as *Time, Newsweek, Esquire,* and the *New Yorker*. Of course, the audience for the book will determine where some of these sets are sent: A biography of John Adams would be sent to *American Heritage* magazine, and so forth.

Some of the remaining sets of galleys are used for the sale of subsidiary rights, which we will discuss later on in this chapter. Others may be sent to the salesmen and even occasionally to wholesalers and chain store book buyers.

**Bound Books.** When bound books are ready, the publicity department will mail out approximately twenty-five to five hundred review copies (this would be for an anticipated blockbuster) though the average number sent is about one hundred. Working from your list, combined with their general list and supplemented by a hand-picked list particularly suited to the subject of your book, these copies will be divided among newspapers, magazines, journals, and syndicates, and sometimes as well to radio and television programs that discuss or review books or interview authors.

The publicity director and others on the staff do not rely merely on mailing out review copies. Part of their job is to see major reviewers in person (actually, they are the ones who delegate reviews), usually by taking them to lunch. Armed with the fall or spring catalog, they will try to generate enthusiasm for some of the books, focusing on those that might particularly appeal to that reviewer as well as on the major books for that season. They may also on occasion diplomatically suggest who might be a natural to review a certain title.

There are a variety of overt as well as covert criteria that determine whether, where, and how a book is reviewed, above and beyond the actual merits of the book. It should surprise no writer that two dozen or so major trade houses may account for more than half of the reviews in the national media. The larger houses have the staff and money to actively promote their titles, spend their advertising dollars in these media, and attract the more glamorous and best-selling authors. Payola, beyond expensive lunches and free books, can be discounted. It is, at most, a rare event. There is, however, a sort of eastern publishing establishment fraternity that is self-perpetuating, and its members, which include authors, do scratch each others' backs.* A certain amount of justifiable paranoia grips smaller publishers, who feel that many of their good

---

*For a chilling, if sometimes exaggerated, analysis of this media manipulation, see Richard Kostelanetz's *The End of Intelligent Writing* (Mission, Kansas: Andrews and McMeel, 1974).

books are unfairly ignored, and especially "alternative" publishers, who feel that they are fundamentally excluded from access to traditional review media, though in the last few years both are gaining more attention for their books. By and large, reviewers and book editors at magazines and newspapers are merely subject to the same crunch as every other channel in publishing, limited space, and it is to their credit that works of scholarly or literary merit, rather than simply what may be assumed the public will buy or read in huge quantities, are generally given a fair amount of review space.

Needless to say, other divisions in publishing are equally active in sending out review copies, though on a smaller scale.

**The Press Release.** Simultaneous with or prior to sending a review copy, the publicity department usually mails out a one- or two-page press release; though publishers are now cutting back on this practice, and many books now get only a "pub. slip," containing author, title, publication date, and price. Originating as an actual news release, the press release continues to use the same format, that is, providing strictly factual information about the book, but it is now commonly "enriched" by blurbs and other promotional statements. One of its functions is to identify the publication date, so that newspapers and other media can review or announce the book at approximately the same time, presumably to coincide with the arrival of the book in the bookstore. In reality, publishers try to get the book out to the stores a month or more in advance of publication date, partly in hopes that it may take hold before it is reviewed, just in case the reviews are negative. While most newspapers and magazines will attempt to honor the publication date, the squeeze for space and the problems of scheduling prevent them from doing this except for a limited number of titles. Most reviews will appear anywhere from a month before to six months after publication date, especially in magazines. Journals are notorious for reviewing books a year or two after publication, sometimes after the book makes its appearance on the remainder tables.

Many more press releases than review copies will be distributed. Not only are they much cheaper, but they can stir up advance interest in the book and permit the review media, which are constantly inundated with written information and books, to decide whether to follow up when the book arrives or to request a copy if none is forthcoming. As many as 1,500 or more releases may be sent to: book editors at 500 or so newspapers and magazines, radio and television book contacts, newspaper syndicates, libraries, salesmen, etc. Since some books are newsworthy, copies may be sent to feature editors, news commentators, columnists, and a variety of "opinion makers." The publicity department will attempt to generate news coverage for the book, often racking their brains for a local or national angle.

As many local newspapers do not have their own book reviewer and do not subscribe to a syndicated review, they may use part of the press release itself for a review, particularly if the book has local appeal. For a hometown author, this may be supplemented by an interview, editorial, or feature story, which is generally accompanied by a photo of the author. Don't be reticent about sending in a photograph with your author's questionnaire. Even if you do not want it to appear on the jacket, it can be a useful tool for the publicity department.

**News Conferences, Press Parties, and Publishers' Parties.** If the appearance of a book coincides with a current event; if the book is particularly topical, political, or worthy of a feature story; or if the book is written by a celebrity, political figure, or notable author, the publicity department may schedule a press or publisher's party or call a news conference. Generally these convocations are limited to "hard" news or celebrities; a publicity director who arranges a non-newsworthy happening for reporters soon finds himself in the same position as the boy who cried "wolf."

**Radio and Television Interviews.** An appearance by an author on national television shows such as "The Johnny Carson Show," "The Donahue Show," or "The Today Show," is a coup for the publicity department, a windfall for the sales department, and a consummation devoutly to be wished by many authors, but it's a rare event. Whereas there are sixty-odd radio shows around the country that delight in interviewing authors (as do some local television shows for hometown authors), most national television talk shows shy away from them unless the author is a notable or a personality, or the topic of the book either has broad appeal (such as gardening, dieting, or raising pets) or timely consumer interest (such as ecology, women's liberation, or self-help). Novelists are rarely interviewed on television unless they happen to be best-selling authors or personalities.

Be prepared for at least two auditions if a television appearance becomes a possibility: Someone in publicity will covertly give you the once-over to see if you would go over well, and someone from the program itself will interview you either in person or by phone. If you pass muster, you may be primed with some printed or verbal instructions on technique, which will include such trenchant advice as "Glance through the book before interview if book has been out a while. See if book is on set."

Since media exposure can often sell a lot of copies of your book, it pays to suggest to the publicity department that for specific reasons you think your book will appeal to a certain local program or interviewer, and that an audience will find you witty, charming and articulate. Even if you think your book has a narrow audience, you might find that certain anecdotes about the topic or what happened to you while researching or writing the book are funny, interesting, or whatever. A book on scrimshaw, for instance, whether a how-to or an illustrated history, might appeal to a television interviewer if you had a sufficiently interesting collection for show-and-tell.

Generally, unless you or your book patently appears to be a natural for radio or television, nothing will happen unless you make the first move—all the more reason to establish a relationship with someone in the publicity department.

**Authors' Tours.** The bane of many a successful author's existence is the author's tour. Unless you enjoy hopping from city to city and from motel to hotel—you will not enjoy a promotion tour. There is also the frustration of finding that in at least half of the cities in which you appear not a single copy of your book can be found. (The publicity director told the local salesman you would be in Omaha on November 16, and he did call the local bookstores and got additional orders, but the warehouse shipped them late, and they will arrive next week when you are in San Francisco.)

Only rarely will a publisher sponsor a national author's tour; it's costly and therefore generally limited to authors of anticipated best sellers; moreover, inflation is slashing this facet of the publicity budget even further. But you may have the time or resources to sponsor your own publicity or lecture tour, locally or out of state, even if it's only to coincide with a vacation. Certainly your hometown and home state will welcome lectures and appearances at local clubs and organizations, and local radio stations and newspapers will be happy to interview you (in the largest urban centers, of course, you may not be welcomed so eagerly; the competition is keener). You can motivate the publicity department to send press releases and copies of the book, as well as to send letters and make phone calls if you indicate your own enthusiasm for cooperating and assisting in arranging these events. These can be coordinated with autograph parties at local bookstores, and often the publisher can be persuaded to place some local cooperative ads in newspapers (the publisher usually pays 75 percent of the cost, and the bookstore pays the rest). It's really not a big deal, and the publicity department knows exactly how to go about it, but without any prodding on your part, the possibility may never be raised. Generating this campaign effectively requires the full cooperation of the salesman for that territory; get to know him and go out of your way to cultivate his good graces. It's a good idea to plan appearances at least six weeks in advance so that you can manage, if possible, to take a month or so off, and so that publicity and sales can comfortably coordinate the arrangements—which will include seeing that books are there when you are (if you drive, put fifty copies in your trunk for insurance).

If you travel out of state on a vacation or can arrange to do so for any reason at all, and are willing to pay for your own expenses (you might ask for a partial rebate), the publicity department will generally assist you as described above. Appearances, media interviews, lectures, and autograph parties at either bookstores or in department stores are an effective means of publicizing and selling your book, but they are often avoided by authors out of fear, timidity, ignorance, or inertia, or shirked by the publisher because of commitments to the major titles on that season's list—or merely because other authors have been more vocal about their interest in publicizing their book and their willingness to cooperate in doing so.

Though authors' tours and other elaborate methods of promotion are usually reserved for that small percentage of books that the publisher thinks have a chance of "taking off," it sometimes happens that a modest book will begin to gain momentum, whether through unusually good or widespread reviews, by word of mouth, or by other means, and sales will dramatically increase months after publication. The publisher may then decide to initiate some of the publicity devices he had skipped, such as an author's tour. Or he may hire an independent publicist to plan and execute a special promotional campaign.

*LMP*, under a section called "Public Relations," lists almost 100 individuals or firms who can perform a variety of publicity functions for a one-time fee or an annual retainer. Publishers can decide to call them in at any of several key stages in the life of a book: before publication, upon publication, or thereafter. A small house may find itself with a potential best seller, feel that it lacks the clout or manpower to follow through, and judiciously invest some of its publicity budget in getting this outside help. These free-lance services are also available to authors. If, for instance, your book unexpectedly gets a rave review on the front page of the *New York Times Book Review,* and you jubilantly phone your editor to find out how the house intends to capitalize on this serendipity—as happened with one of my authors recently—you may find that even though the editor is equally excited, the house has decided to "sit tight" and "see what happens" (meaning it is probably just going to enjoy the extra sales, but may not try to parlay the terrific publicity, as it should). If you can afford to spend $1,000 to $3,000 to hire one of these free-lancers to promote you and your book, in the long run it would probably pay for itself and then some, in additional sales (i.e., royalties). The additional publicity might also, for instance, double the value of a paperback reprint sale. Before committing yourself to such an expensive step, you would want to discuss it with your editor, who will take it up with the house. In most cases, the house will cooperate with you and the free-lancer, and even if it will not share the cost, it may consider some supplementary advertising, or be willing to compensate you for some of the cost if the campaign clearly results in additional sales for the house. It is an option certainly worth discussing.

**Other Publicity Department Functions.** Aside from the obvious need of publicity to help coordinate the general promotion of a title by working in conjunction with the editorial, advertising, and sales departments, they also act as both the "custodian" for the publisher and public relations spokesperson.

Being custodian means keeping any information concerning the author or title in its files, whether it is reviews, advertisements, the author's questionnaire, newspaper clippings, and so forth. Virtually all publishers subscribe to one or more clipping services, and each week the current file of reviews will be passed around the house. Generally a photocopy of each review is forwarded to your editor, who will pass it on to you. Some editors are less diligent than others about this, and a good relationship with someone in publicity will permit you to ask that copies be sent directly to you.

The publicity department sees to it that the trade journals and newspapers are kept apprised of internal changes of personnel, as well as providing newsworthy items about the house, such as a big rights sale, an acquisition of an "important" title or author, or a merger. Finally, in conjunction with the editor, publicity will submit appropriate titles for literary prizes. Do not neglect to inform your editor or someone in publicity if you think your book might be eligible for a certain prize. Generally the more famous contests, such as The American Book Awards, do not solicit submissions, but many of the lesser-known ones—likely to be overlooked without your reminder—do request submissions.

From the variety of tasks that the publicity department performs, two conclusions can be drawn: first, that many of its functions are not just routine, and an imaginative and diligent director or department member can make a big difference in getting the word out (and that does usually mean more sales); and second, that the author who can skirt the line between being a nuisance and a confrere is able and welcome to cooperate and assist in affecting the amount and quality of publicity for his book.

**What You Can Reasonably Expect.** Unless the house has pre-determined that the book is going to be one of their big books for that season—about 10 percent get this designation—either because of the author's track record, his or her celebrity, or the topic of the book, most authors are going to be disappointed; they generally expect more than a publisher can deliver. They are not going to try to get you on the "Today Show," and they are not going to send a copy of your book to every Merv, Edwin, and Barbara who might talk it up. They will probably not throw a press conference or a publisher's party, nor send you on a national tour, invite you to speak at their sales conference, or ask you to autograph copies of the book at the annual American Bookseller's Association meetings. All the more reason for you to be active and cooperative within the scope of your possibilities. Complaints of inadequate or ineffectual publicity generally bear no fruit, while diplomatic suggestions and a note of thanks for tasks accomplished can produce unexpected efforts and results.

Many authors, and even editors, having struggled through the one to five years needed to write and see the book produced, sometimes feel and act as if its appearance is the final curtain for them; it is now out of their hands. One must overcome this inertia; the public does not yet even know the book exists. External developments, impressive early sales, or enthusiastic reviews can all be the occasion for renewed or stepped-up publicity efforts, and it is up to the author as well as the publisher to stay on top of things and be responsive to continuing publicity opportunities.

## What You Can Do Yourself

As I have stressed repeatedly, each author faces severe competition of one form or another at every stage in book publishing, from the initial submission to the book's appearance—God forbid—on the remainder table. To try to avoid this denouement, you must see yourself as an active partner in the entire process, rather than as a passive observer of an event over which you have no control and into which you have no significant input.

Filling out the author's questionnaire in detail is just one of many other steps you can and should take. You can generate local publicity on your own by sending notes to local newspapers suggesting an interview with a "native son" author, by writing to local book reviewers, and by doing the same with local radio and TV stations (of course, you will notify the publicity department about what you are doing, and inform it of your success). By generating interest and sales in your community, you may perk up your publisher's interest and effort. Visit local book-stores; offer to autograph copies of your book or to help arrange an autograph party. Arrange as many lectures as you can for yourself, and don't be timid or lazy about traveling farther afield.

Identify potential ''special sales'' for your editor (or find out who handles this at your publisher's and establish contact with this person). Is there an association that you belong to which might sell the book through its magazine, newsletter, or even send out a special mailing piece, which you or the publisher will provide? Is there a mail-order catalog it would fit into? A manufacturer who might give it away as a premium? An organization or club, local or national, whose members might want to buy and read your book? Are there specialty stores that might carry it? No one knows your book's potential audience as well as you do. If there is any chance at all for a special sale, write a separate letter exploring the possibilities, and make sure to supply the names and addresses of the appropriate people your publisher can contact.

To help interest the publisher's sales reps in your book, since it is unlikely many of them will read it, you can prepare a one-page fact sheet for the sales conference, pointing out what is unique about your book and why it should sell well. Help your editor come up with a ''handle,'' a short, catchy, one-sentence description that either sets the book apart from the competition or links it with a previous best-seller (*Up the Ladder* does for women in business what Michael Korda's *Power: How to Get It. How to Use It* did for men). You may also be able to identify specific areas of the country where your book is likely to do particularly well.

For the sub-rights department, you will want not only to suggest the magazines which might be interested in running a section of the book, but you can pick out the chapters most suitable for the individual magazines, or suggest how certain sections might be adapted or linked together to form a suitable article, or even suggest spin-off articles that overlap with your book's contents. Look over the list of 200 book clubs in *LMP* and see whether one or more of the specialized clubs—which might be overlooked—is a possible market for your book.

Finally, since it is unlikely that your publisher will fully exploit the potential sales or publicity for your book, considering the limited time and budget any publisher has to expend on a single title, you can consider hiring your own publicity agent (talk to your editor first!) and you can place your own coupon ads in specialized magazines (or even in clas-sified sections), filling the orders yourself with copies you've purchased at a 40 percent discount.

With any of these tactics, you will want to be diplomatic, generous in praise for efforts on the publisher's part, and careful not to nag, bug, or overdo it. By providing as much information as you can, and by supple-menting rather than interfering with the publisher's role, you will gener-ally find that your help will be accepted and appreciated. The publisher is as anxious as you are to see that your book is a success, even if he doesn't always behave that way.

**Publicity in Other Divisions.** Paperback originals—whether qual-ity, oversized, or mass market—are generally publicized by the same methods as are used for trade books. In spite of the recent and continued growth in originals, paperbacks still have a harder time getting reviews in the media, though improvements, such as a paperback page in the *New York Times Book Review,* are taking place. As a consequence, the publicity dollar is more likely to be spent in advertising or sales promo-tion. For mass market houses in particular, the problem is compounded by having a small staff turn out a huge number of titles each month, so that it is logistically impossible to expend much effort in publicity on most individual titles. Because of the greater number of consumer outlets for these paperbacks, the built-in market for category books, the lower prices, and, in the case of reprints, the fact that publicity has already been initiated by the trade publisher, publicity is not considered as vital to the success of most books, except for a limited number of blockbuster titles.

Textbook houses tend to restrict themselves to putting in appearances at academic conventions and to sending out copious quantities of com-plimentary (examination) copies of each book. From 250 to 2,500 or more free copies may be sent to professors teaching a course in which they might adopt—require their students to buy—the book. Publicity and advertising are normally combined as a single function, as when the publisher sends out a mailing piece to 75,000 professors who teach Introductory Sociology, extolling the virtues of its textbook (with some blurbs here, too) and urging the teacher merely to write in for a free copy. Textbooks are hardly ever reviewed as such, so that publishers com-pensate by advertising in academic journals.

Professional book publishers also rely almost exclusively on advertis-ing and sales promotion to get the word out. Primarily through mail order brochures, using mailing lists purchased from magazines and organiza-tions as well as their own list of previous customers, by space advertising in technical and professional journals, and by displaying at academic and professional conventions, these publishers are able to zero in on their potential customers.

## *Advertising*

The rule of thumb that most trade publishers use to determine their advertising budget is to allocate 10 percent of the anticipated net sales for any given season or year, and then to apportion that amount among individual titles based on the sales expectations of each particular title. By and large, the major books for a given season claim the major portion of an advertising budget, and the amount of money left to advertise middling titles would never satisfy the expectations of *any* author. An author's concept of advertising is generally limited to consumer space ads, such as in the *New York Times Book Review*. Since the cost of a full-page ad there runs to about $6,450, a book with an anticipated first-year sales of 7,000 copies would shoot its entire budget on about half a page. Aside from the fact that no publisher is convinced this kind of ad will sell a single copy of a book, it would leave no funds for advertising to the trade, the most vital initial market for your book. Very simply, if your book is not on the shelves of a bookstore, there is little point in spending money to attract people to the store to buy it. Of course, a clamor for your book at stores will generate orders, but generally the books will arrive when the demand has passed. The function of advertising, then, begins with an appeal to the trade: to bookstore owners or buyers and wholesalers. In fact, the advertising dollar must be spent in a variety of ways, many of which are unseen by the author, such as on the publisher's catalog, posters, circulars, and on ads in several different trade magazines.

Depending on the size of the publisher, the house may employ a single advertising manager and a secretary, or a department with a staff of up to ten or more people. The advertising manager works in close conjunction with publicity and sales and acts as the liaison between the publisher and the ad agency (scarcely any publisher continues to perform the ad agency's job). Working generally with an information sheet on every title, which contains a description of the book, background on the author, and material from publicity, such as blurbs, this department is also generally responsible for supplying jacket copy, catalog copy, copy for mailing pieces, circulars, and sales letters, as well as supplying book information and suggestions to the ad agency, helping to determine mutually the kind and format of specific ads, the media in which to place them, and the disbursement of the budget in order to get the most mileage from each dollar spent. In doing all this, the advertising manager must take into account and reflect in the ads the ideas of the editorial and sales department, not to mention those of executive management.

While the author conceives of advertising as a means of persuading the consumer to buy his book, there are actually several other equally important goals to be accomplished. The wholesale and retail bookseller is the most important link in the chain between the publisher and the public, so that advertising to the trade, primarily through trade journals such as *Publishers Weekly* and *Library Journal*, is the most important first step. Each summer and winter, these two magazines publish their "announcement" issues, in which most trade publishers take full page (or more) ads to announce all their titles for the forthcoming fall or spring season's books. During the rest of the year, some of the individual issues are devoted to other specific categories or divisions, such as religious, juvenile, or professional publishing, or examine other segments of the industry, such as regional or international publishing. Throughout the year publishers advertise heavily in trade magazines—and generally provide more specific information about the book than is found in consumer ads: the size of the first printing, the sales record of the author, subsidiary rights sales, publicity, sales promotion and advertising budgets and plans, why the book should sell well, etc. Presumably the bookseller is informed both by the size and number of the ads, as well as by the information in them, of the extent to which the publisher is getting behind the book—"$50,000 National Advertising Campaign!"—and will be influenced to stock the book in commensurate quantities. The slant of ads in *Library Journal* and other magazines and journals for librarians will, of course, be more oriented to the quality of the book rather than just its marketability. Successful advance or early season sales for a book will usually result in follow-up ads in *Publishers Weekly*—"Third printing! 20,000 copies now in print!"—to encourage the bookseller to reorder.

In addition to stimulating wholesale and retail book sales, early advertising in both trade and consumer media is expected to have an influence on subsidiary rights sales. Both book clubs and paperback reprint houses are the main targets: The more advertising splash for a title, the more attention is drawn to the book, the more likely it is to be considered for a subsidiary rights sale. Each sale that does take place may be the occasion for another ad—"Main selection of the Literary Guild! To be serialized in *Ladies' Home Journal*!"—in order to stimulate further subsidiary rights sales as well as wholesale or retail bookstore orders. Ideally, the publisher is hoping for a snowball effect: that each event—whether a rave review in *Publishers Weekly*, a first serial sale, a second printing, or a bookclub sale—will generate more interest, excitement, and publicity, which will in turn result in additional orders from bookstores and wholesalers, another subsidiary rights sale (perhaps an option for a film), greater consumer sales, and finally an appearance on the best-seller list. While advertising cannot in itself generate this activity, it is an effective means of parading it and keeping the title alive in the minds of all concerned.

Reviewers, of course, are not totally immune to advertising either. Trade ads, which support the efforts of the publicity department, bring titles to the attention of prospective reviewers. The more splash a publisher makes for a book, the more likely a reviewer is at least to consider reviewing the book. Nor are agents and authors unresponsive to ads. While the effectiveness of advertising, particularly in consumer media, cannot be measured—except for coupon ads, which can be quite effective for how-to and self-help books—authors still believe in it, probably because it is so much more visible than publicity and sales promotion (ads placed primarily to please authors are called tombstone ads). Many successful authors will consider moving from one publishing house to another either because they feel slighted due to the low number of ads for their book or because some other house is heavily advertising its authors and they want some of the same. Agents respond to advertising not only because they know it makes their authors happy, but also because it lets them know which publishers are doing what, occasionally suggesting why and where they might submit their next manuscript.

Each book on a publisher's list requires a different advertising strategy or campaign. If the book is not slated to be a major book for that season and thus does not have a generous budget, the problem of deciding how to reach the greatest possible number of potential customers for the least amount of money is even more crucial. The amount of circulation for a particular magazine, journal, or newspaper is usually not the decisive factor: The publisher wants to reach the hard-core book buyer, not the casual reader. A Ralph Nader book on the automobile industry is obviously much more effectively advertised in *The New Republic,* which has a circulation of 100,000, than it is in *People* magazine, which has a circulation of over two million. As there are more than 10,000 newspapers published in the United States, and almost as many magazines, the problem of targeting the prime audience for the book is particularly difficult with a "general" book. A first novel, for instance, with an average ad budget of $1,500 to $2,500, will generally get an ad or two in large-circulation magazines or newspapers whose audience contains "serious" readers, but its effectiveness is doubtful.

Many nonfiction books have a more clearly identifiable audience, so that advertising in the magazines and journals that cater to this audience can be effective. Your suggestions in the author's questionnaire or in a letter to your editor for advertising media will be considered; you may know the market and the most appropriate media in which to advertise your book better than anyone in the house, especially if the topic is quite specific, such as a hobby, a craft, or a vocation.

One cost-effective method for the publisher is a "P.I." ad (per inquiry). A magazine will run a full- or half-page coupon ad, for which the publisher pays the magazine 30 to 50 percent of the receipts the ad draws. Or the magazine will list or review books that might interest its readers on a "bookshelf" page, and—acting like a book club—will offer these books at list price or for a small discount, while buying the books directly from the publisher at a standard bookstore discount. For both special-interest and new magazines, this helps to inflate the number of advertising pages and brings in some additional revenue, whereas for the publisher it is basically a free ad, since he is still selling his books at a normal discount.

While advertisements in major national newspapers are generally most effective for books with a wide appeal, a book by a local author or a book with regional interest (such as *Libraries of New England*) may warrant ads in a regional newspaper. Publishers may try to coordinate these ads with local interviews, appearances, and autograph parties at bookstores.

Television advertising is costly and used very sparingly. In the last few years, mass market publishers have come occasionally to use spot commercials for books with anticipated sales of a half million or more copies, or for series such as Barbara Cartland's romances, and large chains sometimes share the cost of television ads with some trade publishers for specific "major" titles. The use of late-night nonnetwork advertising, which is considerably cheaper, is also increasing, and publishers are now exploring the benefits of advertising on cable TV. But to date, the cost of television advertising and the inability to measure its usefulness have discouraged publishers from using this medium. A television ad tie-in, however—promoting or advertising a book that is simultaneously appearing as a major film—is becoming more popular. As films are increasingly "novelized," and as novels are increasingly serialized on television programs, the amount of television advertising for books is increasing.

Radio advertising is cheaper, and the number of programs that feature authors is higher, so that books are more commonly advertised on radio. Some programs, for instance, will run a prerecorded interview of an author for a price. In general, though, only a very small proportion of nonfiction books are advertised on either radio or television, since it is felt that hard-core readers can be reached more inexpensively through magazines and journals.

The use of mailing pieces, which might just as readily be identified as a sales function, is particularly effective for professional or highly technical books. These books are generally more expensive (so that the cost of mailings is offset by the higher net receipts), the specific audience is easier to reach, and the percentage of book buyers, per capita, is much higher than for the general population. Trade publishers, who also often publish books for specialized audiences, will use mailing pieces as well, especially when they publish a series or a number of books in a specific field. Textbook publishers, as mentioned before, generally confine their advertising to journals and use mailing pieces—frequently with coupons attached—to solicit requests for examination copies.

A coupon ad, conversely, may be most effective for a book with wide appeal, directed toward an audience that does not consist of hard-core book buyers. A book on how to stop smoking or books on dieting or self-help are examples.

The library market is so vital to the juvenile division, professional publishers, and university presses—as well as to the trade division of many houses—that a separate budget may be set aside for library promotion, which combines advertising, sales promotion, and publicity. There are more than a dozen publications specifically for librarians, such as *Library Journal* and the *A.L.A. Booklist,* and in addition to advertising in these special media, publishers may produce separate catalogs solely for the library market.

Since the ad budget for most books is so limited, publishers frequently resort to group ads, in which several or more titles are combined, sometimes featuring one or more titles and merely listing the others. This holds true for both trade and consumer ads and mailing pieces, whether the book is directed to a broad audience or a narrow one. Authors tend to overlook the group ad when complaining about the lack of advertising for their book.

If you consider the publisher's expectation of selling roughly 6,000 copies of a "middling" book and recognize that money allocated for advertising must also pay for trade ads, catalogs, and a variety of unseen costs (cost of preparation of the ad by the ad agency, for example), the author should not be disappointed to learn that only a handful of ads or less have been scheduled for his book. The time to squawk is when no ads at all are placed for your book, which is not that uncommon. As in all businesses, the advertising department often finds itself over budget before the year is out, and the middling book is the one most likely to be short-changed. Also, unforeseen expenses—additional ads for a book that starts to take off or gets rave reviews—may cut even further into the yearly budget. If the advance sales exceed the publisher's expectations, if a hefty subsidiary rights sale is concluded, if the book gets excellent reviews in trade journals or large-circulation consumer magazines or newspapers, or if the bookstore orders or reorders are heavy, then the publisher will generally follow up with some additional ads. In other words, it is often only when the book succeeds in spite of minimal advertising that the publisher increases the budget for the book, though, of course, a major book will already have a substantial budget. The main reason for this Catch-22 is the publishing lottery: The major books aside, most publishers are still producing more books than they can effectively promote, either through publicity, advertising, or sales promotion—in spite of the current impact of inflation, which has resulted in a trimming of lists at many major trade houses—partly because it's impossible to know in advance which ones will sell and which won't. The only certainty is that less than half will have to support the rest.

## Sales, Sales Promotion, and Distribution

Inflation has also had a crucial impact on the sales department, and the results will be seen through the eighties. Some publishers have cut back on their inside-the-house sales forces and increased their use of independent "commission reps." They are also controlling the itineraries of their sales forces more carefully, and concentrating sales calls on those stores or areas with greater sales potential. The slack is taken up by the increasing use of telephone sales. In selling by mail or through coupon ads, publishers are trying to target the audiences more precisely, and are using test mailings or ads more frequently, in order to make sure that a larger campaign is worth the expenditure.

Obviously no other department is so vital to the life or death of a publishing house than sales; thus in many ways inflationary pressure is felt most keenly here. Publishers are trying to boost sales by opening up more nonbookstore markets, from sporting goods stores to hardware stores to garden supply stores. And special sales, such as selling to manufacturers who may give away a book as a premium, are being pursued with renewed intensity.

One additional result of these pressures is stricter attention to the budget, not only in marketing, but in all the other departments in the house. As a consequence more power and decision making has passed into the hands of the accounting department and the financial people—a trend helped along by conglomerate policies—and so in some ways publishing is beginning more and more to resemble conventional industries, such as those that manufacture and sell soaps or cereals.

**The Sales Conference.** The cycle for selling trade books officially begins at the sales conference. Even though the sales manager, as mentioned before, may have had a decisive voice in determining whether or not to sign up a book and in estimating how many copies it might sell, it is not until this semiannual conference is held that the salesmen are actually presented with the next season's list. In the last ten years, more and more books have come to be published during the summer and winter months, so that the traditional fall and spring lists are actually spread out over twelve months. But the practice of holding the meetings in late May for the fall list and in early December for the spring list still persists.

The conference lasts from one to four days and is generally attended by all the editors and salesmen, as well as by representatives from publicity, advertising, and other departments. The main objectives of the meeting are to inform the salesmen of the next season's books, to outline the publicity and advertising plan for the list, and, in general, to fire up enthusiasm. In addition to the seasonal catalog, salesmen are supplied with dust jackets, if they are ready, copies of forthcoming ads and circulars, press releases, blurbs, backlist information, and sometimes copies or page proofs of one or more of the anticipated major books for the next season.

A medium-size house may publish up to forty or fifty books a season, not to mention the juvenile titles, which are also generally presented at this meeting. As a consequence, each editor is expected to spend no more than three to four minutes presenting one of his books, providing a brief description that emphasizes the book's merits, discusses its potential audience and market, distinguishes it from the competition, and points out salient facts about the author. Lest you should feel overly dismayed that four minutes hardly do justice to your book, observe that when the salesman presents the book to the buyer, he will probably average a minute per book. In an attempt to overcome this handicap, the editor will try to provide a "handle" for each of his books, a one-sentence pitch designed to arrest the attention of the bookseller by pinpointing the book's main virtue and its theme. For a while, "everything you always wanted to know about _____ but were afraid to ask" was quite popular, but that quickly paled. Thinking up a striking handle (or a good title for that matter) is an art, and editors often have to limp along with something like "the most poignant love story since *Love Story*."

As the books are presented, questions and comments arise, from "That cover will kill the sales on the west coast; can't you put some red in it?" to "They won't go for Russian cooking in my territory; nobody's ever heard of borscht in Alabama." The editors' presentations are followed up with a report of the publicity and advertising campaigns that are planned for the forthcoming books. A certain amount of time will also be devoted to the current list and the backlist: What's selling well and what isn't; what additional ads, sales promotion, or publicity are intended; what so and so's appearance on the "Today" show has done for her book; which books are going into second or third printings; which books have been taken as bookclub selections or been sold to a paperback reprinter; and so forth.

A major feature on the last day of the conference is the setting of quotas by the sales manager for "advance sales." Taking into account the original estimate for the first year's sale of a book, the amount of the first printing, the comments of salesmen and others on each title during the presentations and the rest of the meeting (including palavers over lunch and dinner), the initial success or quality of specific subsidiary rights sales, and finally his own educated hunch, the sales manager will set a specific quota for each title of the total number of copies he wants, hopes, or expects the entire sales force to sell on their first trip into the field. Furthermore, he will allocate a specific portion of that quota to each salesman or territory. For a first printing of 7,500 copies, for instance, he may set an advance of 2,500 copies: 250 for California, 300 copies for the southeast, 400 copies for New England, and so forth. The quota may be influenced by the previous regional sales of that author's book, the subject of the book, the author's location, or the nature of the advertising and publicity campaign.

While this quota is obviously as much a fantasy as the estimate of the first year's sale of a specific title, it often takes on the potency of a self-fulfilling prophecy. The higher the quota for a specific title, the more time, effort and attention each salesperson will devote to that title, so that the sales manager's prediction influences the sales rep's exertions, which in turn influences both the bookseller's expectations and his/her order for that title. While many books manage to break the initial mold that is cast for them, either doing better or worse than has been prophesied, the prepublication quota is often a vital determinant in the success or failure of many books. The rationale, and often the result of these quotas, is the oft-mentioned competition for time and space. In this instance, each salesperson knows that a bookseller has only limited shelf space for the 20,000 new trade books published each year, and that he can be turned on by only a handful of titles on that publisher's seasonal list. Thus, the bulk of the sales pitch is confined to the major books; the rest go out on a wing and a prayer. However, as the advance sales are sought prior to actual book publication, an unexpected enthusiastic response on the part of buyers, that is, bigger orders than were anticipated, may not only increase the size of the first printing, but may influence the house to spend additional money on advertising, to expend more time on publicity and sales promotion, and to urge the salesmen to increase their efforts for that title.

**The Sales Staff.** There are two categories of sales reps in trade publishing: those who work solely for that house, and those who work exclusively on commission and represent several publishers. The former are salaried by the publisher, work exclusively for that house, and generally also get a yearly incentive bonus based on their sales and quotas. The latter are independent, work exclusively on a commission of roughly 10 percent of sales, and may represent from five to fifteen publishers. While the bigger houses usually employ house reps, and the smaller houses commission reps, many publishers work with a combination of both. Overseeing the staff is a sales manager, whose other prime responsibilities are to see that accounts are serviced properly and regularly and that major customer relations problems are solved, to set house policy on returns and discounts, to work with other departments for a smooth coordination of overall marketing strategy, to advise on decisions about signing up books, and to see that the sales reps are supplied with any requisite new information or materials that filter in from day to day. The sales manager will also personally take care of, or oversee, the selling to the large chains. At the moment both B. Dalton (with 435 stores) and Waldenbooks (with 650 stores) not only buy in huge quantities—their combined sales of almost $500 million represent almost 20 percent of all trade sales—but their policies and ordering patterns now have a significant impact on some publishing decisions. That they almost never take a literary first novel, for instance, is partly responsible for its diminishing numbers. And trade houses are sometimes swayed for or against a book by the answer a buyer at either chain gives to a phone call asking whether or not he or she thinks a book on X, Y, or Z will or will not sell well.

Each house will divide the country into territories, whose size is determined both by the number of salespersons employed by the house and the volume of business in a specific territory. The biggest houses may have as many as one hundred representatives, and a single territory may be no larger than ten square miles, whereas a smaller house may have one man or woman covering a territory as large as New England.

Most sales reps will service roughly two hundred accounts, which may include individual retail bookstores, chains, wholesalers, and sometimes library systems. On an average, each visits his bookstore accounts four times a year: once before the fall and spring lists are published, and once during the season to check stock and take reorders. At the two extremes are large accounts, such as wholesalers or chains, who may be serviced every month—and once a week by phone—and the smaller retail stores that are visited but once a year, or which may never see a sales rep and are serviced by phone or mail. Armed with his kit—catalogs, dust jackets, ads, circulars, etc.—the sales rep may spend one to three weeks on the road, though, as most of them live in the territory, they generally do not have to be away from home more than a week at a time. In addition to selling the new list, he or she usually checks stock to see which current titles have sold out and ought to be reordered, and will also see to it that perennials on the backlist are on hand. As an average sales call may last two hours, of which half an hour may be spent in checking stock and another half hour on the backlist (a book goes on the backlist the day it is published), the sales rep may have only an hour or less to talk about the twenty-five to fifty new titles. (A commissioned sales rep, who represents several firms, may be taking orders for over two hundred new titles.) From past experience, he generally knows what kinds of books are stocked or go over well for that store and will concentrate on pushing the major titles and a smattering of the others.

To retain credibility, a judicious salesperson will neither oversell his books nor exaggerate the potential sales of a title—nor will he push more books on that store than he thinks it can reasonably sell. Since the returns policy of virtually all publishers permits the store to send back all unsold books for full credit up to a year after purchase—and now more commonly for as long as the book remains in print—the temptation exists to overload the store by pointing out that "you can always return what you don't sell." But the paperwork for processing returns is time-consuming and complicated (partly to discourage returns), the store's shelf and storage space is limited and the buyer must pay the shipping charges on both the incoming order and the returns, which, due to escalating postal rates, can eat up slim profits. Thus the buyer exercises restraint for these reasons, and the salesman, who will visit the store several times a year, ideally controls his impulses to oversell so that his advice and suggestions are respected on future calls.

**The Bookstore.** Out of over 20,000 hardcover book outlets in the U.S., there are roughly 15,000 that carry trade books, which includes specialty stores (religious, medical, etc.), rare and second-hand bookstores, college and department store concessions, and book chains; about 9,000 general bookstores actually stock and sell new trade books. Unfortunately, one can count on one's fingers and toes the number of individual stores in the United States that have a truly representative stock of hardcovers, from an edition of Jung's *Mysterium Coniunctionis* to John Ashberry's latest book of poems, not to mention your own book. Only about 2,000 stores have a fair sampling of trade publishers' spring and fall lists. The remaining 7,000 general bookstores will carry several hundred current, popular, best-selling, and perennial titles (such as Gibran's *The Prophet*), and the rest of the stock will consist of trade and mass market paperbacks, and remainders, always a high-profit genre.

**Wholesalers and Jobbers.** Though the bookstore may not order your book from the publisher's representative, he does have access to another supplier. The major wholesalers or jobbers, of whom there are about fifteen spread around the United States, will stock a huge inventory of trade books from most commercial publishers—not only the major titles, but the middling and backlist books, too. These fifteen or so are backed up by almost 1,000 smaller regional wholesalers, many of whom are flourishing because they provide personal service and direct sales calls, which publishers are now supplying by computer or phone. Often in competition among themselves, the small wholesaler may be more imaginative and aggressive in opening up and servicing nonbook outlets, such as toy stores. Some jobbers primarily service trade book accounts; others specialize in library and school sales; most service both. If a customer requests a title that the store doesn't carry or has run out of, the store can generally get the book from the wholesaler within three days, no matter where the store is located. A bookstore in Montana might have to wait three to five weeks to get a shipment of books from an eastern publisher. They may order forthcoming titles from the publisher's representative, but once the season is started, they will generally rely on the wholesaler to supply them with current books. The wholesaler often works closely with the publisher to provide the local store with other materials and assistance: He may supply advice on forthcoming titles, copies of book reviews, a list of best sellers, and help coordinate promotional appearances of authors.

**S.T.O.P.** As big an inventory as a wholesaler may carry, he cannot possibly stock copies of each of the approximately half million titles that are currently in print in the United States. The Single Title Order Plan, sponsored and administered by the American Booksellers Association, permits the bookstore to order one or more copies of any single title and still receive the standard trade discount, 40 percent, though prepayment must be included with the order. Many publishers have individual plans for single-copy orders, but S.T.O.P. is the most widely used service. Often inefficient—it can sometimes take anywhere from three to five weeks or more to get a single book through S.T.O.P. or the publisher— it is one of the prime examples of the inability of the publishing industry to provide adequate distribution of its products.

**Mass Market Wholesalers.** While many wholesalers now also stock mass market paperbacks, the major suppliers for the over 100,000 paperback outlets—that include drugstores, airline terminals, magazine stands, variety store chains, and supermarkets—are the 550 or so "independents," whose primary business includes magazine distribution (only about 400 carry books). Sales reps for mass market publishers service both bookstores and independents, but since the majority of outlets are businesses for whom paperbacks are a sideline, so that no one on the staff is likely to have or develop the expertise to select paperbacks judiciously for their particular outlet, the book selections are often made by the publisher or the independent distributor; this trend is increasing during the eighties. As consumer buying patterns tend to vary, depending on both the regional location and the type of outlet, some independent distributors have paperback experts who choose and prepack a representative selection and quantity of new titles, based on the previous sales history and volume of business for a particular outlet. Some distributors are not expert at this, choose stock carelessly, overstock their outlets, and service the book racks with minimum attention to what's moving and what isn't, what should be returned and what re-ordered. This accounts in part for the staggering industrywide average of 35 percent returns for mass market paperbacks.

Publishers also have a variety of automatic allotment systems for both nonbookstore outlets and independent distributors who are either less knowledgeable about current paperbacks or don't have the time or personnel to buy carefully or prudently. Keeping track of the bewildering array and huge output of new titles, not to mention the backlist, is not a task for the dilettante.

**College Textbooks.** The textbook sales rep has a special moniker, college traveler, perhaps in recognition of the fact that his job is more public relations than salesmanship. The largest firms employ upwards of sixty sales reps, while the smallest may rely on catalogs and other mailing pieces to promote and sell their books. Each traveler's itinerary consists of a territory in which he visits a specific number of community and four-year colleges and universities. Most textbook firms publish both basic texts—single comprehensive books that presumably cover the entire syllabus for a one-semester course, such as an Introduction to Psychology textbook—and a variety of anthologies or supplementary texts (usually in paperback editions).

The traveler's task is to help persuade a professor to adopt a textbook for his students, that is, to place an order through the bookstore for as many copies of the book as will cover the anticipated enrollment for his forthcoming course. For virtually every standard course in the curriculum, whether undergraduate or graduate, there are anywhere from four or five to forty or fifty competing basic texts. As most professors generally know much more about the subject matter than the traveler, his role is essentially to see that the teacher is apprised of forthcoming texts in his field from the traveler's firm and to prevail upon him to examine a free copy. Prior to the 1970s, required courses with large enrollments, such as a two-semester survey of American history, may have been taught to as many as 2,000 or more students per semester in a single school, and it was common practice for a committee of several teachers to choose a single text for all sections of this course (this is known as a blanket adoption). An adoption of this size did encourage salesmanship, high-pressure tactics, and occasionally fomented departmental politics and factionalism. In the seventies, however, not only did individual course requirements diminish, but most professors, and even teaching assistants, were free to choose their own texts, thereby reducing the traveler's role as salesman while simultaneously driving college bookstore managers crazy—imagine forty different instructors ordering four or five different paperbacks for their Introduction to Literature class. But now, in the eighties, the pendulum is swinging back in the other direction: more required courses, more basic texts, less use of supplementary paperbacks, and more blanket adoptions.

Concomitantly, a more independent attitude, shall we say, on the part of undergraduates is reflected in higher returns of textbooks, as students no longer purchase (or read) all the books assigned by the professor. Returns now average 15 to 20 percent. Students also are now more inclined to sell their textbooks after the course is over, so that secondhand sales (controlled by a few large used text outlets) cut heavily into the textbook market within a year after the book is published. Partial results are a decline in the number of books signed up, an increase in list prices, and more frequent revisions of successful basic texts.

In addition to the use of travelers, sales are pursued through frequent mailings of catalogs and fliers and by displays of texts at annual academic conventions. Since 1970, telephone sales have become a conventional means of selling textbooks. Instead of sending a traveler from school to school, which costs a publisher roughly $14,000 in salary and close to $9,000 in expenses, he can hire an inexperienced clerk with a pleasant voice to call individual professors or committee members and make a pitch over the phone. In this way, the publisher can reach more schools at a much lower cost per sales call. The use of commission sales reps to sell texts is also a growing phenomenon of the eighties.

During the last decade, the increased use of trade and mass market paperbacks in the classroom, either to supplement or replace the textbook, has resulted in a windfall for paperback publishers that has prompted them to develop and publish titles particularly for the education market and to devote time, attention, and money to educational sales and promotion. In addition to a barrage of catalogs and mailing pieces, many paperback publishers also provided professors with free sample copies of books that might be adopted or recommended, attended and displayed at academic conventions, and a few even had their own college travelers. But as the swing back to basic texts has increased, these publishers have also cut back on their publishing programs.

**Professional Book Sales.** Books specifically written for professionals, academics, or specialists are primarily sold by mail order. The three basic markets are individuals, libraries, and foreign sales (which accounts for a surprisingly high 20 percent of total sales). By means of the house mailing list, lists purchased from journals, professional organizations, and companies that sell specialized mailing lists, the publisher is able to direct his sales efforts to prime potential customers. Professional, reference, and technical book clubs have burgeoned in the last ten years. Macmillan, for instance, runs no fewer than twenty-one different clubs, from the Behavioral Science Book Service to the Lawyers Literary Club. These book clubs now account for a hefty percentage of professional sales, and several other publishers have started their own clubs. Library, academic, and professional conventions provide another outlet for the professional or reference publisher to display and sell his list. There are very few specialty bookstores for professional books, and while the 3,000 or so college bookstores stock a handful of titles, most general bookstores will not carry a single title, nor will most wholesalers stock them in representative quantities (though there are now a few specialized wholesalers who cater to this audience). The main reason for this is a discount problem, a thorny thicket we have wittingly managed to avoid so far, but one that should be discussed even if briefly and superficially.

**Discounts and Distribution.** The discount schedule in publishing is so far from uniform that the American Booksellers Association annually provides a thick looseleaf collection of hundreds of different publishers' discount schedules for its members; in fact many publishers offer different discounts on different books, or offer different discounts on the *same* book on different occasions, regardless of the quantity ordered. The gremlins introduced into publishing by the computers are usually responsible. Similarly fragmented are the archaic and confusing means and methods of book distribution, ordering and returning procedures and policies, combined with the lack of an industrywide systematic method of inventory control that would link the publisher, the wholesaler, and the retailer. Contributing in no small way to this problem is the staggering number of books now in print and available to order (400,000). Automation has yet to deliver this branch of publishing from the Middle Ages, though it certainly will someday, since the lack of a comprehensive, uniform, industrywide system for marketing books is costing every publisher more than he would care to admit—if he were able to figure out what it was costing him. Merely to note the average returns of unsold books—15 to 20 percent for trade and text publishers; as high as 40 percent for mass market publishers—is sufficient proof of the seriousness of the problem. Let us therefore not delve too deeply into all these matters for fear that we drown. In an effort to reduce these punishing figures, some publishers are now offering an additional 5 to 10 percent discount to bookstores on initial orders if they agree to take the books on a nonreturnable basis. In fact the notion of selling trade books on a nonreturnable basis is gathering increasing support throughout the industry, as is attested to by a recent and persuasive article in *Publishers Weekly*. The whys and wherefores go beyond the scope of this book, but it seems as if this gigantic and costly headache could be cured simply by giving bookstores larger discounts, and having them remainder those books that they might normally return.

In a recent study by Benjamin Compaine, *The Book Industry in Transition* (1979), the author identifies five major problems contributing to current dilemmas in marketing and distribution: (1) the cumbersome and inefficient distribution network itself; (2) insufficient funds to adequately support each individual title published; (3) the lack of "hard-nosed business practices in publishing house management and bookstore proprietorship"; (4) the paucity of retail outlets for books; and (5) the fact that too many books are being published.

With regard to distribution, technology is now making some inroads into these massive problems, and most publishers are eagerly incorporating new methods and systems of distribution, which are helping to increase the standardization of practices in the industry. The use of machine-readable symbols on books, for instance, supplemented by the use of scanners—such as those now seen in many supermarkets—will provide useful data for both the publisher and the bookseller. Publishers know what they sell to bookstores and wholesalers, but they are often in the dark about what these firms are selling to *their* customers. By knowing more quickly what titles are moving in the stores, publishers can more efficiently and rapidly decide which titles to reprint; guesswork has been one reason for big returns. Computer-to-computer communication via tapes of orders, invoices, and price changes, between publishers and their customers, will not only expedite orders—so that sales are made rather than lost because interest waned before books arrived—but will reduce the number of man-made errors in billing, filling, and shipping orders (though computer errors at least equal man-made errors as this book goes to press). With regard to royalty statements, some publishers may jointly use or sell computer systems which will provide more standardized, readable, and informative statements; many of the current ones are confusing, cryptic in detail, and not uncommonly contain simple mathematical errors. During this transitional period, as publishers increasingly employ automation, authors (and publishers) may find that the problems created are equal to the problems solved, but in the long run it is assumed that the computer's ability to store and retrieve large amounts of information will benefit all the players in the industry.

But as we were saying, the professional book publisher does not get his wares displayed in general bookstores, not primarily because the audience is limited, but mainly because he offers his books to the bookseller at a "short" discount, that is, in the 20 to 33⅓ percent range (depending on the individual publisher and the quantity of titles ordered). Booksellers feel that the mark-up is not high enough to warrant having the book in stock. Textbooks, which are generally sold to the bookseller at a 20 percent discount (although 25 percent is becoming increasingly common), are therefore also excluded from general bookstores and are only stocked by college bookstores when a professor adopts a title.

Trade books, however, as well as mass market books, are sold at a "long" discount, which ranges from 40 to 50 percent, again depending on the publisher and the quantity ordered. A typical trade discount schedule would be:

> 40 percent on 5 or more assorted titles
> 42 percent on 50 or more assorted titles
> 44 percent on 250 or more assorted titles
> 46 percent on 500 or more assorted titles

The wholesaler and the independent, who order from publishers in larger quantities, receive higher discounts, ranging from 42 to 50 percent for trade books and going as high as 55 percent for mass market paperbacks. Of course, the individual bookstore or outlet must pay for the convenience of buying from the wholesaler instead of the publisher by receiving a lower discount, which averages 33⅓ percent, though it may go as high as 40 percent for large orders. In other words, the wholesaler stays in business by buying at an average 47 to 50 percent discount and selling at an average 37 to 40 percent discount; what he lacks in margin he makes up in volume.

**Library and Institutional Sales and Promotion.** The revenue from library sales is so important for virtually all categories of publishing that a separate department or school and library consultant devotes full time to this market. This department promotes and sells its books both to the library and to the el-hi (elementary–high school) market. The reasons are twofold: The teacher (and department chairman and principal, or the district curriculum committee) have a say in what books are purchased for the library, and some of the books—particularly juveniles—may be used in the classroom. We are not talking about textbooks *per se*. The el-hi publisher or division is separate and has its own sales staff and methods of sales and promotion. *Educational sales* in this context refers specifically to the spillover into classroom use of juvenile and trade titles, hence the combining of library and educational sales efforts. This spillover has stimulated the sales efforts and even refocused the editorial policies of some mass market publishers during the last decade. Many mass market paperbacks are now written for and adopted in the el-hi classroom. Juvenile publishers also issue many of their titles in paperback, sell paperback reprint rights to mass market houses, or initiate paperback originals themselves.

Look at the library figures: There are about 9,000 public libraries, 8,000 special libraries (technical, business, scientific, medical, law, etc.), 49,000 elementary school libraries, 13,000 junior high school libraries, 18,000 public and private high school libraries, and 3,000 college and university libraries. All combined, they buy a lot of books! Large library systems, for instance, may buy as many as 500 copies of a best seller. Unfortunately, federal funding and school library budgets have been cut back significantly in the last twelve years or so, but inflation is equally the culprit. Library materials budgets are over $2 billion, but higher and higher list prices for books have cut into the quantity of books libraries can afford to purchase. The professional book publisher who used to be able to count on selling 1,500 copies to libraries (which for certain kinds of books was the difference between profit and loss) is no longer sure of selling even 500 copies. Recent statistics indicating the percentage of total book sales that are accounted for by libraries reveal their importance:

Juveniles—over 80 percent
University press—roughly 25 percent
Professional and technical—25 percent
Trade books—20 percent (up to 50 percent or more for first novels)

It is apparent that many publishers could not exist without library sales. University presses in particular have felt the squeeze over the last decade: Some have folded, most have cut back their lists, and many are now passing up marginal scholarly books, regardless of their quality or potential contribution to scholarship. Instead, some are now signing up trade books—nonfiction with a wide potential audience and even fiction.

Surprisingly, over 75 percent of the orders from libraries are filled by jobbers and wholesalers. The explanation is simply that publishers give libraries discounts of 10 to 20 percent, whereas wholesalers—some of whom specialize exclusively or primarily in library sales—offer discounts as high as 39 percent. Nevertheless, both the publisher and the wholesaler are active in promoting books for library sales.

The publisher exerts his sales efforts in several ways. Direct sales calls to wholesalers and to library systems are supported by a variety of catalogs, mailing pieces, and even newsletters. As the library represents the major market for most publishers of juveniles, many will prepare separate library and educational catalogs, broken down by subject, grade levels, or both. These catalogs and mailing pieces will be sent not only to librarians, but to school principals, district-level media specialists, curriculum committees, etc. A variety of prepackaged "standing order" buying plans for groups of books is available for both the school and library, and the practice of sending a free review copy to the committee or buyers for a school or library system is conventional, as some systems purchase up to one hundred copies of a book. Classroom adoptions of juveniles, of course, can run into the thousands. Multiple-order library purchases are often made six to eight months after publication, since librarians either wish to review the books themselves first or want to see reviews in the various specialized journals and magazines, such as *Library Journal, School Library Journal*, or *Booklist*, before making their decisions. Advertising for this market is concentrated in these magazines and journals and in ads and listings placed in wholesaler's catalogs. The publisher's library consultant may clip and send out copies of good reviews, along with notices of awards and prizes or nominations for them—the coveted Newberry or Caldecott juveniles awards may boost an anticipated 10,000 copy sale up to 40,000 or 50,000 copies.

The publisher, but even more consistently and effectively the wholesaler, will also provide the library with Library of Congress catalog cards and check-out cards and will put shelf numbers on bindings, though for these services and higher discounts most wholesalers require an exclusive contract with a library system. In fact, for most trade publishers, the sales and promotion efforts encourage libraries to buy from wholesalers. The cost of the paperwork involved in billing and shipping the individual orders and in servicing library accounts is more headache than profit. The task is obviously more efficiently managed by wholesalers, who can supply an individual library with titles from a wide variety of trade publishers.

Lastly, a number of annual national and regional conventions, whether for professionals, academics, teachers, or librarians, provide the publisher—whether juvenile, professional, trade, mass market, or university press—an opportunity to display, promote and sell to the library and educational markets.

**Special Sales.** One method of compensating for current inflationary problems, reduced net profits, and diminishing sales figures is to open up new markets. Special sales are those made to any outlet other than a bookstore or library. While this method is not by any means new to publishers, there is now an intense and renewed effort made to exploit these markets more thoroughly and systematically. Hitherto most publishers merely filled requests that came in unsolicited, such as when a mail-order house would ask for quotes for multiple copies of a book it wished to offer through its catalogs. Now some publishers are either hiring someone to go after these sales, assigning the task to someone in-house, or setting up a separate department to handle them.

Premium sales are both the most difficult to make and the most potentially lucrative of special sales. Manufacturers, banks, insurance companies, or any other firm with a product or service to sell to a huge number of customers may be a suitable market. Warner Books, which published the paperback edition of *How to Prosper During the Coming Bad Years,* noticed that the author recommended stocking up on dehydrated food. The editor contacted one manufacturer of such foods, who wound up taking thousands of copies, which were offered through its catalog; over thirty other manufacturers later followed suit and contacted Warner's to order multiple copies.

The other major avenues for special sales are mail-order catalogs, special-interest stores (health, sports, crafts, gourmet, computers, and the like), associations and their publications, and direct-mail campaigns initiated by the publisher, either through its own mailing lists or those rented outside of the house.

Publishers will now be particularly receptive to suggestions from authors on where and how to make a special sale for their books. While selling novels this way is a slim possibility, many nonfiction books are appropriate, particularly how-to and craft books. By writing a letter to your editor, accompanying the author's questionnaire, and by identifying the potential "special" audience, you may be able to turn your modest book into one that unexpectedly sells thousands of additional copies.

**International Sales.** There are two ways a publisher markets books outside the United States: either by exporting the English-language edition in the "open market" throughout the world, or by selling British or translation rights (which we will discuss shortly). Some of the larger U.S. publishers have their own subsidiaries or representatives in foreign countries which sell and distribute directly to foreign wholesalers, libraries, and bookstores. Many publishers, however, rely on the handful of firms that act as middlemen and specialize in overseas sales and distribution. The most well known of these is Feffer and Simons, which identifies itself as "Publishers' Export Representatives."

The percentage of total sales that foreign sales represent for any publisher varies considerably and is directly related to the type or category of books published. For university presses and professional book publishers foreign sales represent an average of 15 percent of total sales, while for trade publishers the amount averages 5 percent, and an additional 5 percent in Canadian sales. Foreign mass market and college text sales, surprisingly high, fall somewhere between these two. The complexities of marketing English-language books throughout the world —consider bill collecting problems with a New Zealand firm, for instance—make obvious the benefit of local representation, and a firm like Feffer and Simons has either its own local sales agents or offices or is in partnership with a variety of wholesalers throughout the world. For an average 10-percent-of-list commission and exclusive territorial rights for designated countries, they sell, distribute, ship (occasionally), and bill for more than two hundred major U.S. publishers. By means of sales-men, mailings of catalogs, appearances at foreign book fairs and exhibi-tions, an export representative markets books in much the same way as do U.S. publishers. The cost of the export representative's commission, as with the added operational costs of U.S. publishers' own foreign sales subsidiaries and representatives, is reflected in the author's reduced royalty rates for export sales.

Canadian sales are generally excluded from the open market territory; U.S. publishers invariably employ Canadian wholesale distributors, most of whom are publishers in their own right, and they sometimes publish a separate Canadian edition of a U.S. book. But the export representative does sell the book in the rest of the British Common-wealth—provided the U.S. publisher has not sold British rights to a British publisher—and in virtually every other English-speaking as well as non-English speaking country, including Communist-controlled countries, where any purchase is generally made by the government itself. A full-time salesman based in the Philippines, for instance, may cover Hong Kong, Thailand, Singapore, etc. One very promising new development, expected to expand during the eighties, is the recent opening up of China as a market for English-language books and transla-tions, both technical and nontechnical. With close to a billion people, the potential sales are stimulating many marketing fantasies.

**Remainder Sales, Out-of-Print Decisions, and Reprints.** Since the advent of the computer in publishing, weekly printouts permit the publisher to maintain precise inventory control, that is, to know how many copies of your book still remain unsold in the warehouse. At some predetermined level of inventory depletion, a symbol on the printout (or some similar procedure) will indicate to the sales manager that a decision must be made to reprint the book or to let it go out of stock (or out of print) by continuing to sell it until the last remaining copy is gone. On the other hand, the publisher's inventory may remain at a high level because the book, for whatever reason, is not selling or selling very slowly. Then a decision may be forthcoming to dispose of all or most of the remaining copies at a much reduced price, with the books subsequently sold to the public as "remainders," or "overstocks."

Several factors determine whether and when a publisher decides to remainder or to let a book go out of print, and these factors vary depending on the category of publisher. Keeping any book in print involves certain ongoing costs: warehousing, recordkeeping, royalty reporting, etc., not to mention reprinting. After the first year, as sales diminish beyond a certain point, the publisher must decide whether the anticipated future sales warrant keeping the remaining stock and justify the aforementioned costs. If a trade book has been sold for paperback reprint rights—in which case the paperback edition is generally issued one year after hardcover publication—the publisher knows that sales of the cloth edition will plummet close to zero once the paperback appears. Whether the cloth edition has been successful or not, he may be stuck with 500 to 10,000 or more copies at that point (book clubs can also overprint and be stuck with potential remainders). As determining the first print run and predicting first-year sales are based on educated hunches, many books do not live up to initial expectations. Good reviews or big advance sales, for instance, may prompt the sales manager to hastily order a second printing, but once the book is actually sent to the stores, it may not sell well; returns may be heavy, and the second printing may go begging. Christmas books are particularly vulnerable to this calamity. Since the shelf life for most trade books is often now less than three months, and since the appearance of the paperback will cut off future sales, the only sensible option in many cases is to remainder the book if the warehouse inventory greatly exceeds anticipated sales over a one- to three-year period. Paperback reprinters, incidentally, may stipulate in their contracts that a book cannot be remaindered for at least six months or a year or more after the appearance of the paperback, since the remainder price may be lower than the paperback cover price and cut into sales. However, even if all the clothbound copies are remaindered and none are available for sale, the existence of the paperback means that the book is still in print, so that the author usually cannot reclaim the rights.

Even if no paperback reprint right is sold or the publisher himself has no intention of issuing a paperback, he is still faced with a similar decision: Will future sales warrant keeping the book in print? The publisher's backlist, the titles that he keeps in print over a period of years, is a vital source of revenue, and it keeps many publishers afloat. The books require no publicity, scant advertising, promotion, or sales efforts, and the cost of reprinting each copy is often only two-thirds as much as the cost of the original edition, as all plant costs have been paid off. So a publisher's first preference is to keep your book in print.

But there are the costs we mentioned, and the additional problem of higher unit-costs for smaller reprint orders. As the unit-cost for reprinting a book is dependent on the size of the print run, most trade publishers do not find it economical to reprint less than 2,500 copies at a time, but a run as low as this means a high unit-cost. Furthermore, the lower the list price of the book (and thus the less net income per sale), the more likely the publisher is to consider that keeping the book in print is not worth the costs. This means that whereas on a $10 title he may consider 2,000 copies a year the minimum number it must sell to warrant stocking and reprinting, on a $20 title he may consider 1,000 copies sufficient. Other factors in the decision may be: keeping a house author happy, stocking a classic or important book as a "service to the profession," or the anticipation of a revival of interest. Unfortunately, the recent trend is towards a decrease of backlist-title sales, which have dropped from a high of about 50 percent of total sales during the 1960s, to the current average of 20 percent. Two recent factors that affect this trend in the eighties are the escalating costs of reprinting—up approximately 30 percent in the past 18 months alone—and the recent I.R.S. ruling concerning the tax writeoff of inventory, which makes it economically difficult to keep slow-moving books in stock, placing the publisher under pressure to remainder the book.

Other categories of publishers use different rules of thumb. Mass market houses will generally not keep a book in print unless they can sell a minimum of 5,000 copies a year, and will not reprint less than 15,000 copies; quality paperback houses (or lines) generally not less than 3,000 copies for either sales or reprintings (though some go as low as 1,000 and some as high as 5,000). Both these amounts are for absolute minimum numbers of sales and reprintings. Many paperback houses have higher standards. On the other hand, juvenile divisions commonly expect the life of the book to stretch over ten to twenty years, so that reprinting in smaller quantities is a way of life, so to speak; however, owing to inflation, the cost of printing juveniles in low quantities has become prohibitive, and many of these publishers are letting slow-selling books go out of print. Professional book publishers and university presses may be content to reprint as few as 500 or 1,000 copies. The cover price is generally high, the sales normally tend to spread out over a number of years, and the publisher's operation is geared to expect and handle a smaller volume of sales. One option, most frequently exercised by textbook publishers, is to revise the book and publish a second revised edition. Bringing certain kinds of books up to date often breathes new life into diminishing sales. The keen competition for introductory-course adoptions often necessitates a revision every three or four years; an expected fringe benefit is that it temporarily eliminates the second-hand market.

But if the sales of a book in any category have gradually trickled down to under 500 or so copies a year and there is no reason to expect that matters will improve, the publisher will normally declare the book out of print once his stock is exhausted, or do so upon remaindering the copies left in the warehouse. It's not a general public declaration, he just discontinues listing it in his catalogs, does not file the title with annual bibliographies such as *Books in Print,* may publish a list of discontinued titles in the classified section of *Publishers Weekly,* and will return requests for the book by stamping letters or invoices "out of print." He may not, in fact, as we mentioned in Chapter 3, even notify the author.

If sufficient stock remains to warrant remaindering, the publisher has the choice of selling the stock at reduced prices directly to bookstores, or selling it to a "remainder house," a specialized wholesaler who deals exclusively in remainders.

As the list prices of clothbound titles have escalated, the remainder business has skyrocketed, especially in the last ten years. A huge market exists for those clothbound books that the average consumer is unable or unwilling to pay $15 to $50 for, and many bookstores now thrive on remainder or "budget" sales. Though the bookstore usually makes only a 40 percent mark-up on these books (many remainder houses offer the bookstore an additional 10 percent discount provided it is spent in advertising these titles), the sale tables often draw in the nonhabitual book buyer and build traffic. The number of remainder wholesalers has tripled in the last decade, and some of them now also buy "cheap cloth edition" reprint rights from the original publisher. When the $19.95 edition, which has been remaindered for $9.95, is sold out, the wholesaler can reprint 10,000 to 25,000 copies on cheaper paper, with inexpensive bindings, and put a list price of $7.95 on the book or put a list price of $12.95 on it and mark it down to $7.95. A number of publishers have traditionally done this. Others have recently caught on to the gambit and will reprint their own cheap edition to sell on the remainder table. Art books and illustrated film books are the prime candidates. Best sellers, though, are rarely reprinted in cheap clothbound editions because of the inevitable appearance of the later paperback edition. The author, unfortunately, does not receive a fair share of profits from this second life. The convention is to pay a 5- to 6-percent-of-list royalty for the cheap cloth edition, even though the costs and profits would permit the publisher to pay a higher royalty.

Once the publisher has decided to remainder the stock for several titles, he will generally notify a number of different remainder houses by mail, listing the titles and number of copies available, and solicit a bid, either for specific quantities or titles or for the entire list. Some titles may be sold in bulk directly to bookstore chains, as the publisher generally gets a higher price from the chains than from the wholesaler. Or, as is happening more recently, the publisher will merely remainder his titles through his own sales staff and with mailing pieces. Instead of soliciting bids, he will set a wholesale remainder price on the book so that individual stores can buy in any quantity they wish.

The remainder wholesaler, in turn, will market the book in several different ways: mailing catalogs to retailers, inviting buyers to a show-room where samples are on view, and by means of direct sales calls. For some individual book outlets throughout the country, but particularly for variety stores and supermarket chains, the "prepack" is popular—buying in quantity a preselected mix of remainder titles. Some remainder houses, such as Barnes & Noble Books, have retail bookstores, act as remainder wholesalers, and sell remainders directly to the consumer by mail order. Professional-book publishers and university presses will occasionally hold a warehouse or clean-out sale and remainder their books directly to the professional or academic consumer by mail. Obviously remainders are sold by a variety of overlapping methods and firms.

How do the finances work? Based on market savvy, the kind of book, and the quantity available, the remainder house may, for example, bid as low as $.25 or as high as $1 for a book that lists for $10. Then, considering both what was paid for the book and what the traffic will bear, the remainder is offered to the retailer at a wholesale price with an implicit retail price. The $10 book, for which the remainder house has paid $.25, may be offered to the retailer at $1.20, implying—at a 40 percent mark-up—a $2 retail price. Of course, the retailer can sell it for $1.75 if he wants to, or even $1.50—if he doesn't have competitors nearby who are selling it for $1.35. The price the remainder house pays the publisher for a book can vary so much, as can the price the traffic will bear, that the profit margins are frequently very high, which accounts for the fact that many publishers are now marketing their own remainders directly to the booksellers.

The author, of course, doesn't fare well amidst these shenanigans. On remainder sales (*overstock* is the euphemism in the contract), the author generally gets 10 percent of the amount received by the publisher, but only if this amount is higher than the publisher's manufacturing costs—that is, his manufacturing unit-cost per book—which it usually isn't. In other words, if the unit-cost of your $10 book was $1.50 and the publisher sells it as a remainder for $1.25, you receive no royalty or share of this sale.

**One More Reprinter.** As mentioned earlier, authors should see to it that their contracts permit them to reclaim the rights to their out-of-print book, in the event that at a later date some publisher may express interest in reprinting the book. Particularly in the area of professional and scholarly books, a book that is either in the public domain or has been out of print for many years may find a small and select library or professional market when reissued by a reprinter who specializes in these types of book.

Generally this reprinter publishes books in series, such as in the history of science or volumes of eighteenth- or nineteenth-century legal documents or classics in British and Scottish folklore. By reprinting as few as 250 copies, charging extremely high prices (from $20 to $50 for books that may have originally sold for from $5 to $10), and by mail order marketing to libraries and select lists of professionals, some of these firms have been able to earn huge net profits because of their low overhead costs. The seventies saw a mushrooming of titles reprinted and a huge increase in the volume of sales, as well as the appearance of many new reprint houses, some of whom expanded their concepts of a typical reprint to include more recent nonfiction books and fiction classics or oddities (early nineteenth-century romances by women, for instance). Even some of the remainder houses branched out into this area of reprinting. But due to reduced library budgets, and perhaps a now-oversaturated market, these kinds of reprint sales have begun to decline.

**Sales Promotion.** The word *promotion* is bandied about so much in publishing that it is difficult for the casual outsider to get a fix on it. Nevertheless, *sales promotion* refers to the materials the publisher or wholesaler supplies to help the retailer at the point of sale to the consumer.

A variety of display materials may be furnished free to the retailer, most of them reserved for the major titles: posters, bookmarks, window stickers, counter cards, blow-ups of dust jackets, and sometimes even buttons, bumper stickers, and shopping bags. As many retail stores have mailing lists of steady customers, particularly for use during the Christmas season, the publisher and wholesaler supply a number of different mailing pieces with the bookseller's name and address imprinted on the material, though these fliers are mostly for ''general market'' or expensive gift books. The mailing pieces may range from a statement stuffer—a one-page flier that is included in the customer's monthly bill—to an elaborate four-or-more-page circular already prepackaged for mailing that has been test-marketed for its drawing power.

With rising costs and declining sales, publishers in the eighties are more than ever attempting to gain attention and additional sales with new promotional gimmicks. New American Library, for example, launched a recent romance, *Wine of the Dreamers,* by imprinting wine glasses with the book's title and then distributing them to key direct accounts. To encourage floor displays, it also randomly packed twenty-seven gift certificates worth twenty-five dollars in thirty-copy-display dump-bins. Each certificate could be redeemed by the bookstore employee or manager who found it. Furthermore, random books in the display contained coupons for customers to enter in a drawing for twenty-five pairs of crystal wine glasses.

Examples of other materials available to the bookseller include, for instance, a retail chain catalog called ''Book Chat,'' which is distributed bimonthly to over half a million consumers; individual publishers may purchase space ads in the catalog for recent titles. A variety of similar mailing pieces and catalogs are available to bookstore owners from both publishers and distributors. Some publishers are active not only in supplying promotional materials to wholesalers, but in educating them on how to reach and expand their markets. Bantam, for example, publishes a twenty-two-page pamphlet for wholesalers containing ''effective tips and suggestions on how to sell educational paperbacks to the new and expanding school and college market.''

Display racks for books, primarily for paperbacks, may be offered to the bookstore either by the publisher or the wholesaler, and the rack jobber—the independent mass market paperback distributor—will supply racks for variety and chain stores, supermarkets, and other outlets carrying paperbacks. Or publishers and distributors of mass market books may give new bookstores a ''rack allowance'' of sixty to seventy cents per ''pocket,'' depending on the percentage of titles the store will carry from that particular publisher or distributor. For instance, a new store with 10,000 pockets may intend to fill about 400 with Ace paperbacks and thereby have $240 deducted from its first bill(s). Some quality paperback publishers will extend the same offer. Dump-bins, cartons of books that can be opened and folded out to be used as both a display and a container for best-selling paperbacks, are widely furnished by paperback publishers. As publishers and wholesalers are competing so keenly for display space in bookstores, it is obviously to their advantage to be imaginative, generous, and diligent in supplying a variety of free promotional materials to book outlets.

## Subsidiary Rights

The day-to-day operations of the subsidiary rights department are belied by glamorous tales of the million-dollar paperback-reprint sale that is followed up by the sale of movie rights to Francis F. Coppola Productions for a sum "in the high six figures," as the trade magazines like to say. These highlights are infrequent events at most trade houses. The day-to-day reality is that many trade books do not get sold for a single subsidiary right, and most of those that do ring up considerably more modest revenues.

**Permissions.** The rights department generally includes permissions under its aegis, that is, granting either an author, a publisher, or a magazine the right to excerpt a passage, paragraph, page, chapter, short story, or poem for use within another work. If the use is incidental or for critical purposes, such as using a stanza for an epigraph or quoting a paragraph to make a point, then permission is generally granted gratis. Though many of these requests are covered by "fair use," permission is often solicited anyhow. A request for permission to reprint a poem or a short story in a textbook anthology, or a chapter from a nonfiction book in a collection of critical essays, will require a fee. The permissions person generally works from an informal and flexible house "going rate," which depends on several factors: the reputation of the author; the manner of publication intended, whether cloth, paper, or both; the size of the extract; the territory requested, whether United States and Canadian, English-language or world; and what the traffic will bear. These are postpublication requests, and you may not be consulted if permission to use an extract from your book is requested and sold, but will find out only when the sale is listed on your royalty statement and your 50 percent share included in the royalty check.

But the major task for the subsidiary rights department is the attempt to sell first serial, bookclub, paperback reprint, and foreign rights. Radio, television, film, and dramatic rights are generally not aggressively pursued, since the great majority of writers whose works might naturally be attractive to those media have agents already who have retained these rights for their clients. However, when they do have these rights and the book seems particularly suitable for a "performance" rights sale, they may use a sub-agent (usually one on the West Coast) to handle them. Some smaller houses don't have their own sub-rights department, but use instead one of a handful of independents who specialize in rights sales.

Subsidiary rights possibilities, as mentioned before, are discussed at the time the decision is made to sign up the book. Occasionally the house will canvass a mass market reprint house before signing the book if the author or agent is asking for a very large advance, but generally the sale of these rights does not begin until the completed manuscript is in house. If expectations for rights sale are high, the department may begin sending out photocopies of the manuscript even before it has been copyedited. Magazines, in particular, require considerable lead time in order to serialize a book in several installments, so that a historical romance, for instance, may be sent to *Ladies' Home Journal,* the same week it arrives in house. Book clubs and paperback reprinters generally work from bound galleys, but there is no hard and fast rule: Any stage from manuscript to galleys to page proofs to bound books may be used by the subsidiary rights department. The ideal schedule is to sell first serial rights, then bookclub rights, then paperback rights, and then film rights—all accomplished before the book is in the stores—using each one to help stimulate interest in the next, as well as to boost the price. Most books do not follow this pattern, though, and a rights sale for a paperback edition after book reviews appear is conventional. In the case of a very few books, most of which are agented, first serial, paperback, foreign, and even film rights may be sold just as soon as an outline has been accepted by a trade house, but these are rare exceptions.

**First Serial Rights.** The halcyon days of serializing books for huge sums has come and gone, such as when *Life, Look,* and *The Saturday Evening Post* bid for William Manchester's *Death of a President,* which *Life* scooped up for an immodest $650,000. Not only have prices come down, but so has the amount of space available in large national-circulation magazines; many more have folded than have arisen to take their place. The major women's magazines, such as *Ladies' Home Journal, Redbook* and *Cosmopolitan,* are now more inclined to serialize novels (or use abridgments) in two issues, rather than six or seven, buy second serial rights (after publication) for roughly half the price, or perhaps just buy a chapter. Occasionally these magazines will still bid the price for an expected best seller to over $100,000, such as for Betty Ford's or Lauren Bacall's autobiography, but the much more common price for serializing either a novel or a nonfiction book is in the $10,000 to $15,000 range, with excerpts of 3,000 to 9,000 words going for an average of $2,000 to $4,000. Other top magazines, such as *Playboy, Esquire,* and the *New Yorker,* pay in the same range, with *Reader's Digest* going a little higher, whereas *The National Enquirer* often pays huge sums—$25,000 to $100,000—for small excerpts provided they are sufficiently "newsworthy." The actual condensing, whether of a chapter or an entire book, is generally performed by an editor on the magazine's staff. If serial rights for a condensation of an entire book are sold to one of these magazines, the publisher will generally shift the book's publication date, if necessary, so that the book comes out shortly after it has appeared in the magazine. Most people in publishing circles, by the way, do not feel that serialization severely cuts into sales of the book. The additional revenue and the wide exposure are considered to more than compensate for any loss of sales.

The bulk of first serial rights, however, is sold to magazines with modest circulations and payment rates. The topic of your book will generally determine where the rights department will send a chapter(s), though there are so many specialized and small-circulation magazines to keep track of that any suggestions from you may be useful, and in the case of those magazines or journals that do not pay, you may be better off suggesting to submit it on your own. Obviously, even if the fee is small or nonexistent, the author is getting free publicity; any first serial publication is worth your time and effort, if not the publisher's.

**Second Serial Rights.** Some magazines are now more active in acquiring postpublication rights, particularly since the going rate is half the price or less. *Cosmopolitan,* for example, now commonly serializes novels after publication. Newspapers almost always serialize after publication. The rights department may sell these rights directly to a newspaper or, as is more common, to a newspaper syndicate, which will in turn sell the book to individual newspapers. The fees are nominal: Even a large-circulation newspaper may pay as low as $50 to $100 per excerpt. The syndicate takes 50 percent for its services, and your publisher takes half the rest, which leaves you with 25 percent. Still, it can add up if the book is widely serialized, and the exposure is generally believed to increase sales.

**Book Clubs.** It is not difficult to account for the phenomenal success of book clubs when one considers the paucity of bookstores in the United States. Close to half the population does not have ready access to a bookstore, and for those book buyers who do, only a very small selection of clothbound books is available. Consequently, bookclub sales now account for almost 8 percent of the total book sales in the United States.

Currently there are roughly 200 book clubs, catering to both a mass readership and a diversity of special-interest groups from gamblers to gardeners. Membership ranges from a high of almost two million for the Reader's Digest Condensed Book Club to as low as 2,500 for some of the more esoteric newcomers. The two other giants are the Literary Guild, with a membership of close to one and a half million, and the Book of the Month Club, which has more than 1.25 million members. While a number of firms run more than one club, such as the Macmillan book clubs (twenty-one) or Prentice-Hall (twenty-seven), with quite impressive combined memberships, the actual membership figures per club dip to 200,000 and under after the big three, and the average medium-sized club has about 100,000 members.

Most clubs have a board of judges that select the main and sometimes the alternate selections after all of the submissions have been winnowed down by the editorial staff to a manageable number of recommended titles. About thirteen to fifteen times a year each club offers a main selection, two to five alternates, and up to one hundred additional titles. The bigger clubs print their own books, using plates or negatives supplied by the publisher, whereas the medium- and small-sized clubs usually join in on the publisher's first print run—or occasionally buy stock directly from the publisher if the decision is made too late for the first print run.

A typical main selection will sell about 200,000 copies for Literary Guild and Book of the Month Club, which drops to an average of 10,000 copies for the medium-sized clubs. Most book clubs pay a guaranteed advance against a 10 percent of bookclub-list-price royalty, which the publisher shares equally with the author. (Literary Guild pays an average of 7½ percent, whereas Reader's Digest, since it includes four books in one volume, pays 2 percent per book). Royalties for premiums for the four-for-$1.00 type are reduced to 5 percent of the bookclub list. Advances are negotiable. If the two major clubs are bidding for the exclusive right for a main selection, the advance can go as high as $250,000, but commonly the advance will average $85,000 for a main and anywhere from $13,000 to $25,000 for an alternate. For medium-sized clubs, the average advances for main selections are in the $5,000 to $10,000 range. Obviously the amount of an advance varies considerably, depending on whether the book is a main or an alternate and on the size of the club.

There are two schools of thought in publishing regarding the influence of book clubs on trade sales and the author's income. The major school feels that the added exposure, advertising, and sales are a boon for both publishers and authors. The minority dissenters point out that the book club cuts heavily into trade sales and the author's royalties (which are reduced *and* cut in half) and fosters the notion that publishers are ripping off the public. When a $25 dictionary is offered as a premium for $2.00 it is hard for the layman not to conclude that he is being gouged by the publisher. But the income for the publisher is irresistible; not only is he guaranteed before publication to recoup all or part of his investment, but even a small sale increases the size of his print run and thereby reduces his unit-costs. In fact, a sale to a book club can have a considerable influence on marketing strategy and trade sales. When Mary Gordon's *Final Payments*, for instance, was chosen for a main selection by a major club, the publisher increased his own first printing considerably, and stepped up advertising and publicity plans; there is little doubt that the bookclub selection was instrumental in making the book a best seller.

**Paperback Reprints.** The big paperback auction is the rights sale that gains the most attention in publishing circles. A typical scenario goes something like this: Copies of galleys, or even the manuscript, have been sent to the eight major paperback reprinters, followed up by intermittent letters from the publisher announcing that first serial rights were sold to *McCalls,* that Book of the Month Club has taken the book for an alternate, that additional printings have been ordered to meet the huge prepublication demand, and that *Publishers Weekly* has given the book a rave review. Finally the closing date is announced, that is, the date for the actual bidding, and a $50,000 "floor" or minimum bid is set. Fawcett calls a week before the auction date, offers the minimum bid, and is given "topping" privileges, the right to take the book for 10 percent higher than the last best offer. The day of the auction the phones are buzzing; five out of eight reprinters want the book. Having bid $65,000 at 11 A.M., Avon finds that by 4 P.M. they will have to bid over $150,000 to stay in the running. At 5:45 the game is still on, and it is carried over to the following day. The editor-in-chief at Bantam thinks the bidding may go as high as $750,000 and calls the company president—who is sunbathing in Jamaica—to get an authorization to go that high if necessary. By noon the following day, Pocket Books has offered $560,000, Bantam decides to pass, and Fawcett declines to top the final bid. The subsidiary rights director and the editor-in-chief go out for an $80.00 lunch after calling the author's agent, who turns around and calls his client. To say he is stunned is an understatement.

The final deal includes the following extras in addition to the $560,000 advance: another $50,000 if a movie sale is consummated; $20,000 additional if the cloth edition appears on the *New York Times* best-seller list, plus $5,000 to $100,000 for subsequent appearances on the list, depending on the number of weeks and the book's position on the list (these are called escalators).

Needless to say, 99 percent of the reprint sales do not follow this pattern. In fact, the median price paid for mass market rights is closer to $4,000 to $7,500, even though most of the books are auctioned off, or offered to a number of reprinters at the same time. The same is true in selling quality paperback rights, though the median advance is even a bit lower. The conventional royalty the mass market house pays is 6 percent for the first 150,000, 8 percent for the next 150,000 copies, and 10 percent thereafter; for a quality paperback, 6 percent for the first 15,000 copies sold, 7½ percent thereafter. Both are negotiable, and books with high-priced auctions or by well-known authors will generally command higher royalty rates. The originating publisher generally licenses the reprinter for a period of five, seven, or ten years, after which the reprinter may have to renegotiate the contract if he wishes to continue to carry the book or may just be given the nod by the publisher to carry on.

Several recent developments have cut back the number of high-priced auctions and have slightly altered the situation for the eighties. A number of mass market houses have developed their own hardcover lines, such as Warner Books and New American Library, or have been acquired by conglomerates with hardcover houses, as were Popular Library and Fawcett by CBS, which already owned Holt, Rinehart & Winston. In the former case the mass market house may buy "volume" rights; i.e., it will publish the book in both formats without selling any reprint rights (and even in a third, "trade paperback," format, if the potential sales warrant it). In the latter case it may also buy "volume" rights, or may license a "reverse" rights sale—an option open to all mass market houses, and now occurring more frequently, as paperback houses step up the number of originals they publish—in which the hardcover rights are sold to a trade cloth house by the paperback reprinter for book publication a year or a season prior to paperback publication, or simultaneous with it. Another growing phenomenon is a "joint rights" sale, in which a cloth house and a paperback house jointly buy the rights, share the cost of the author's advance, and then work together on the entire marketing strategy. This ad hoc arrangement may become formalized, as Morrow has done with Bantam in setting up Perigord Press specifically for occasional joint ventures. These arrangements are particularly advantageous for successful authors with track records, because they receive full royalties on both editions—instead of sharing the revenue from an auction sale with the originating publisher—and they still get a six-figure advance.

**British and Foreign Rights.** Most publishers employ agents overseas to represent them in British and foreign rights sales, though some of the larger publishers handle these rights themselves. Often the publisher or the author's agent will send galleys overseas to sell British rights, so that the British publisher can get in on the print run, as only a few minor typesetting changes are necessary. If the book, as is more common, is sold once bound books are ready, the British publisher will buy negatives or positives from the U.S. publisher, paying an offset (shooting) fee of approximately 30 percent of the U.S. composition costs, which averages $800 to $1200, in addition to the advance and royalty. British advances, as you might expect, are generally lower than U.S. advances: A book that commanded a $6,000 advance here might be sold for $2,500 for British rights, though royalty rates are roughly equal. In fact, the British publishing scene is quite comparable to that in the United States, insofar as general operating procedures and subsidiary rights are concerned. One new development is in the banding together of several trade houses to set up their own mass market paperback subsidiaries, thereby paying the author a full royalty on paperback editions.

**Translation Rights.** Here, too, most U.S. publishers and literary agents use foreign agents to represent them. Sending bound books, rather than galleys, is generally the rule, though for the major books, manuscripts or galleys may be sent. Publishers follow these overseas by attending the Frankfurt Book Fair, held once a year in early October, in order to negotiate deals in person with editors from foreign book publishers. Though foreign publishers buy and translate our books in much greater proportion than we do theirs—so that on an Italian publisher's trade list, for example, 10 percent of the books may be translations from various languages, whereas most U.S. publishers can scarcely point to more than one book a year—the amount is still negligible when compared to the number of books published in the United States every year. When a book is sold, discounting the blockbusters which may be auctioned off for big sums as they are here, the advances are quite low, averaging $500 to $2,500, and the royalties are also reduced, starting as low as 5 to 7 percent, to compensate for the additional cost of translating. (In the United States, most translators are still paid coolie wages, averaging $35 per 1,000 words, whereas overseas the average rates for translators are almost double.) Foreign publishers generally ask for and receive a two-month option in which to consider a U.S. book.

**Television, Film, and Dramatic Rights.** In the world of the visual media, your book is known as a property, perhaps because fidelity to its contents is so rare that it might as well be identified as a parcel of land, distinguished only by dimension rather than substance. The conventional advice from agents and subsidiary rights directors is to "take the money and run," since most authors are dismayed to see the final results, over which they have little control even if they are hired to write the script. The greatest number of rights sales are for options, that is, the right to hold on to the property for six months to two years just in case enough money can be raised by the producer to put it into production or, in the case of television, to sell the idea to an independent packager, network, or sponsor. Often the author's agent, or even the subsidiary rights director, will join forces and split the commission with a dramatic agent, many of whom are based on the West Coast, as these specialists are more adept at threading their way through the eccentricities of the show business subculture.

Options are purchased cheap: The going rate is anywhere from $500 to $2,500, and the vast majority, perhaps as much as 90 percent, are never exercised. Usually the option stipulates the pick-up price, the price to be paid if the option is exercised, which averages $25,000 to $50,000 for a film plus, on occasion, a small percentage of the gross. For a television movie or one-hour special, the price will average 10 percent of the total production costs, thus anywhere from $5,000 to $50,000. Best sellers or hot properties, of course, can command much higher figures, especially if several producers or studios are bidding for the rights.

# 8

# *Alternatives: Small Presses, University Presses, Vanity Presses, and Self-Publishing*

A small press is an attitude, a kind of anti-commerciality. The dollars come second, the talent and quality of the writing come first. If the presses wanted to make money, they'd be out there selling cookbooks.

—Bill Henderson

In spite of the vast number of trade books published every year, you may find, to your dismay, that your manuscript or proposal is rejected out of hand by every commercial publisher you approach. Some writers give up more quickly than others, succumbing to defeat after four or five rejections, while others have stronger egos. As an agent, I have sometimes submitted the same proposal to over thirty publishers before giving up, when I firmly believed in the merits or sales potential of the project. At other times I have desisted after eight or nine submissions, primarily because the editors were consistent in their criticism, and I was finally persuaded that their cumulative intuitions were more accurate than my own. Each writer, however, has to decide for himself when it is time to stop, but to curl up in despair after three or four rejections is a sign of being in the wrong field.

Too small a market or a poorly conceived and executed idea are probably the most common and justifiable reasons for the failure to find a publisher, though you might not think so from scanning the shelves of a bookstore. But the competition in every phase of the publishing industry is fierce, and nowhere more keenly experienced than in passing the first hurdle. If you are trying to place your first book, particularly a first novel or collection of poems, the odds are heavily stacked against you, no matter what its literary merits or potential market. At some point, you will sit back and take stock. The proposal or manuscript has been turned down by a dozen or more publishers, two years have passed, and you have had it. Before considering some of the alternatives to commercial publishing, perhaps you ought to try a different gambit.

If the manuscript is a novel, a book of poems, or a collection of short stories, you should try to publish an excerpt or selections in magazines or journals before approaching a publisher. Almost every book editor will be more receptive to fiction and poetry that has been accepted for publication elsewhere, even in small-circulation literary magazines. The number of these that exist and the quantities of material they use provide much better odds for getting published; if you cannot get a story or a poem published in a magazine or journal, you probably have little chance of finding a commercial book publisher. The references that have already been mentioned—*Literary Market Place, Writer's Market,* and the *International Directory of Little Magazines and Small Presses*—contain the names and addresses, and the latter two clearly identify the type of material used, the preferred manner of submission, etc.

The same advice holds for nonfiction. There is generally at least one chapter in any nonfiction book that is suitable as an article, even if it requires some editing, cutting, or adapting. Approaching a publisher with an offprint or copy of an article, which is culled from a proposed book or is appropriate as the genesis for one, immediately increases the writer's chances of at least being taken seriously, even if he or she is not ultimately offered a contract.

But though you succeed in publishing an excerpt, some poems, or a piece of fiction, you may still eventually find the doors of commercial book publishing closed to you. Assuming that the fiction or poetry is imaginative and worthy, or that the nonfiction is informative and original, chances are that an editor or publisher predicted the market just wasn't there: They intuit that not enough people will buy the book to compensate for the efforts and expense required to produce and sell it. Maybe they are shortsighted or dead wrong; an impressive tradition of self-published writers, from Thomas Paine to Zane Grey to James Joyce, is testimony to the frequent initial myopia of commercial publishers. Maybe they are right. What if under ideal conditions your book of poetry would only sell 500 or 750 copies? Even then it doesn't follow that you should automatically forego attempts to get it into print.

The alternatives to commercial book publishing have been in existence for a long time. The university press, for example, identifies an esoteric biblical commentary published by Oxford University Press in 1478 as its first publication. Small-press publishing, self-publishing, and vanity or subsidy publishing constitute, in a sense, the origins of book publishing. During publishing's infancy, books were produced either by small local printers or by individual authors and were usually financed or subsidized by the author or a patron. (The poet William Blake took all matters into his own hands and wrote, designed, printed, and sold his books.)

One of the problems in discussing the alternatives is defining them clearly and locating their boundaries: Small presses may overlap with trade publishers; subsidy publishing is sometimes a component of small-press (and even university press) publishing; and a self-publisher can become a small press merely by assigning an imprint to his or her first publication. Three major factors that help to distinguish the alternatives are: who pays the costs, who owns the book, and who distributes it. Since the small presses *in most cases* finance, distribute, sell, and license rights for the books they publish, and since they are initial logical alternatives for a writer, let us examine them first.

## The Small Press

"A small press is a state of mind." In the course of interviewing small-press publishers and in gathering information about these presses, this definition evolved as the only one that was even vaguely accurate. A series of characteristics generally hold true for most small presses, but an all-embracing definition is impossible. These characteristics are: publishing less than fifteen titles a year, a list that has a narrow focus (such as poetry only), small first print runs, limited publicity and advertising, separate distribution channels, reduced sales expectations, and whether, unintentionally or not, small presses are usually nonprofit-making organizations. It will be useful as well to state what a small press is not. As a generic term, *small press* does not mean merely that the publisher's annual list is smaller in number than a medium-size press. Many religious book publishers, textbook publishers, professional book publishers, and even commercial trade publishers produce in the neighborhood of five to twenty-five books a year. They may be small publishers, but they are not small-press publishers. *Literary Market Place*, for instance, makes no distinction and will list any firm as a publisher as long as they produce three or more books a year; yet many of the small presses are not listed in *LMP*. (While we are constructing definitions, *Books in Print* will list as a *book* any publication it receives that is available for sale at more than twenty-five cents and is over forty-eight pages in length, Webster notwithstanding.)

There are two basic kinds of small presses: regional publishers and "alternative" or, loosely speaking, literary or counterculture publishers. In one sense, what separates both of them from the mainstream of commercial book publishing is that, in the various processes we have described so far, they tend to forego traditional methods, either in favor of truncating them, such as in reduced expenditures for publicity and advertising, or in devising alternate methods of marketing, such as in forming their own distribution cooperatives. Depending on which sources you wish to quote and what criteria you use to define a small press, there are anywhere from 1,000 to 2,000 of these publishers, with newcomers cropping up as fast as others are lying down. For a representative sampling, one would turn to the pages of the *International Directory of Little Magazines and Small Presses*, which contains an annotated list of more than 1,500 of these publishers, as well as over 1,500 little magazines.

**Regional Publishing.** The regional publisher is quite traditional in his motives and methods, more closely resembles the commercial publisher, and generally makes a living if not a profit for his efforts. Typically, a firm consists of no more than five employees, and the publisher himself may perform the majority of the tasks, such as acquiring, editing, estimating, interior design, and preparing catalog copy. He will often farm out to free-lancers such tasks as copyediting, proofreading, and jacket design. The yearly list, about eight to twelve titles, will contain a high percentage of regional interest titles. One New Hampshire publisher, for example, has a number of titles, such as *More Than Land: Stories of New England Country Life and Surveying*, which indicate the flavor and thrust of the list. Regional poetry and fiction, regional histories, regional flora and fauna, and regional craft are the mainstay of the typical list.

In addition to regional books, these publishers will frequently fill out their list with small market "bread and butter" titles, ranging from bottle collecting to quilt-making to a manual on making maple syrup. The diversity of the list is subject only to the interests and whims of the publisher, and many of the titles might be suitable for a commercial trade house. The publisher's only constraint is a nominal sales expectation: Can the book sell over 1,000 copies? His costs and his overhead are geared to return a profit on as small a sale as 750 copies. For him a best seller is a book that sells over 7,500 copies. On rare occasions a commercial house will buy the rights, either cloth or paper or both, if the initial sales figures are impressive and the book comes to their attention. In the spring of 1981, for example, Fireside—a paperback division of Simon & Schuster—published Dale Alexander's *Arthritis and Common Sense*, which a small regional publisher issued in 1951. During this time the book has sold a total of 950,000 copies, and was followed by *Healthy Hair and Common Sense* and *Dry Skin and Common Sense*, both of which have sold over 100,000 copies, and are also being rereleased by Fireside.

The publisher usually acquires manuscripts from local authors, either over-the-transom, by word of mouth, or by initiating book ideas and then locating a writer. As a one-man editorial board, the publisher's decision-making process is quite simple: If he likes both the idea and the sample chapters or manuscript, if he thinks it is suitable for his list, and if his preliminary estimate of the costs indicates that he can make a profit on a sale of roughly 1,000 copies, he will sign the book up. A contract may consist of a simple one- to two-page form or just a letter of agreement. Generally, no advances are given, though some regional publishers can be persuaded to part with $250 to $1,000. Royalties tend to be a flat 10 percent of list price for clothbound books and 6 or 7½ percent for paperbacks. Occasionally the publisher will request or be offered a subsidy for a specific book. For instance, if a local historian has produced a town history for which sales expectations do not exceed 400 copies, either the author, the Chamber of Commerce, or even a local patron may subsidize part of the production costs.

In the production of the book, from copyediting to design to typesetting to manufacturing, the publisher can reduce a portion of the normal direct and indirect costs by doing much of the work himself. He may, for instance, in working closely with a local printer, paste up the production proofs by himself. He can save on typesetting costs by choosing to set with "cold type" or prepare camera-ready copy from an IBM Executive typewriter. He can cut corners in other ways. He can, for instance, go directly from manuscript into page proofs, skipping the first galley stage. Because of low overhead, and by maintaining close personal control over every stage of the book and by performing many of the tasks himself, he lowers the conventional break-even point to make a small printing feasible. This is not to imply that the final book looks like a home-made or cottage industry product. Many regional presses will produce books that are indistinguishable in quality and appearance from their commercial trade counterparts.

In marketing the book, the publisher generally follows traditional procedures, though specific elements are reduced in scope. Working with an author's questionnaire, the publisher will solicit blurbs and send out advance review copies to trade magazines. Using the same kinds of lists as a trade house, promotion and review copies are sent to major review media, though the publisher will concentrate on regional media and specialized magazines and journals and will mail out an average of fifty rather than one hundred review copies.

Advertising expenditures are equally reduced, but simple fliers as well as press releases are frequently employed, and most publishers will prepare a yearly general catalog that is sent to mail-order customers, individual bookstore accounts, wholesalers, and libraries. Though reviews in national media are rare, the trade magazines such as *Publishers*

*Weekly* and *Library Journal* will occasionally review worthy titles, and an enthusiastic notice there may result in 400 to 500 copies sold to regional libraries—a market that is particularly vital to the small publisher. Feature articles and even radio and television appearances by authors are not infrequent.

Distribution and sales for regional presses can be handled in several different ways. While scarcely any publishers employ their own house salesmen, the line may be carried by one or more regular commission men who operate in that particular territory and who represent several regional press lines along with their normal trade lists. There are more than a dozen small-press wholesale distributors in the United States who confine themselves to specific regions such as the midwest, the south, or New England. Some of these distributors represent a combination of trade publishers, regional publishers, and alternative presses, and they operate in a highly professional manner. No two are alike: Some distribute periodicals and books; some specialize, such as in feminist or radical literature; some are merely bookstores that carry small-press books and produce joint catalogs and mailing pieces for libraries and previous-customer lists. Some carry the books on a consignment basis only, while some may not actually stock small-press titles but, rather, buy them from the publisher only after they receive orders. The different kinds of arrangements, discounts, and methods are too various to enumerate here. Nationwide commercial wholesale distributors, such as Baker and Taylor, often carry regional press books, too, though only in that specific regional office.

The regional press augments these sales efforts by mailing catalogs or individual fliers to libraries, lists of previous customers—both individuals and bookstores—and to mailing lists purchased from magazines, journals, or organizations. They also put in appearances at regional book fairs and exhibits.

Subsidiary rights or international sales are generally a very minor source of income and are not pursued with any consistency or aggressiveness.

In sum, the regional press resembles the commercial trade house and differs primarily in the limited scope and size of its list, its expectations, its overhead and expenditures, its ability to gain attention for itself in national media, and in its cumulative sales record. For the author whose book may have a limited audience, the regional press may be an ideal solution. While the publisher may not be a prestigious one or a household name, you will not feel that you or your book have been lost in the shuffle or that the book was taken to fill a slot on some publisher's semiannual list only to be summarily dumped on the market to sink or swim.

**The Independent Press.** While there have always been a number of small presses to accommodate "uncommercial," avant-garde, or radical writers, the true flowering, or more accurately, mushrooming, of these presses dates from the early 1960s, coinciding with the eruption of political and social activism that characterized the period. Lacking access to national media or commercial book publishers, except for lurid, newsworthy, or dramatic events, the members of the New Left began to print their own broadsides, pamphlets, and newspapers. Their immediate literary forerunners, the Beats, had already signaled the renaissance in the 1950s: Writers such as Kerouac, Ginsberg, and Corso began to see print from new "alternative press" (and so called through the sixties and seventies) publishers such as City Lights Books, founded in 1953 by poet Lawrence Ferlinghetti. Thus the ingredients out of which the alternative presses brewed this reincarnation—a voice for society's dissidents, political and social ferment, lack of an establishment platform from which to be heard—continue to infuse the rhetoric of alternative publishing, even though much of its current output is by no means radical, controversial, or even innovative. Major social movements during the last decade or so—e.g., back-to-the-land, "natural" this and that, Orientalia, and feminism—have contributed both to the burgeoning number of presses and the counterculture ideology that often represents editorial policy.

The reformist, anti-establishment, and somewhat defensive tone of this major arm of the small-press movement can be gleaned from the following excerpt, taken from the introduction to *Alternatives in Print: Catalog of Social Change Publications.**

> The alternative press in this period of economic decline offers the vitality, the variety, the essential information needed at a low price; this cannot be provided by a literary-industrial complex run for maximizing profit alone. We vigilantly support the movement's attempts to increase its control over the publishing/distribution system vital to political and economic democracy. To counteract the built-in censorship of the publishing establishment's distribution system is to move toward intellectual freedom—just as to counteract unequal distribution of wealth is to move toward a more democratic society; they are intimately connected.

The oversimplification inherent in this statement is the implication that alternative publishing at its best, and commercial publishing at its

*The newly revised edition is now available from Neal-Schuman Publishers, 64 University Place, New York, N.Y. 10003 for $39.95.

worst, is what publishing is all about. While it is true that commercial publishing is now governed primarily by profit-making motives, it would be more accurate to focus on the problem of the limited audience—as for radical polemical writings, for instance—as the reason many activists are neither published by commercial houses nor have their work distributed to or sold in most bookstores. Omitting the question of the quality of the work, the reality of commercial publishing is that if a large enough audience exists, an Eldridge Cleaver or a Jerry Rubin will get a contract from a Random House or a Simon & Schuster.

The most admirable and praiseworthy trait of the independent presses is that many of them are intentionally nonprofit-making organizations dedicated to disseminating—at a reasonable price—literature or information that is either truly innovative, unavailable elsewhere, or which documents political and social problems and grievances: They do provide an alternative voice. In actual fact, many of these presses also publish poetry and fiction, ranging from bad to mediocre to excellent, the authors of which are primarily motivated by the desire to see their work in print, rather than to reform society. Given the option, most of these writers would welcome the opportunity to publish with Doubleday, for instance, as a chance to have their work widely read and to provide them with the means to write at greater leisure. Equally so, most of these presses, if the sales figures warrant, will readily move into that gray area of production, sales, and distribution in which commercial and small presses overlap.

The diversity of independent-press methods of operation and range of publishing interests—say from abortion to Zionism—are too numerous to inventory, but the aforementioned catalog, which contains a list of titles from over 1,500 "groups," will indicate the amazing variety of books and pamphlets available.* Most of the independent presses can also be found in the *International Directory of Little Magazines and Small Presses*.

What primarily distinguishes the independent presses from the regional presses are editorial policy and book content, and methods of sales and distribution, and lack of profit. Though virtually any category of books can be found in browsing through a list of independent-press titles, there tends to be an emphasis on certain topics and genres. Foremost are poetry and fiction, which constitute more than 50 percent of the total output. One could safely say that there is no famous American poet of the twentieth century, from Pound and Williams to Lowell and Rukeyser, who doesn't have at least one volume that has been published

---

*The Small Press Record of Books (9th ed., 1980, $17.95), listing over 7,000 titles and authors from 1,500 small presses, is a more representative catalog. It is available from Dust Books, P.O. Box 1056, Paradise, Calif. 95969.

by one of these presses. Many distinguished poets, novelists, and prose writers have been, and continue to be, published by independent presses. Capra Press, for example, has titles by Henry Miller (including his recent posthumously published study of D.H. Lawrence), Anais Nin, Lawrence Durrell, and Ross MacDonald. Often these presses will publish the less commercial works of successful trade writers—their poetry or collections of short stories or essays. "Chapbooks," small hand-bound pamphlets averaging forty-eight pages, selling for a modest price, and usually consisting of poetry, are as commonly published as books; they may be the most suitable format for publication of a first book of poems. For the poet, novelist, or short-story writer who does not, for one reason or another, scale the walls of commercial publishing, the independent press is the most ideal option.*

In nonfiction, the emphasis is on militancy and social change—feminism, Third World movements, gay liberation, peace movements, etc.; alternate or improved life-styles—back-to-the-land, pollution and ecology, gardening and farming, health, etc.; mental, physical, and spiritual self-help—from astrology and acupuncture to vegetarianism and Yoga; and how-to's of all types. But virtually any topic can be found in the subject index of the *A.I.P.* and is grist for the small-press mill.

Some of the independent presses, such as the Black Sparrow Press, have a long, stable tradition and reputation for publishing only first-rate work. By virtue of consistent high quality and staying power, Black Sparrow and others like them now occupy a position in the publishing hierarchy that straddles the small-press/commercial press world. Their books can be found in many standard trade bookstores and are carried by many of the commercial distributors. The majority of these presses, however, operate within a framework that is the outgrowth of small-press history, development, and custom.

The primary clearinghouse and professional organization for the little-magazine and small-press field is C.O.S.M.E.P., the Committee of Small Magazine Editors and Publishers.** Membership (currently over 1,000) is also open to self-publishers—or even "just-interested" parties. Through its monthly newsletter, C.O.S.M.E.P. keeps members informed of grant opportunities, new developments in production and distribution, lists of stores and libraries that carry small-press publications, and pertinent regional and national fairs and conferences. It also lobbies for small presses, both in Congress (against rising postal rates, for instance) and in national review media for greater small-press cover-

*\*Coda: Poets and Writer's Newsletter*, published five times a year, is the most informative and professional magazine for this audience. Subscriptions available for $7.00 from: Poets and Writers, Inc., 201 West 54th Street, New York, N.Y. 10019.

\*\*Send away for details and a sample newsletter to: P.O. Box 703, San Francisco, Calif. 94101.

age. C.O.S.M.E.P. has also produced a number pamphlets on vital "how-to" phases of small-press publishing.

Lack of money is obviously one of the small presses' biggest problems. Undercapitalized to begin with, the income from book sales rarely manages to cover the costs and overhead. Most of the literary small presses are subsidized either out of pocket by their owners, by contributions solicited from their own authors, by private grants (including patrons, among whom are a number of successful and best-selling authors, some of them originally published by small presses), or by federal grants. In 1980 alone, the National Endowment for the Arts (N.E.A.) gave out 130 grants totaling over $700,000 for small presses and literary magazines. Out of this, fifty-eight small presses received over $400,000 in grants ranging in size from $1,100 to $10,000. They are given for specific projects, not for general support, but can also be used for promotion and distribution as well as book production.

Virtually all literary small presses operate at a deficit, and most can finance only about 50 percent of their operating costs from the sales of books. One reason is that in an effort to reach as wide an audience as possible, most books are published as paperback originals, and sold at more-than-reasonable list prices; the median is about $3.00. The other 50 percent of their operating costs comes from grants, donations, "family money," or the publisher's own pocket(s). Making a profit is the exception, not the rule. As Bill Zavatsky of Sun Press says, "For me, break-even is Nirvana." Grantsmanship, then, often becomes a crucial factor in keeping a number of the better literary presses afloat, and grant "politics" is an ongoing game. Grants are sought not only from the N.E.A., but from state arts councils, the Coordinating Council of Literary Magazines, various government agencies, and from successful authors, most of whom remain anonymous donors (how would you like to have 1,000 small presses asking for a donation?). Several years ago James Michener donated $160,000—which was matched by equal donations from several major trade houses—to support the publication of poetry, although this didn't actually help small presses, as the money is being used to subsidize trade publication of poetry.

Some of the manuscripts are acquired through local supporters and friends, and a small percentage of the titles are the works of the staff of each press, but "casual acquaintance" is the most common entry to small presses. As each press grows, however, the range of manuscripts published broadens to include over-the-transom submissions. A typical literary press may receive as many as 2,000 manuscripts a year, out of which it may choose to publish three to five books (so you can expect a high rate of rejection slips here too). The ability or inclination of the author to promote, publicize, and sell his or her own book (as at poetry readings) is sometimes a key factor in deciding whether or not to take on a book. Small presses are quirkier in their decisions, since their own tastes rather than commercial considerations generally determine their choice of what to publish. Good work may be turned down only because it doesn't suit the tastes of the editors. And with 2,000 submissions a year and an average yearly list of ten books, writers must be as persistent, and as careful in their selection of houses, as they should be with trade houses. Many small publishers are looking to discover new writers, rather than publish small-press "professionals," even those with good track records. So the novice may have a step up on the pro. Prospective authors can consult the *International Directory* or *A.I.P.* catalog to decide which presses might be suitable for their books, or can write directly to these publishers for current catalogs or flyers.

Authors accepted for publication should be prepared for very informal contracts or letters of agreement. You may get a token advance of $50 to $250, but no advance at all is more common. The royalty terms range from the conventional to the conditional; for example, royalties will be paid only after a requisite number of copies are sold to recoup expenses. More common as a royalty is to give the author 10 percent of the books from the first print run and 10 percent of any reprints. For authors who expect to give readings, this can add up to a 10-percent-of-list royalty (also a conventional royalty for small presses). In fact, these two rates are not only recommended in the N.E.A. "Grant Guidelines," but are now required of houses who receive their grants. If you hope or expect to generate sales on your own, as from poetry readings, you should ask for a 50 percent discount on copies you purchase; this, of course, adds up to a hefty royalty if you sell them. While a handshake is as common as a contract, you should at least expect or ask for a letter from the press, stating its intention to publish a book ("within one year," preferably), what kind of royalty it will pay, and what your share of the subsidiary rights are. Sub-rights sales are rare—presses don't generally send galleys to book clubs or mass market reprinters, as trade publishers do—and very few books are sent overseas. In compensation, many small presses will only take 10 percent of these unexpected rights sales, or will gladly let you keep—and spell out in the letter—first serial, performance, British, and foreign translation rights, and even second serial rights (for a short story or a poem to be reprinted in an anthology or magazine is obviously not as remote a possibility as a film option or even a bookclub sale). Most small presses hardly think about subsidiary rights, but you don't have to be quite as casual; there is always a possibility for a sale, and you may be more likely to see it happen if you initiate it yourself. Provided the press doesn't object, you might try selling the sub-rights on your own, or at least recommend to the publisher where a sale is a possibility; there are several hundred small book clubs, for example, that are particularly receptive to nonfiction, even from obscure presses.

The appearance and quality of the bound book can be of prize-winning stature, or it can look like a mimeographed broadside handed out on a street corner. Tight budgets, however, are frequently compensated for by loving care: Many of the small-press publishers have a strong and abiding interest in the aesthetics of book production, which is reflected in the final product. Many, in fact, have their own typesetting equipment. An I.B.M. composer can now be purchased for about $3,000. The in-house labor, of course, whether editorial, production, or marketing, is donated. No profits also generally means no salaries.

The average first printing for a novel, book of poems, or collection of short stories is in the range of 1,500 copies, but it may go as low as 500 or as high as 2,500. This is calculated to cover the first eighteen months' to two years' sales (in contrast to trade houses, who rarely print for more than one year's sales, and now often print for only the first six months' estimated sales). Books from small presses sell more slowly, and it takes more time to get them publicized and distributed.

Though restricted by small budgets, the majority of alternative presses will carry out traditional publicity functions. Review copies (though maybe not advance page proofs, but up to 10 percent of the first print run) will be sent to trade magazines such as *Publishers Weekly, Library Journal,* and *Choice,* who are increasingly taking note of small-press books.* Review copies will also go out to local and regional newspapers, as well as to a variety of special interest magazines, though only the top or more optimistic presses will gamble on sending copies to national consumer media such as the *New York Times,* even though they do occasionally review small-press books. The most receptive review media are the "little magazines," the small-circulation literary journals and reviews that are the magazine counterparts to the small presses. Many of them review small-press books regularly, and a few are devoted almost exclusively to the small-press industry and book reviewing, such as *Stony Hills: The New England Alternative Press Review,* or *Small Press Review,* which "seeks to study and promulgate the small press worldwide."**

Press releases are common, as are active attempts to get local cover-

---

*In *Library Journal,* a monthly column is devoted to little-known magazines and small presses; once a year an entire section provides an annual round-up. *Booklist,* a bi-monthly review journal published by the American Library Association, has a "Small Press Scene" column in each fifteenth-of-the-month issue. *The San Francisco Review of Books* also has a column, by Steve Vincent, on small presses and the small-press literary scene.

**For a free sample issue of this monthly write to P.O. Box 100, Paradise, Calif. 95969, or subscribe for $10.00 per year.

age, whether in newspapers or on radio or television. Some small presses are quite successful in arranging local lecture tours or poetry readings. Catalogs are produced, usually once a year, and are sent to libraries, bookstores, and mail order lists of previous individual customers. Individual fliers for specific books are often sent to lists of potential customers provided by the author, and also to relevant special interest groups and specific magazine and journal subscribers.

Advertising is minimal, but ads in little magazines and literary quarterlies, local newspapers, library publications, and even national media are not uncommon, while ads for appropriate nonfiction titles may be placed in classified sections.

The major problems for alternative presses are sales and distribution. For poetry, for example, even a sale of 500 to 750 copies can be considered a success. (Curiously, there seem to be more writers of poetry than buyers or readers.) Ideally each book requires and will get a separate sales strategy. Within a radius of one hundred miles or so, the publisher may make direct calls on and service the local bookstores. This is especially true in college towns. Cities such as Austin, Berkeley, Cambridge, Iowa City, New Orleans, and Northampton are heavily populated by students and professors, who are a prime audience for literary presses. One successful ploy in developing new bookstore accounts is to give away a free copy of one or two or more titles. Assuming they sell—and the bookstore has been able to pocket the entire amount—the store will now presumably be more receptive to stocking new titles from that press. Another promotional device is to give a store one hundred or more copies of a slow-moving book, which the store will use as a free premium in its Christmas catalog. Most stores send these catalogs to their charge-account customers, and the free copy is sent out with any order. A key salesman, however, in any marketing strategy is the author, who is usually expected to sell a hefty number of copies of his or her work, since many poets, novelists, and short-story writers teach, lecture, or give readings at colleges, coffee houses, and so on.

The more financially successful small presses are those which prepare individual marketing plans for each book, carefully identify and seek to reach a specific audience, try to sell sub-rights, and concentrate on nontraditional markets; for example, publishing regional trail guides and then selling them directly to ''outdoor'' and sporting-goods stores, such as Eastern Mountain Sports.

Since many independent-press books will not be carried by commercial jobbers and distributors, nor in most bookstores, a variety of solutions has evolved. At one extreme are the very few presses that have made sales and distribution arrangements with a commercial publisher, such as has the Shambhala Publications, which is distributed by Random

House. As mentioned earlier, about a dozen scattered wholesale distributors now exist, e.g., The Book Bus in the east and Book People on the west coast, who represent both a number of small presses as well as some commercial publishers (in 1980, there are about 110 distributors who will handle small-press books, down from 140 in 1979). In recent years, a number of small-press regional associations have sprung up to provide collective distribution facilities; membership numbers range from roughly fifteen to fifty publishers. Half are full-service distributors—that is, they will stock, bill, and ship titles—and the other half act as clearinghouses that forward orders to the individual presses. These collectives are eligible for grants, and some are even eligible for non-profit, tax-exempt status. Member presses, if geography permits, share in the work; otherwise, one member coordinates and the rest contribute operating capital. The value of collective or wholesale distribution, aside from the obvious benefits to the individual publishers, is felt more strongly by the bookstore and the library. The abundance of publishers and small-press titles, their limited sales potential and audience, and the occasional here-today-gone-tomorrow syndrome discourages libraries and bookstores from stocking titles or dealing individually with any but the top 10 percent of the field. But the professionalism, stability, and convenience of dealing with distributors makes buying books more attractive and less complicated.

Nevertheless many independent presses have often been cavalier about—if not downright disdainful of—the sales and distribution side of publishing. A sign of change in attitude is evident in the growing number of publishing seminars on marketing for small presses sponsored by C.O.S.M.E.P., Knowledge Industries, and others. After all, sales + grants = survival. Three problems that continue to plague some small press distributors are "antibusiness" prejudice, which still permeates much of the small-press world; the meager amount of income actually generated by their sales (the average book of poems lists for $3.00, of which the distributor nets 10 percent, that is, 30¢); and the difficulty in collecting on bills to bookstores, who are now either paying in 90 to 120 days, making heavy returns, or not paying bills at all. This last set of issues, incidentally, is a problem which now extends to trade-book publishing as well.

The production and distribution of a joint mail order catalog is the most effective tool of both the wholesale and cooperative distributor. Libraries and lists of individual consumers are as much a target as bookstores, since few of the latter stock titles on a regular basis. Many of the larger bookstore chains, however, such as Waldenbooks and B. Dalton, are becoming less resistant to ordering individual titles, though poetry and fiction are still the lowest priority genres. The larger small-press wholesalers, such as Bookpeople, employ sales representatives, follow up catalogs with individual mailing pieces and fliers, and exhibit at major publishing industry meetings. The collectives are less rigorous: If there are sales people, they may be working part-time or they may be individual small-press publishers who voluntarily rotate sales calls. As collectives, with very low budgets, the necessity for communal cooperation and free voluntary services are vital to their continued existence.

Four recent experimental ventures in the area of sales and distribution are indicative of the continuing growth and potential of the independent presses: 1) a new distributor, Quarto Book Service, which sells just poetry and only by mail order; 2) The Small Press Book Club,* which now has been incorporated into the monthly *Small Press Review* (thus twelve "mailings a year"), and which has offered books for as low as twenty-nine cents (members do not have to make a specified number of purchases); 3) an on-again off-again traveling distributor, "The Book Bus," which stocks a variety of small-press titles, displays at college campuses and book fairs, and calls on libraries and bookstores;** 4) annual regional small-press book fairs, which in New York City and San Francisco, for instance, have drawn standing-room only crowds in the last few years.

One important word of caution. Since many poets and writers of fiction publish excerpts in little magazines prior to small-press publication, their work frequently appears in print without due regard to copyright formalities; though pirating of uncopyrighted (and even copyrighted) poetry is uncommon, writers should nevertheless take care to protect their "property." Generally, a periodical registers copyright for an issue as one complete unit and will assign and transfer the individual copyright back to the writer after publication, upon request, by means of a simple letter containing the relevant details and signed by the publisher. The author should then file the letter with the Register of Copyrights, enclosing a $10.00 registration fee and making sure to retain a copy of the letter. If the publisher does not copyright the magazine, the writer should insist that the excerpt be followed by the copyright symbol, date, and the author's name (©1981 by John Doe) and should then obtain and file form "TX" with the Copyright Office, along with one copy of the "collective" work, and a fee of 10.00.† Small presses, as opposed to little magazines, will invariably file the proper copyright form for your book.

*Write for a free current catalog to: P.O. Box 100, Paradise, Calif. 95969.

**Several small-press distributors were running buses as this went to print.

†Since January 1978, contributors to periodicals have additional copyright protection. An explanatory leaflet is available from the Copyright Office, or see the February/March 1977 edition of *Coda* magazine for details, or buy their recent *Writer's Guide to Copyright* for $5.00.

Authors who have published with the better small presses are generally surprised and delighted by the quality of book production, but are frequently frustrated and disappointed by the length of time it takes for books to appear in the stores or to get reviews, and by the modest sales. Keep in mind that the operation of almost all small presses is a labor of love, and that the motives of those who run them are rarely found in commercial publishing today. Small-press people are often juggling full-time jobs and raising families and are usually not rewarded for all their efforts with so much as a bus token. They generally deserve your gratitude, no matter how many copies of your book they sell.

Though shoestring budgets and other problems remain, the independent presses are growing, thriving, and developing new techniques for solving their inherent limitations. Fed up with what many writers and small-press impresarios feel is the growing bottom-line mentality of the publishing industry—"Make your living at anything *except* with the biggest literary cesspool called commercial publishing"—the independent presses are providing an opportunity for a growing number of unpublished or disillusioned writers.

## The University Press

Many university presses are now existing in a state of siege. Since about 1970, when college enrollments began to decline and universities started to feel the pinch of recession and inflation, the university press has become a principal target for balancing or cutting the school budget. Traditionally, most U.P.'s were run at a deficit, although they all attempted to break even. Considering their goals, among which are the production of scholarly works that contribute to the advancement of knowledge in specific fields, and the reflection of prestige upon their parent institution, the directors felt neither a sense of ignominy nor failure in the need for continuing subsidy from the university. But in addition to the university's financial problems, the presses also became victims of a declining economy: In the space of two years, the average U.P. book was selling about 1,300 copies instead of its former average of 2,300, and this dip had devastating results for its operating statements. In 1971, for example, Harvard University Press had a $500,000 deficit. One consequence was that its editor-in-chief was replaced by a commercial press editor. Sales have fallen off primarily for four reasons: a reduction in college and university library budgets, a cutback in federal funds available to higher education for book acquisition, a decline in the student population resulting in a loss of text adoption sales, and because scholars are buying fewer books.

One of the results of this debacle has been a shift in editorial policy.

Though they have not abandoned their traditional motives and goals, many university presses are now publishing more poetry, fiction and nonfiction that was hitherto considered—if not exactly commercial—more suitable for trade houses, that is, a profit might be realized from publication. Furthermore, university press doors have opened wider to non-university-affiliated writers.

In 1981, for example, Grove Press will be issuing the paperback edition of *A Confederacy of Dunces*, by John Kennedy Toole, a southern writer who died by his own hand when he was thirty-two. Twenty years ago the book was turned down by eight houses; the author went into a shell and gave up on the book. After his death his mother continued to make submissions and pile up rejection slips. Years passed, until she persuaded Walker Percy to read it. He was so smitten with the book that he submitted it to his own publisher, Farrar, Straus & Giroux, who turned it down because the author, being dead, "could neither help to promote it, nor follow it with another." Percy then sent it to L.S.U. Press, who published it, sent out over 300 review copies, garnered rave reviews, have sold over 35,000 cloth copies (it is currently on the shelves), sold the paperback rights to Grove Press, and have just concluded a rights sale to 20th-Century Fox for a film.

Two other ways in which university presses hope to compensate for rising inflation and declining sales are to expand their cooperative efforts, especially in advertising, promotion, sales and distribution, and to attempt to increase their international sales. China, for instance, has become a significant new potential market; Chinese publishers are now compiling a list for a catalog of 1,000 new university press titles—in the social sciences and humanities as well as the sciences—which will be mailed to libraries and other book outlets. The recent merger of New York University Press with Columbia University Press suggests a possible future course for other presses.

As in any other segment of the publishing industry, the range of U.P. interests, methods, and relative prosperity are diverse. At one extreme are, surprisingly enough, two British-sponsored university presses, Oxford and Cambridge, both of which are highly profitable operations whose U.S. branches bear much closer resemblance to commercial presses than to university presses. Of the 100 or so current American university presses (73 are accredited members of the A.A.U.P.) which produce a total of about 2,000 new books a year, a handful are particularly prestigious, large (bring out over 125 titles a year), and publish both scholarly and trade-oriented books: Princeton, Harvard, the University of Chicago, and the University of California head the list. Considering their numbers, an unusually high percentage of their books are The American Book Award winners or nominees, and a few, such as T. H. White's *Book of Merlin* or Yale U.P.'s *Edwardian Country House*, occasionally make the best-seller lists. Some of the presses gain a reputation for their particular specialties, such as Indiana University Press's folklore and film titles, the University of Texas Press's translations, and the University of Oklahoma and Nebraska presses' many titles by and about American Indians. The majority of the presses are small, produce approximately twenty to thirty titles a year, and publish mostly scholarly and regional interest titles. In recent years, some presses, such as those of the University of Illinois and the University of Massachusetts, have expanded their lists to include more poetry, novels, and collections of short stories, not all of which are written by college professors.

Listed on a recent brochure from the University of Missouri Press were no less than one dozen short-story collections by contemporary writers (in addition to two dozen collections of poetry). The University of Illinois Press recently had four new short-story collections reviewed in the *New York Times Book Review*, and the University of Pittsburgh Press has just announced a prize consisting of publication plus $5,000 for a collection of short stories. As this book goes to press, it appears that university presses are now the most probable place for short stories in book form to find a home.

Practically all of the editorial staffs are encumbered by faculty boards consisting of from six to twelve professors who must approve publishing projects. Due to the outside academic critiques that are solicited for each manuscript (usually two to three) as well as the faculty board review, the presses often take from two months to a year to make a final decision about signing up a book—a factor to be weighed carefully before submitting your manuscript.

As scholarly books generally sell modestly, first printings average but 2,000 to 2,500 copies, and there is little money to spare for advances. The larger, more solvent or commercially oriented U.P.'s will sometimes pay advances of from $500 to $1,500, and royalties are similar to those for trade books, though about a third of the presses pay on net receipts rather than list price. Some presses now consistently require a subsidy to help defray the cost of production. It may come from out of the author's pocket, from private or federal grants, or from university research funds. Other presses may do this only on occasion, but particularly when a project required years of preparation and results in a multivolume set, such as Princeton's forthcoming collected papers of Albert Einstein, which garnered over a million-dollar grant.

The quality of design and production is consistently high and frequently superb: The books are usually a delight to hold, to look at, and to own. Due to financial pressure, some of the presses are now cutting corners, but the list prices of the books remain, nevertheless, very high.

With regard to publicity and advertising, most U.P.'s follow the conventions of commercial presses, although on a reduced scale. Since the audience and market for many of their books are largely composed of scholars and libraries, review copies and ads are concentrated in scholarly journals, library publications, and special interest magazines.

Many of the presses are represented by commercial distributors, whether regionally or nationally. Some have jointly hired a salesman to represent them exclusively, while others employ commission men who normally represent a number of commercial presses as well. The more scholarly books are found mainly in college bookstores, whereas the trade-oriented books can be found in traditional bookstores.* Mail order sale to libraries, scholars, and professionals is a primary emphasis of marketing efforts, in addition to foreign sales, which represent an unusually high percentage of total book sales. Equally important in promoting sales are the regional and national academic and professional conventions where the presses display and take orders for their books.

A decision to submit a manuscript (proposals with samples are frowned upon, except from scholars with previous publications) to a university press must take into consideration the specific interests and informal guidelines each press maintains. The *A.A.U.P. Directory*, which can be found in most libraries, contains a list of its seventy-three members (those university presses that do not meet A.A.U.P. criteria do not belong) with a description of their publishing interests; a similar list can be found in *Writer's Market*. Several of the presses are known for their poetry contests, such as "The Yale Series of Younger Poets," whose awards consist of book publication, occasionally supplemented by nominal advances of $500 or $1,000. The competition is very keen, and the standards are very high: The criterion for publication is excellence, not saleability. A listing of these contests can be found in the *Annual Grants and Awards Available to American Writers*.** This publication, incidentally, is an invaluable resource for writers seeking scholarships, grants, and awards; more than 500 are listed.

In general, the presses will only consider "serious" nonfiction and literary fiction; before submitting a manuscript, it would be advisable to write the individual presses for a copy of their current catalog, to determine the kinds of books they publish as well as the audience they aim for. While the presses are not opposed to signing up books that might have an impressive (for them) sale, they are usually more concerned with the quality of the writing, the originality of the research data, the contribution to the advancement of knowledge in a particular field, and the regional potential.

*The current sales breakdown is: 25 percent general bookstores; 25 percent text adoptions; 25 percent libraries; 15 percent export; 10 percent mail order.

**Copies can be purchased for $3.00 (11th edition) from: P.E.N. American Center, 47 Fifth Avenue, New York, N.Y. 10003.

## *Publishing for Hire*

There are several instances in which a writer might decide to pay for the cost of publishing his or her book. Foremost is the blunt fact that no commercial house, small press, or university press will take on the manuscript. But there are other sensible reasons for considering this option. A writer could spend a lifetime canvassing publishers (*LMP* rents a mailing list of over 6,000) and most are unwilling to do so. If seeing your work in print is the primary goal and you are fully prepared to write off the investment—since the odds are that you will recoup only a small portion of it—then you might as well consider taking the plunge. Perhaps you have written a history of your family,* a book of light verse, a novel, or even a polemical denunciation of capital punishment. You may have an avocation or vocation from which you collected a considerable body of specialized or technical data or information that might interest only a few hundred readers, or even more. Incidentally, this is the most appropriate genre for self-publishing, and the one most likely to earn you back your investment. You will not be in isolated company paying for book publication: The so-called vanity presses alone publish about 2,000 books a year.

There are two basic choices for the writer who travels this route, and the decision of which to make should hinge on two simple factors: time and money. Now that you have been exposed to the fundamental operations of publishing, it should be clear that there are a limited number of skills and procedures that, with a certain amount of patience and effort, can either be learned or purchased, or a combination of both. You may not want to learn how to become a typographer and then rent or buy your own Linotype machine, but you can, for instance, learn how to prepare your manuscript for composition, how to design the interior of the book, and how to assemble or buy mailing lists for review copies and library sales. If you have the time, the inclination and the confidence, and wish to keep your costs to a minimum, you should seriously consider publishing your own book. If money is no object, or if you cannot spare the time or are intimidated by the thought of tackling the job on your own, then you may want to look into the vanity presses. One reason the decision is a simple one is that there is no indication that the vanity press will sell more copies of the book —all claims notwithstanding—than you can.

**The Vanity Press.** There are about a dozen nationally known and advertised firms, such as Exposition Press, Dorrance, and Vantage, that

---

*Since the huge success of *Roots*, editors and agents have been flooded with memoirs, auto-biographies, and books of family letters; the chances of finding a trade publisher for these are as slim as for a first book of poems.

actively solicit or advertise for authors. They refer to themselves as subsidy publishers, shunning the designation *vanity*, although that is the term people in the publishing industry continue to employ. They advertise their services frequently in writer's magazines and national media, and a headline such as "Publisher Seeking Authors" will serve to identify them. The larger companies will often also advertise in local newspapers, stating that a publisher's representative will be in town for several days to talk to prospective authors, and so forth.

Practically everyone in publishing wrinkles his nose when you mention vanity presses; unfortunately, that includes reviewers, bookstore buyers, distributors, and libraries. One of the major reasons for the conventional disdain (aside from the generally poor quality of the writing) is the variety of misleading claims purveyed by these presses. The Federal Trade Commission has come down on these firms several times during the last three decades, so that their ads, brochures and contracts are now no more misleading than those of used-car dealers. Since in a capitalist society we are all exposed to the hawking of services or wares that do not quite measure up to our expectations, there is really no reason to single out the vanity press for an extra dose of condemnation. Just remember that if you are going to consider doing business with them, you are well advised to keep your eyes wide open, read contracts and other documents very carefully, and make sure not only that you understand exactly what goods or services you think you are buying, but that you have a written document to detail them.

Vanity presses will publish virtually *any* manuscript for a fee, provided that it is not racist, pornographic, excessively violent, patently subversive, or so out of bounds that for one reason or another the publisher might expose himself to a lawsuit. In preparation for this book, I sent copies of an unpublished manuscript of roughly 300 pages to two of the leading vanity presses. Within ten days I had a glowing report from each publisher, praising my work in superlatives and indicating that it had been accepted for publication. Within less than a week after that, I received a contract from each firm—very complicated ones, I might add—along with catalogs and fliers with testimonials from satisfied customers. There were numerous case histories of books that had gone into multiple printings, sold in huge quantities, and had earned their authors thousands of dollars. One book had actually made the best-seller list of the *New York Times* (in 1954), one author had allegedly published 300 books (none of which are currently listed in *Books in Print*), one book was written by a Nobel Prize winner, and another author had gone on to become a Pulitzer Prize winner. Very impressive! Both the contracts and the author's questionnaires (which were included) looked infinitely more professional than the ones I normally get from commercial publishers. In order to appreciate the optimistic and enthusiastic vapors with which these documents intoxicate the potential customer, you will have to send a vanity press a copy of your manuscript and receive your own set of blandishments. The only apparent thorn in this bouquet of roses was on the last page of the contract: "In consideration of the advantages to accrue to the author . . . he agrees to pay $9,000" (the other read $7,700).

Vanity presses will only accept a completed manuscript, since they cannot calculate the actual costs or your fee without it. Simply put, they will publish your manuscript in a cloth or paper binding at a cost to you which enables them to make a very handsome profit whether or not they ever actually sell a single copy of the book. According to all the literature on vanity presses, about 10 percent of their authors recoup their entire investment. For the other 90 percent, the average return is roughly 25 percent of the total payment. In other words, out of my $9,000 investment, I could expect to kiss $6,750 goodbye.

Some of the conditions and services pertinent to the vanity press agreement are worth considering here. Obviously the cost of publication will depend on the size and complexity of your manuscript, as well as on the number of copies printed. The manuscript I submitted was 300 pages long; a 64-page book of poems in a paperback edition would have cost considerably less. According to the terms of the contract, the publisher generally sends the author fifty to seventy-five free copies and mails out approximately seventy-five review copies. Yearly catalogs are produced and sent to distributors, bookstores, and libraries, and a press release is also produced. A mailing piece will be sent to a list of potential customers provided by you and to "any other appropriate list" (you would want some clarification here). On all copies sold of the first printing (roughly 3,000, although only about 400 to 600 are actually bound—the rest remain in "sheets" unless sales warrant binding), the publisher pays a royalty of 40 percent of the list price; for subsequent printings, 20 percent. Some of the contracts stipulate that the publisher will spend 10 percent of your payment in direct mail, space, or cooperative advertising. While the quality of the design, the print, the jacket, the binding, and the paper will not win any awards, they are practically indistinguishable from many trade books. The presses work fast: They will generally bring the book out in six months or less. Books of a certain ilk, such as local histories or technical manuals, will receive more promotional attention if the publisher actually feels that the sales potential is there.

So far, so good, but here's the rub. The author receives virtually no editorial guidance; only gross grammatical and spelling errors are corrected. Reviews, whether in trade or consumer magazines, are as common as needles in haystacks, and space ads do not pull many orders, even though the largest houses frequently run list ads in *The New York Times Book Review* to impress you. Sales prospects are dismal: In most cases only local bookstores will carry the book; distributors or chains will rarely touch them. Aside from copies purchased by your own friends and acquaintances, mail order sales and library sales are miniscule. In other words, if the book is going to sell, you will have to be the salesman. A final drawback is the stigma attached to publishing with a vanity press. If you ever hope to publish a second book with a commercial press, you would only damage your chances by referring to your first (unless the sales were extraordinary, say, over 3,000 copies).

Two conclusions to be drawn are that vanity presses stimulate unrealistic expectations, and for the goods and services they offer, they charge a higher price than they should. If they actually bound all the copies of the first printing and then turned the remaining stock over to the author after, say, a year, the arrangement would be almost equitable. But in fact, when and if the contract is terminated (usually after two years), the author must purchase the remaining stock, if he wants it, though most of it will still be in unbound sheets.

Nevertheless there are a number of satisfied customers, particularly among the 10 percent who recoup their investment. If you decide to look into the prospect of publishing with a vanity press, send for a free offprint of "Does It Pay To Pay To Have It Published?" from *Writer's Digest*,\* which contains a checklist of twenty-two points to consider or clarify before signing a contract. Shop around. Submit a copy of the manuscript to several firms and see who offers the best deal. Be sure not to negotiate for more than a 1,000-copy first printing, and keep in mind that a paperback may cost a lot less than a clothbound edition.

## Self-Publishing

There are more famous and eventually successful self-published writers than any vanity press would care to shake a stick at. In this country alone, one of the best sellers of the eighteenth century, Paine's *Common Sense*, has ultimately sold over half a million copies. Whether you consider reference books, such as Bartlett's *Quotations* or Robert's *Rules of Order*; novelists, such as Twain and Crane; poets, such as Whitman, Pound, and Sandburg; inspirational writers, such as Mary Baker Eddy (whose estate of over $2 million was derived from numerous editions of *Science and Health*); or, for that matter, America's head

---

\*9933 Alliance Road, Cincinnati, Ohio 45242. Enclose a stamped, self-addressed envelope.

yippy, Abby Hoffman (*Steal This Book*), you can find a stalwart who was willing and determined to take a chance. Thoreau took the plunge somewhat unsuccessfully with his first book, *A Week on the Concord and Merrimack Rivers*. For $290 he had 1,000 copies printed. Four years later, having given away over 250 copies and having actually sold about fifteen dollars' worth, he packed and shipped the remaining 700-odd volumes to his mother's house in Concord, where she stored them in the attic (a copy of this first edition today is worth more than Thoreau's entire printing bill). Alas, this tale is as common today as it was then.

Conversely, consider the success story of *How to Keep Your Volkswagen Alive*, self-published in 1967 by its author, John Muir. Unable to find a publisher, Muir did it on his own, managed to get Book People to distribute it, and after its twenty-third recent reprinting, has sold over 1,300,000 copies. John Muir Publications now has a list of over twenty books, among which is a guide to Mexico that has sold over 100,000 copies.

However, that the tradition is still alive and well is suggested by some current phenomena: the unusual success of *The Publish-It-Yourself Handbook*, edited by Bill Henderson, which has received national media attention and has sold over 40,000 copies to date; a recent monthly newsletter, *Publishing in the Output Mode*, which contains useful and often witty articles and tips for self-publishers and small presses*; the publication in the past two years alone of at least half-a-dozen how-to's on self-publishing (the best two I have looked at are listed in the bibliography); and some current success stories of self-publishers. Robert Ringer, for example, self-published *Winning Through Intimidation*, which sold over 200,000 copies in cloth, and then also became a best-seller in paperback. He followed this with another best seller, *Looking Out for #1*, which sold almost as well; his third and most recent book, *Restoring the American Dream*, has sold over 150,000 copies in cloth so far (Harper & Row is distributing it for him), and is still going strong.

But self-publishing is not a step to be taken lightly; there are a number of detailed and time-consuming tasks, and the rewards are more apt to come from a job well done than in high sales figures and profit. The procedures to be faced are evident by now: final preparation of the manuscript, copyediting, design, typesetting, proofreading, manufacturing, registering copyright, publicity, advertising, sales, and distribution. There are time-saving and cheaper ways to accomplish some of these, such as preparing camera-ready copy with an IBM Selectric

*Write for a sample issue to: Padre Productions, P.O. Box 1725, San Luis Obispo, California 93406.

typewriter, and there are more elaborate and expensive routes, such as hiring a free-lance specialist in book publicity. For starters, you will want to look over *The Publish-It-Yourself Handbook*,\* which contains an excellent reference section with names and addresses and various other how-to tips, and you might take a look at a very useful, if slightly out-of-date, article, "Roll Yr. Own," which explores the pros and cons of self-publishing and contains a hefty annotated bibliography (*Chrysalis* #7, August, 1978).

There are three basic ways of going about it. The easiest one is to work with those few printers and manufacturers who are willing not only to print in short runs, but also to midwife your book from manuscript to bound books. Two reliable firms, which also publish manuals on self-publishing, are Adams Press (*How to Publish, Promote & Sell Your Book*, $4.50) and Harlo Press (*How to Publish Your Own Book*, $4.95).\*\* There are several other full-service firms to be found in the "Book Manufacturing" section of *LMP*, all of whom will do business by mail. This includes, by the way, some of the major vanity presses, who offer these manufacturing services as a sideline, at a competitive price.

A more complicated and expensive method is to free-lance separately most of the tasks involved, from copyediting to advertising. Again, refer to the pages of *LMP*, which contain listings of virtually every kind of service the self-publisher would require. In this instance you would be acting, more or less, as your own managing editor. One advantage of this method is that you can procure the highest quality professional work, and your final product will be indistinguishable from that of a commercial press.

Lastly, you can work with a local printer who will provide some advice and help, but on most phases of the process you will be on your own, and the amount of time, care, and effort you put in will determine how handsome the final book is. This can be the most inexpensive method *if* you do most of the work yourself, shop around carefully for supplies, such as paper, and services, such as binding, and publish a small first print run. Though the plant costs are the same whether you print 100 or 1,000 copies, you can save a considerable amount of money on your first printing by only binding a portion of the print run, say 500 out of a 1,000-copy print run. If sales warrant, you can always bind the remaining sheets and then reprint.

Commercial publishers themselves constantly send out for bids for different publishing tasks. The more you shop around, the better the prices you will get, and the lower your total costs will be.

\*The 1980 2nd edition is available as a Harper & Row paperbook for $6.95.
\*\*Send away for free brochures to: Adams Press, 30 West Washington Street, Chicago, Illinois 60602; Harlo Press, 16721 Hamilton, Detroit, Michigan 48203.

The hardest and most frustrating part of the process may be the marketing of your book; if you refer to the various small-press and self-publishing publications mentioned or listed in the bibliography, you can learn how to go about it. But the number of choices to be made are manifold—where to send review copies and press releases, where to advertise, which mailing lists to buy or rent, and what newspapers to advertise in and how (space or classified?). Selling your own book requires stamina and brass, especially if you are going to call on bookstores . . . and you should.

Others have done it, done it well, and done it successfully. With a bit of luck, and the right book, you might be shocked one day to find a letter in the mailbox from a commercial publisher who has come across the book and decided to make an offer for paperback rights. Or maybe, because of reviews and ads or by word of mouth, the book will somehow catch on and sell out its first and second and third printings, and you will decide to become a small-press publisher. Dan Poynter, of Parachuting Publications, was so successful with his first book that he became a small-press publisher, and now has over ten books on his list, including an extremely informative how-to on self-publishing. Only 10 percent of his sales are to bookstores; the balance are sold via sky-diving schools, parachute shops, mail order, and so forth. This is the secret of successful self-publishing: a special topic sold to special markets. But the chances are you will attempt to publish your own book mostly because you want to see it in print. However many books you sell, nothing can surpass the feeling of triumph and pride that comes from holding that first copy in your hands.

# *Appendix*

## A Sample Book Proposal

Prospectus
WORKING IN REAL ESTATE
A Guide Especially for Women

by Carolyn Janik

In the 1979-80 *Subject Guide to Books in Print* there are nine full-page columns devoted to books on the real estate business. In that list there is only *one* book written specifically for women, Margaret Crispen's *How Any Woman Can Get Rich Fast in Real Estate* (Andrews & McMeel, 1978, $9.95). It is a get-rich-quick book, however, and leaves unanswered essential questions about the advantages, the problems, the risks, and the rewards that go with being a woman in a fast-paced, high exposure, competitive, and often emotionally appealing career.

Of course the most logical question is, "How is being a woman in real estate different from being a man in real estate?" It is different. In the first place, the numbers add up into sexist columns. The majority of brokers are men and the overwhelming majority (an estimated 75 percent!) of the residential sales agents are women. Yes, there *are* women brokers, and women office managers, and women in commercial sales, and appraisals, and property management, but they are the few. In general, women sell *houses*, and a discussion of and for women in real estate leads to a book focused upon residential sales.

It cannot, however, be a book on sales and listing techniques alone, there is much more. A book for women in real estate must deal with the problems of women working in a field with erratic hours and intense pressure, and trying at the same time to be responsible wives and mothers. It must suggest ways to overcome the long-established stereotypes and clichés about women and money since real estate women deal with escrow deposits, and mortgage qualification, and negotiating, and closing procedures, all of which are frightening financial question marks to most home buyers and sellers.

A book for women in real estate, women who routinely conduct total strangers through empty houses, must also deal with the possibilities of theft, rape, and violence, all of which are occupational hazards that to this date have not been discussed adequately in print. Yet it should not sacrifice optimism and a positive outlook to the delineation of problem areas. It must shed equal light on the specific strengths of women in the field, their ability to empathize with the homemaker concerned with buying the right "home," their ability to give a woman's point of view to the male corporate transferee out house hunting without his wife and family, and their firsthand knowledge of the life styles and community services in the areas in which they live.

Some space must also be given to "positive negatives." Erratic hours can also be looked upon as a flexible schedule, a schedule that allows time off for personal needs and the ability to vacation at any time throughout the year. Salary by commission means no weekly paycheck, but it also means no set limit on earnings.

In short, there is a need for an inside view of the profession by a woman for women. *Working in Real Estate* will be that book. In the readable style of *The House Hunt Game* and *Selling Your Home* (both Macmillan, 1979 and 1980 respectively), it will explore what it means to be a woman in the real estate business today. It will outline the drawbacks and pitfalls of the job, and spotlight the techniques and secrets of success.

Its potential market is huge. There are 754,000* members of the National Association of Realtors in this country and well over half of them are women. To this add the data that in 1978 (the last year for which collected figures are currently available) over 544,000** people in the United States made applications to take state examinations for a real estate salesman's license, and again *far* more than half of these were women. And to this annually increasing figure we must add yet another factor, an unknown, the hundreds of thousands of housewives who go house hunting each year and think as they watch their real estate agent work, "Now that's a career I would enjoy."

The market for *Working in Real Estate* is nationwide and cuts across socio-economic lines from the ambitious woman striving to climb out of a routine working class job to the upper middle class housewife who looks for an occupation out of boredom. It will be read by women who did not finish high school and by women with a college degree. It should be included in the libraries of the more than 500 colleges and universities

---

*National Association of Realtors membership figure as of November 30, 1979.
**Annual report, National Association of Real Estate Licensing Law Officials, 1980.

across the country that offer courses or degrees in real estate. It has a potential market to the career counseling offices of high schools and junior colleges. It will be recommended by the men and women who run the real estate schools, and the franchise training programs, and the small independent real estate offices across the country.

*Working in Real Estate* will be between 60,000 and 70,000 words. It will be complete by September 1, 1980.

## Working in Real Estate

### (Outline)

Introduction—A Personal Note

#### PART I — GETTING STARTED

*1. It's a Job.* A candid look at the work day and the work week: showing houses, looking at houses, looking for houses, canvassing, floor time, paper work, qualifying, negotiating, financing, attending closings, extras.

*2. Are You the Type?* A picture of some real estate women; a discussion of the personality traits that make up the typical profile: aggressive, assertive, or competitive; self-reliant; active; risk-taking and creative; decisive; energetic; candid and tactful; intelligent and responsible; at ease with people.

*3. The License.* A state-by-state survey of license requirements.

*4. First Decisions.* Choosing the right office for you; descriptions of typical training programs available among various types: the national franchise, the multi-office firm, the single office firm, the mavericks.

*5. Beginnings.* The effective interview: presenting yourself, appearance, skills, goals; evaluating the office, floor time, commission splits, incentive programs, group insurance, the working contract. The paperwork of beginning; initial expenditures.

#### PART II — GETTING AHEAD

*1. Selling Good Service.* Being paid for knowledge and efficiency. Know the communities you work in, know what makes a "good" house, know the needs of your customers and clients, know comparative property value, know the mortgage market, know the local lawyers and the law. Efficiency: take listings carefully, use office facilities; make appointments in advance, allowing sufficient time, follow-ups.

*2. The Listing Farm.* Your "territory"; door-to-door canvassing; phone canvassing; clubs, hobbies, and your neighbors; home-owner ads; what makes your agency special; the presentation.

*3. Customers.* Answering the phone; qualification and conversation; working with "out-of-area" buyers; working with local buyers.

*4. Negotiating.* The requirements of an agency relationship vs. the art of playing the game. Keeping everyone cool and finding mortgage money.

*5. Headaches and Hazards.* Floor time, office meetings, illness, days-off, caravans and open houses, weekend duty, disputes between salespeople, disputes with the broker, legal entanglements, partnerships between salespeople, the draw, driving hazards, car insurance, safeguards against physical harm (theft, rape, violence).

*6. A Woman First.* Separating your life from your job: if you're single, if you're married, if you're the mother of young children, if you're a "senior citizen." Organizing time and priorities; leisure.

*7. Other Directions.* Opening your own office; office management; relocation specialist; training new agents; commercial speciality; rentals, property management; appraising; public relations; leaving the field.

*Glossary — The Words of the Trade*


## A Sample Reader's Report

Inadvertently, one publisher to whom I submitted my original proposal and sample chapters for this book enclosed his reader's report when he rejected the book and returned the materials to me. The contradiction evident here—the enthusiasm and then the suggestion to decline—is not uncommon.

To RL from SH
HANDBOOK TO PUBLISHING (Preface, two chapters, Contents)
by Richard Balkin
October 12, 1975

The author proposes a book which, if successful (very good likelihood as he has good background experience as both editor and agent), will cover every area for a prospective author from manuscript to printed book and after, in fact, with inclusion of material on subsidiary rights, expectation of reviews and sales.

Like:

Do I need/can I get an agent? How? What do they do?
How a publisher evaluates and makes a decision on one's proposal
How to read, understand and negotiate a contract (what an author can expect financially; what riders can be added to a contract)
How to prepare your manuscript for the publisher (not at all how to write, exclusively how to prepare: typing, style books suggested; front and back matter; permissions and copyright rules; who pays the fees for permissions; tables and illustrations; additional tips)
What happens to your manuscript at the publishers (a discussion of the various departments and functions in the house—why it takes the time it takes to publish a book)
What happens to your manuscript upon publication (sales, promotion, publicity, how and why a book gets remaindered)
Alternatives—university presses, vanity presses and self-publishing
Bibliography (books on style, various aspects of publishing, LMP)

I can see how this kind of book would be very helpful but I do personally see it as an agent's obligation to inform an author of his rights; an editor's to give his author a basic understanding of all the information contained above. I may be optimistic. To be truthful, if I were an author I think I would prefer to get it from my editor rather than from a book.

On the other hand, I do think that this book, in paperback form, would sell very well—and perhaps not only to prospective authors but to people involved in the publishing business itself.

I am not sure what information is contained in a new book, just out, an original paperback, entitled something like "How to Publish Your Own Book." The material in this proposal may overlap, but, as I say, I do not know.

My basic inclination is to decline.

## A Sample Contract

The following contract is quite conventional in both format and terms, as commercial trade contracts go. At the author's and the publisher's request, I have deleted their names.

**AGREEMENT**   dated as of the twenty-eighth day of   January      19  80

between

whose residence address is

and whose Social Security Number is:
who is a citizen of          United States   hereinafter called the 'Author' and
                                                                New York, New York
10016, a Delaware corporation, hereinafter called the 'Publisher,' with respect to the
work tentatively entitled

hereinafter called the 'Work.'

**AUTHOR'S GRANT**   1.   The Author hereby grants and assigns to the Publisher during the full term of
copyright and all renewals thereof all rights in the Work, including book publication
rights and the rights hereinafter specifically referred to in this Agreement, ~~throughout~~
~~the world.~~ in the United States, its possessions, Canada, and elsewhere in the world, except for the British Commonwealth, excluding Canada.

**COPYRIGHT**   2.   The Publisher shall have exclusive right to take out copyrights in the Work
in the name of the author        in the United States of America and such other
countries as it may deem expedient; and the Author agrees to take or cause to be taken,
as provided by law, all necessary steps to effect renewals of the copyright in the Work
on the expiration of the term thereof and to grant and assign the same or the rights under
the same to the Publisher. In case the copyright is in the name of the Author, the Author
hereby grants to the Publisher the right to bring, in the name of the Author, any action
or proceeding for the enjoining of any infringement of the copyright in the Work and
for any damages resulting therefrom, and all rights under said copyright and all renewals
thereof subject to the terms of this Agreement.

**MANUSCRIPT**   3.   The Author agrees to deliver to the Publisher not later than  1 February  1981
two copies of a legible manuscript of the Work in form and content satisfactory to the
Publisher and ready for the Printer. The manuscript shall contain about 100,000
words and, in addition, the following material:   50 halftones

**ROYALTIES**     4.  The Publisher agrees to pay to the Author, subject to the provisions of the succeeding paragraphs of this Agreement:

(a)  On regular sales in the United States

```
Ten percent (10%) of the list price on the first
five thousand (5000) copies sold; twelve and one-
half per cent (12½%) of the list price on the next
five thousand (5000) copies sold; fifteen per cent
(15%) of the list price on all copies sold thereafter.
```

```
The publisher further agrees to pay the author as an
advance against all earnings accruing under the terms
of this agreement the sum of six thousand dollars
($6000), half of which is payable on the signing
of this agreement and half of which is apyable on
delivery of the final manuscript.
```

```
The publisher agrees to pay the author the sum of
one thousand dollars ($1000) to prepare the illus-
trations for the Work, the sum to be charged
against the author's earnings.
```

No royalty shall be paid on free copies furnished to the Author or on copies used for review, sample, or other similar purposes, or on copies accidentally damaged or destroyed, or on copies returned.

(b)  On sales of a special edition at a reduced price, or on sales of the regular edition at reduced prices for special use, or when, in the opinion of the Publisher, the remunerative sale of the regular edition has ceased, a royalty of 10% of the gross price obtained; but if the Publisher shall sell copies of the Work at less than manufacturing cost (which it shall not do prior to one year after publication of the Work) no royalty shall be payable to the Author on such sales.

(c)  On all copies of the Publisher's regular edition sold for export in unbound sheets or in bound form a royalty of 5% of the United States published price.

(d)  On all copies sold through the medium of mail-order or coupon advertising a royalty of 5% of the United States published price.

(e)  In order to keep the Work in print as long as possible, on all copies sold from printings undertaken after sales of the Work have fallen to 500 copies or less per year, one-half the then prevailing rate of royalty.

**INEXPENSIVE EDITION (1)**  5.  The Publisher shall have the exclusive right, at the Publisher's option, to publish at a published price no greater than two-thirds of the published price of the regular edition an inexpensive edition of the Work. The Publisher agrees to pay to the Author the following royalties on such an edition:

```
Seven and one-half percent (7½%) of the list price
on all domestic sales; five per cent (5%) of the list
price on all export sales.
```

**INEXPENSIVE EDITION (2)**  6.  The Publisher shall have the exclusive right, at the Publisher's option, to license reprint publishers to publish and sell inexpensive editions of the Work. If rights of publication in the Work are so licensed, the Publisher agrees to pay to the Author 50% of the Publisher's net receipts after deduction of any expenses arising from the licensing of such rights.

**BOOK CLUB EDITIONS**     7.  The Publisher shall have the exclusive right, at the Publisher's option, either to license rights of publication or sell copies of the Work to a book club. If rights of publication in the Work are so licensed, the Publisher agrees to pay to the Author 50% of the Publisher's net receipts after deduction of the costs of any necessary plate manufacture, transportation, or any other expenses arising from the licensing of publication rights to the book club. If copies of the Publisher's regular edition are sold to the book club, the Publisher agrees to pay the Author 50% of the royalty paid to the Publisher by the book club.

**SUBSIDIARY RIGHTS (1)**    8. ~~The Author hereby grants to the Publisher motion picture, dramatization, radio, television, and first serialization rights, and agrees that 75% of the net proceeds from the sale of such subsidiary rights shall belong to the Author and 25% to the Publisher.~~

**SUBSIDIARY RIGHTS (2)**    9. The Author hereby grants to the Publisher the exclusive right to license the following subsidiary rights in the Work and agrees that the net proceeds received from the license of such subsidiary rights shall be divided equally between Author and Publisher: digest, abridgment, condensation, adaptation, visualization, selection, anthology, quotation, second serialization, syndication, ~~translation,~~ recorded readings, microphotographic reproduction, visual projections of the Work as a book, adaptation of the Work for use in facilities employed in information transfer and retrieval, and Braille transcriptions.

**AUTHOR'S WARRANTY**    10. The Author represents and warrants that he is the sole author and proprietor of the Work and has full power to make this Agreement and grant; that the Work has not heretofore been published in book form; that it contains nothing of an obscene, libelous, injurious, or unlawful nature; and that neither the Work nor the title will infringe upon any copyright, proprietary right, or other right. The Author agrees to indemnify and hold harmless the Publisher from and against any and all suits, claims, damages, and liabilities, based on or in respect of any violation or alleged violation of any copyright, proprietary right, or other right or any obscene, libelous, injurious, or unlawful matter in the Work, whether actual or claimed. The control of the defense of any action against the Publisher in respect of the Work shall be exercised jointly by the Publisher and the Author but at the expense of the Author.

**PREVIOUS PUBLICATION**    11. The Author agrees to notify the Publisher promptly in writing of any arrangement heretofore made for publication of the Work in any form in whole or in part prior to book publication by the Publisher, to secure copyright protection therefor in the United States of America, and to deliver to the Publisher legally recordable assignment or assignments of such copyright or copyrights in order that the Publisher may comply fully with all copyright requirements in the United States of America.

**PERMISSIONS**    12. The Author agrees to secure at his own expense the necessary permission to reprint in the Work any material included that is under copyright, or is subject to any proprietary or other right of others, and to transmit such permissions in writing to the Publisher with the final manuscript.

**MANUSCRIPT REVISION**    13. If, in the opinion of the Publisher, the manuscript is not properly prepared for publication, the Author shall have the option of revising it to the Publisher's satisfaction or of commissioning the Publisher to have it properly prepared or revised at the Author's expense. Unless otherwise mutually agreed, the Publisher shall make the manuscript of the Work conform to its standard style in punctuation, spelling, capitalization, and usage. If the Author fails to supply all necessary illustrative or other special material, it is agreed that the Publisher shall have such material supplied at the Author's expense. If the Author fails to deliver the manuscript to the Publisher as agreed, the Publisher shall have the right to rescind this Agreement by written notice to the Author, and the Author shall thereupon repay to the Publisher any and all amounts theretofore received by the Author in connection with the Work.

**PROOF**    14. The Author agrees to read, revise, and correct and return to the Publisher all galley and page proofs of the Work within a reasonable time. If the Author makes alterations in such galley, page proof, or illustrative material, other than corrections of printer's errors, then the expense thereof in excess of 10% of the cost of original composition shall be charged against any sums accruing to the Author under this Agreement, except that if the Publisher so requests, payment shall be made in cash. In this event the Publisher shall mail to the Author an invoice for said excess alterations promptly after receipt of the printer's bill for the same, which invoice shall be subject to review for a period of not more than thirty days after such mailing thereof, and both the Author and Publisher shall be bound by the amount of the printer's bill.

**INDEX**    15. The Author agrees to prepare and deliver to the Publisher, if requested by the Publisher, an index to the Work, in form and content satisfactory to the Publisher, within a reasonable time after receipt by the Author of the page proofs of the Work, failing which the Publisher may have such an index prepared at the Author's expense and charge the cost thereof against any sums accruing to the Author under this Agreement.

**SIMILAR PROJECT** 16. The Author agrees that he will not during the continuance of this Agreement without first obtaining the written consent of the Publisher, write, print, publish, or cause to be written, printed, or published, any revised, corrected, enlarged, or abridged version of the Work, or in any way become interested in any such version or in any book of a character that might interfere with or reduce the sales of the Work covered or contemplated by this Agreement.

**PUBLICATION** 17. The Publisher agrees to publish the Work at its own expense and in such style and manner and at such price as it deems best suited to the sale thereof.

**AUTHOR'S COPIES** 18. The Publisher agrees to furnish the Author with ten free copies of the Work and to permit the Author to purchase a reasonable number of additional copies for his own use, but not for resale, at the best trade discount then prevailing.

**ATEMENTS OF ACCOUNT** 19. The Publisher agrees to render semiannual statements of account with respect to the Work as of the 31st day of March and the 30th day of September in each year following the publication of the Work and shall deliver the same to the Author on or before the 1st day of July and the 2nd day of January following, together with the amount due.

**REVISION** 20. If, in the opinion of the Publisher, the Work needs revision at any time during the term of this Agreement, the Author, without charge therefor, shall revise the Work or supply such new matter as in the judgment of the Publisher may be needed to keep the Work up to date. If for any reason the Author does not revise the Work or supply the new matter required after a reasonable opportunity has been given him to do so, the Publisher may cause such revision to be made or such new matter supplied and may deduct the expense thereof from the royalties first accruing from the sales of such revised edition. In the event of the publication of an abridged, expanded, or revised edition necessitating the resetting of 20% or more of the Work, such revision shall be considered a new work and this Agreement shall be automatically renewed on the same terms as for the original edition.

**TERMINATION** 21. In the event that the Work shall at any time be out of print, the Author may give notice thereof to the Publisher, and in such event the Publisher shall declare within thirty days in writing whether it intends to have a new printing of the Work. If the Publisher shall declare its intention to have a new printing, it shall publish such printing not later than twelve months from the date of such notice. If within thirty days the Publisher shall not declare in writing that it does so intend, or if it shall not within such twelve months period bring out a new printing of the Work, or in case after two years from the date of first publication of the Work it gives three months notice to the Author of its intention to discontinue publication, then this Agreement shall terminate and all rights granted hereunder shall revert to the Author, together with any existing property originally furnished by the Author. In the event of any termination of this Agreement, the Author shall have the right for thirty days thereafter to purchase any remaining copies or sheets at one-half the manufacturing cost thereof, in default of which the Publisher may dispose of the stock as it sees fit, without prejudice to royalties due the Author, as elsewhere provided herein. If the Work is on option for publication within two years from the date of the demand hereinabove referred to, or under contract for publication, or on sale in a reprint or inexpensive edition, it shall be considered in print. Notwithstanding anything to the contrary herein contained, if the Publisher shall at any time determine that there are not sufficient sales of the Work to enable it to continue publication profitably, it shall have the right, after first giving the Author an opportunity to purchase the overstock at cost, to dispose of such copies as are on hand as it sees fit subject to royalties hereinbefore specified.

In the event of any termination of this Agreement as herein provided, the respective rights of the parties hereto accrued to the date of termination shall not be affected thereby but shall survive such termination, and rights accrued or to accrue under any license or sale made prior to such termination shall not be affected by such termination.

**ASSIGNMENT** 22. No assignment of this Agreement except by operation of law shall be binding upon either of the parties hereto without the written consent of the other; provided, however, that the Author may assign or transfer any monies due or to become due under this Agreement upon giving to the Publisher written notice of such assignment.

**NOTICES** 23. Any notice required under any of the provisions of this Agreement shall be in writing and deemed to have been properly served by delivery in person or by mailing to the party sought to be charged at its address set forth above or at such other address as may have been furnished in writing to the other party.

**SUCCESSORS** 24. The provisions of this Agreement shall be binding upon the Author and his legal representatives, successors and assigns, and shall inure to the benefit of and upon the Publisher and its successors and assigns.

**INTERPRETATION** 25. This Agreement shall be construed in accordance with the laws of the State of New York.

**OPTION** 26. ~~The Author grants to the Publisher an option to publish his next book on terms to be negotiated.~~

**SUPPLEMENTARY PARAGRAPHS** 27. Paragraphs    29              , annexed hereto, are hereby incorporated herein by reference.

WITNESS TO SIGNATURE OF AUTHOR OR PROPRIETOR:

AUTHOR OR PROPRIETOR:

......................................................................    ..........................................................................

......................................................................    ..........................................................................

......................................................................    ..........................................................................

......................................................................    ..........................................................................

WITNESS TO SIGNATURE OF PUBLISHER:

......................................................................    By ..........................................................

PRESIDENT

Mr. Richard Balkin
The Balkin Agency
403 West 115th St.
29. The Author hereby authorizes his agent    New York, N.Y.   100
to collect and receive all sums of money payable to the Author under the terms of this Agreement and the receipt of such agent shall be a good and valid discharge in respect thereof. The said agent is hereby fully authorized and empowered to act on behalf of the Author on all matters in any way arising out of this Agreement.

30. ~~It is agreed that on any sale of the motion picture or television rights made within two years of book publication and regardless of where the rights are sold or by whom the sale is made, the Publisher shall receive, as acknowledgment of its contribution to the value of said rights, in addition to the Publisher's share of the net proceeds from such sale, one-half the amount it has spent for advertising and promoting the sale of the Work; provided, however, that the amount received by the Publisher under this sentence shall in no event exceed 10% of the Author's share of the net proceeds from such sale. Futhermore, the Publisher's share of any additional money under the so-called escalator clauses in motion picture contracts based on book and/or book club sales shall be 10% thereof; provided, however, that the total amount accruing to the Publisher under this sentence shall in no event exceed 15% of the Author's share of the net proceeds from the sale of motion picture rights.~~

## A Publishing Fable

**The Author's Tale** — "The editor was so enthusiastic and supportive, I never thought there would be so many problems with getting the book out and getting it into the stores. Before it ever came out, she quit the publishing house and opened her own literary agency. I wrote her and called long distance, but she never calls back. I feel I was romanced."

**The Editor's Story** — "It was a good idea, with some fresh scenes, but the line editing took forever and the author didn't follow some suggestions that were crucial. Nevertheless, we went to press on schedule, and I'm sorry the house didn't follow through after I left. They're so disorganized. I still love the book and if X ever does anything more I want to see it, but. . . ."

**The Publisher's Story** — "She was recommended by one of our investors, you know, and she was good at grammar and spelling and punctuation even if she didn't have the editorial background. But she made these crazy deals. I think she was having a breakdown. We didn't let her go; it was her decision. And the book was one of a half-dozen we were left with. We put it out and gave it a push, but nothing happened. Have you seen the new book on running we have out?"

**The Production Manager's Story** — "It was a great design and seemed like an interesting subject, but the manufacturer made a last-minute switch in the text stock, and there were bindery errors, and the shipment was two days late. You can't be looking over the vendor's shoulder every minute. . . ."

227

**The Printer** — ''If the book was selling well, you wouldn't hear a murmur. But when it bombs in the bookstores, they look around for someone else to sell the books to, and the first person they think of is the printer. So they want credit for 23 cases of books because it was two days late and one page was out of order in two dozen copies. This happens every day. . . .''

**The Promotion Director** — ''The ads and the reviews and the promo were right on schedule, but we didn't have books in the stores because of the late delivery. And the author didn't proof it right, so there was a glaring error on page 93, and one page was out of order. That killed us for TV.''

**The Reviewer** — ''I never heard of the book before. Do you know how many books come in here in one day? I'll look for it, but why not send me another copy; it may be too late to write anything, but at least I'll look at it.''

**The Chain Buyer** — ''We'll fill any orders that come in, but we can't stock new titles just now. Things are just too tight. Try after the ABA, after Christmas, after you get a Book Club sale, after you get on the Tonight Show, etc. etc.''

**The TV Show Talent Coordinator** — ''If it isn't in all the stores, we can't touch it.''

**The Mom & Pop Stores** — ''Is it a local author? Will you leave, uh, one, on consignment? Can I have a reading copy?''

**The Author's Mother** — ''It looks nice. I put it on the coffee table. You were always so good with words. Not like your brother, but it seems all he can do is make money, no matter what he touches it turns to. . . .''

**Moral:** Really, we are all good people . . . but we each have our own ways of doing things . . . and explaining them . . . and it all adds up to the publishing business we would rather be engaged in than anything else. If any of the foregoing seems like looking in the mirror . . . let's try in the future to be a little more helpful, more responsible, and more aware of the other person's story.

# Selected Bibliography

## BOOK PUBLISHING—GENERAL

Adelman, Robert H. *What's Really Involved in Writing and Selling Your Book*. Los Angeles: Nash Publishing Co., 1972. Using a question-and-answer format, a successful author provides some straight-from-the-shoulder advice on writing and dealing with publishers.

Appelbaum, Judith and Evans, Nancy. *How to Get Happily Published*. New York: Harper & Row, 1978. Chatty, but down-to-earth and supportive advice geared to novice writers on the how, what and where of breaking into print, with an elaborate and useful "resource" section of books, people, places, programs, etc.

Dessauer, John P. *Book Publishing: What It Is, What It Does*. New York: R. R. Bowker, 1974; paper, 1976. A thorough, and authoritative survey of the components of the book publishing industry and its practices.

Geiser, Elizabeth A., ed. *The Business of Book Publishing: 39 Experts on Every Phase and Function of the Publishing Process*. Boulder: Westview Press, 1981. The successor to Chandler Grannis's classic *What Happens in Book Publishing*, now out of date. This should be the definitive overview of the publishing industry for the beginner; all of the contributors are top-notch experts in their specialties. Look for it in late 1981.

Greenfeld, Howard. *Books: From Writer to Reader*. New York: Crown Publishers, Inc., 1976. A clear and simple guide of special use to those interested in a publishing career and helpful to anyone wanting to know about book production.

Gross, Gerald, ed. *Publishers on Publishing*. New York: Grosset & Dunlap, paper, 1961. A hefty compendium of writings about publishing by thirty famous publishers, replete with advice, insights and reminiscences.

Henderson, Bill, ed. *The Art of Literary Publishing*. New York: Pushcart Press, 1980. A lively collection of essays by a melange of editors from trade houses, literary journals, and small presses, which blends personal recollections with practical advice.

Hill, Mary, and Cochran, Wendell. *Into Print: A Practical Guide to Writing, Illustrating and Publishing*. Los Altos, Calif.: Wm. Kaufmann, 1978. Primarily for scientists and engineers, but equally suitable for serious nonfiction writers, this lucid guide is especially useful for its excellent advice on securing and preparing illustrations, charts, maps, photographs, etc.

## FINDING A PUBLISHER

Brady, John, and Schemenaur, P.J., eds. *Writer's Market*. Cincinnati: Writer's Digest, annual. The most complete and up-to-date listing of markets for writers, interspersed with tips on how, what, and where.

Brewer, Annie M., and Geiser, Elizabeth A., eds. *Book Publisher's Directory*. Detroit: Gale Research Company, 2nd edition, 1979. A 668-page directory listing 3,400 "hard-to-find" presses, such as government, institutional, private, avant-garde, and special-interest publishers. Particularly useful for scholars, researchers, and writers on specialized or limited-audience subjects.

Burack, A. S., ed. *The Writer's Handbook*. Boston: The Writer, Inc., 1980. Eight hundred pages of useful articles by writers and experts in publishing on how to do it and then what to do with it, followed by a listing and brief description of markets for the writer.

*Literary Market Place with Names and Numbers*. New York: R. R. Bowker, annual. Comprehensive directory of publishers and personnel, as well as of various services in publishing.

Reynolds, Paul R. *A Professional Guide to Marketing Manuscripts*. Boston: Writers, Inc., 1968. A detailed guide for the writer on marketing manuscripts to book publishers and to other media, by a top agent. The figures are somewhat out-of-date, but the facts hold up.

*Writers' and Artists' Yearbook*. Boston: The Writer, Inc., 1980 (annual). The standard reference for the British publishing market, listing magazines, book publishers, agents, etc. An amalgam of the kind of information found in *LMP* and *Writer's Market*.

## CONTRACTS AND COPYRIGHT*

Baumol, William J., and Heim, Peggy. "On Contracting with Publishers: What Every Author Should Know." *A.A.U.P. Bulletin*, Spring 1967. Primarily for textbook, professional, and university press authors. The figures are somewhat out-of-date, but the survey of contract provisions and terms—as well as the advice—is still sound.

Crawford, Tad, *The Writer's Legal Guide*. New York: Hawthorn Books, Inc., 1978. A practical how-to and guide on legal matters, contracts, new copyright provisions, tax breaks, etc. Thorough, readable, and the most up-to-date reference.

Johnston, Donald. *Copyright Handbook*. New York: R. R. Bowker, 1978. Fourteen exhaustive chapters on all aspects and implications of the new copyright law. If you can't find it here, you probably won't find it.

Madison, Charles, A. *Irving to Irving: Author-Publisher Relations, 1800–1974*. New York: R. R. Bowker, 1974. The evolution of contracts, copyright agreements, and other arrangements between authors and publishers.

Wincor, Richard. *Literary Rights Contracts: A Handbook for Professionals*. New York: Harcourt Brace Jovanovich, 1979. More suitable perhaps for lawyers, agents, and publishers' contracts departments, but the attention to detail, the sample forms and clauses, and the discussion of current trends are particularly useful for the do-it-yourselfer not intimidated by contracts.

Wittenberg, Philip. *The Protection of Literary Property*. 2nd rev. ed. Boston: The Writer, Inc., 1978. Thorough exploration of the laws and regulations on copyright, as well as the ownership and use of literary property. Revised from the 1968 edition to include the new copyright legislation.

*A free "Copyright Information Kit" is available from the Register of Copyrights, Library of Congress, Washington, D.C. 20540. It contains copies of copyright forms, as well as several circulars on various aspects of current and forthcoming copyright provisions.

## EDITING AND COPYEDITING

Barzun, Jacques. *On Writing, Editing and Publishing*. Chicago: The University of Chicago Press, paper, 1971. A discursive collection of nine essays by one of America's foremost *hommes de belles lettres*; worth reading for its stylistic elegance alone.

Gross, Gerald, ed. *Editors on Editing*. New York: Grosset & Dunlap, paper, 1962. Over two dozen articles and miscellanea by well-known and successful editors detailing both how they feel about their work and how they do it.

Nicholson, Margaret. *A Practical Style Guide for Authors and Editors*. New York: Holt, Rinehart & Winston, paper, 1970. The most lucid and concise style guide available in paperback. More than adequate for authors outside of academic and professional book publishing.

*Reference Books*

All three of the following style manuals are comprehensive and authoritative classics.

Jordan, Lewis. *New York Times Manual of Style and Usage*. New York: Quadrangle Books, 1976.

*A Manual of Style*. Chicago: University of Chicago Press, 12th ed., 1969.

Skillin, Marjorie E., and Gay, Robert M. *Words Into Type*. Englewood Cliffs, N.J.: Prentice-Hall, 3rd ed., 1974.

## DESIGN AND PRODUCTION

Lee, Marshall. *Bookmaking: The Illustrated Guide to Design and Production*. New York: R. R. Bowker, 2nd ed., 1979. The designer's classic ABC. Comprehensive instruction on book design and production.

*Pocket Pal*. New York: International Paper Co., 11th ed., paper, 1975. A concise introduction to the graphic arts; everything the beginner might want to know about printing.

Wilson, Adrian. *The Design of Books*. Salt Lake City: Peregrine Smith, reprint ed., paper, 1974. Simple and detailed advice for the novice designer; the best concise basic introduction to book design.

## OTHER CATEGORIES OF PUBLISHING

*Children's Books*

Colby, Jean Poindexter. *Writing, Illustrating and Editing Children's Books*. New York: Hastings House, 1967. A thorough and detailed examination of all phases of children's book publishing, including the author's and illustrator's roles.

McCann, Donnarae, and Richard, Olga. *The Child's First Books: A Critical Study of Pictures and Texts*. New York: H. W. Wilson, 1973. A thematic and conceptual analysis of picture story books, showing both their effectiveness and impact on children.

Whitney, Phyllis A. *Writing Juvenile Stories and Novels*. Boston: The Writer, Inc. 1976. Chatty but solid advice on how to write and market fiction for young adults, by a seasoned pro with thirty titles to her credit.

*University Press*

Hawes, Gene R. *To Advance Knowledge: A Handbook on University Press Publishing*. New York: A.A.U.P. Services, Inc., 1967. The how, why, and wherefore of university presses.

*Small Presses and Self-Publishing*

Burke, Clifford. *Printing It: A Guide to Graphic Technique for the Impecunious*. Berkeley:

Wingbow Press, 1972. Clear, concise, and encouraging, it stresses typewriter composition and photo-offset techniques.

Chickadel, Charles J. *Publish It Yourself*. San Francisco: Trinity Press, 1980, revised edition. One of the best of the current spate of how-to's. Informally yet practically and sensibly Chickadel leads you through the step-by-step process from manuscript editing to sales and promotion. The illustrations are unexpected and charming. Well worth the $5.95 price.

Fulton, Len, ed. *International Directory of Little Magazines and Small Presses*. Paradise, Calif.: Dustbooks, 16th ed., 1980. As complete a listing of markets as can be found for little magazines and small presses, with descriptions of what they publish, what they pay, and how to submit.

Henderson, Bill, ed. *The Publish-It-Yourself Handbook*. 2nd ed. Yonkers, N.Y.: Harper & Row, 1980. An anthology comprised of articles by those who did it themselves. Good reading, long on reminiscences, and a must for the tyro self-publisher.

Huenefeld, John. *How to Make Money Publishing Books*. Bedford, Mass.: Vinebrook Publications, looseleaf, 1974. A reference book for small-press publishers; completely detailed instructions on how to run a small press.

Poynter, Dan. *The Self-Publishing Manual: How to Write, Print and Sell Your Own Book*. Santa Barbara: Parachuting Publications, 1979. On most topics, as much detail as you would need to do it yourself. Sometimes oversimplified or overoptimistic, but essentially an ideal handbook.

*Paperbacks*

Smith, Roger H. *Paperback Parnassus*. Boulder, Colo.: Westview Press, 1976. An exploration of the history and marketing of paperbacks, with an emphasis on the distribution, structure, and economics of the mass market paperback industry.

### MISCELLANEOUS

*The Business of Publishing: A PW Anthology*. New York: R. R. Bowker, 1978. Forty-five articles taken from *Publishers Weekly* over the past five years. Covers many aspects of the economics, issues, and problems in publishing as seen by the insiders for the insiders. Straightforward, practical, and informative; well worth the professional writer's attention.

Committee on Professional Education for Publishing. *The Accidental Profession: Education, Training and the People of Publishing*. New York: Association of American Publishers, 1977. A survey of job opportunities and current in-house practices and external programs for the recruitment and training of publishing personnel, with specific recommendations for more coordinated industry-wide efforts.

Congrat-Butler, Stefan, ed. *Translation & Translators*. New York: R.R. Bowker Co., 1979. An exhaustive and thorough encyclopedic reference for translators, containing sections on associations, conferences, awards, contracts, etc., along with a register of "professional" or accredited translators.

Melcher, D., and Larrick, N. *Printing and Promotion Handbook*. New York: McGraw-Hill, 3rd ed., 1966. The classic guide to planning or preparing advertising and publicity and to buying printing and direct-mail services.

Shaffer, Susan E. *Guide to Book Publishing Courses*. New Jersey: Peterson's Guides, 1979. A comprehensive survey of all U.S. academic and professional programs and courses related to publishing, replete with detailed information. An excellent and thorough guide, except for the somewhat out-of-date bibliography.

Spikel, Sina. *Indexing Your Book*. Madison: University of Wisconsin Press, 1954. A practical and comprehensible 28-page pamphlet on how to prepare an index.

Weber, Olga, ed. *Literary and Library Prizes*. New York: R. R. Bowker, 1976. A comprehensive listing of 370 book awards, including the history of and eligibility requirements for each.

# Index

*233*